**ALSO BY
MICHAEL STREISSGUTH**

*Eddy Arnold:
Pioneer of the Nashville Sound*

*Like a Moth to a Flame:
The Jim Reeves Story*

RING OF FIRE

THE Johnny Cash READER

Edited by

Michael Streissguth

Da Capo Press
A Member of the Perseus Books Group

A list of credits for individual articles appears on page 287.

Designed by *Brent Wilcox*
Set in 11-point Janson Text by the Perseus Books Group

Cataloging-in-Publication data for this book is available from the Library of Congress.

First Da Capo Press edition 2002
ISBN 0-306-81225-8

Published by Da Capo Press
A Member of the Perseus Books Group
http://www.dacapopress.com

Da Capo Press books are available at special discounts for bulk purchases in the U.S. by corporations, institutions, and other organizations. For more information, please contact the Special Markets Department at the Perseus Books Group, 11 Cambridge Center, Cambridge, MA 02142, or call (800) 255-1514 or (617) 252-5298, or e-mail j.mccrary@perseusbooks.com.

3 4 5 6 7 8 9—06 05 04 03

For Leslie

CONTENTS

Acknowledgments xi
Introduction xiii

I. Arkansas Train

Excerpt from *Winners Got Scars Too: The Life of Johnny Cash* 5
Christopher S. Wren, 1971

"Fork in the Road" from *Man in Black* 25
Johnny Cash, 1975

"Johnny Cash: The Sun Sound" 35
Hank Davis, *Goldmine*, December 20, 1985

"Johnny Cash Achieves 'Life's Ambition,' Wins Opry Hearts" 41
Ben A. Green, *Nashville Banner*, July 16, 1956

"It Looks as if Elvis Has a Rival—from Arkansas" 46
Ralph J. Gleason, *San Francisco Chronicle*, December 16, 1956

"Gleason Signs Cash for 10 Guest Spots" 47
Robert Johnson, *Memphis Press-Scimitar*, January 7, 1957

"Write Is Wrong" 51
Time, February 23, 1959

"Johnny Cash" 55

Peter La Farge, *Sing Out!*, 1965

"Seven One Night Stands" from *Man in Black* 59

Johnny Cash, 1975

II. Apogee

"When Johnny Cash Visited Leavenworth" 77

Albert Nussbaum, (Charleston, WV) *Sunday Gazette Mail*, October 7, 1973

Excerpt from *The Nashville Sound: Bright Lights and Country Music* 83

Paul Hemphill, 1970

"Something Rude Showing" 87

Richard Goldstein, *Vogue*, August 15, 1969

"First Angry Man Of Country Singers" 90

Tom Dearmore, *New York Times Magazine*, September 21, 1969

"Johnny Cash: 'I'm Growing, I'm Changing, I'm Becoming'" 109

Dorothy Gallagher, *Redbook*, August 1971

"Cash's 'Gospel Road' Film Is Renaissance for Him" 124

George Vecsey, *New York Times*, December 13, 1973

"Interview with Johnny Cash" 127

Peter McCabe and Jack Killion, *Country Music*, May 1973

"*Penthouse* Interview: Johnny Cash" 143

Larry Linderman, *Penthouse*, August 1975

III. Legend

"What Now, John Cash?" 165
Patrick Carr, *Country Music*, December 1974

"Cash Comes Back" 171
Patrick Carr, *Country Music*, December 1976

"Johnny Cash's Freedom" 186
Patrick Carr, *Country Music*, April 1979

"Johnny Cash: Still Free" 199
Noel Coppage, *Stereo Review*, March 1983

"Hard Talk from the God-Fearin', Pro-Metal Man in Black" 201
Mary Dickie, *Graffiti*, October 1987

"Heroic Survivor" 206
David Sinclair, *The Times*, London, May 15, 1989

"The Mystery of Life" 209
Alanna Nash, *Stereo Review*, April 1991

"Johnny Cash's Best Performance Was Off Stage" 211
Dan McCullough, *Cape Cod Times*, April 9, 1989

IV. Back in Black

"Chordless in Gaza: The Second Coming of John R. Cash" 221
Nick Tosches, *Journal of Country Music*, Vol. 17 (3), 1995

"Johnny Cash, Austerely Direct from Deep Within" 247
Jon Pareles, *New York Times*, September 16, 1994

"Cash Conquers" 251

Chris Dickinson, *Chicago Reader*, September 16, 1994

"Johnny Cash: American Music Legend" 255

Bill DeYoung, *Goldmine*, July 19, 1996

"Cash, Back" 261

Ben Ratliff, *Rolling Stone*, October 26, 2000

"Rays of Light from the Man in Black" 264

David Brinn, *Jerusalem Post*, October 31, 2000

"Johnny Cash: *American III: Solitary Man*" 265

Michael McCall, *Country Music*, February/March 2001

"Hello, This Is Johnny Cash" 267

Peter Cooper, the *Nashville Tennessean*, October 22, 2000

Bibliography 273
Credits 287
Index 291

ACKNOWLEDGMENTS

Many individuals helped me complete the *Johnny Cash Reader*, and I thank them.

At Le Moyne College, Wayne Stevens, the head of interlibrary loan and denizen of the Dinosaur Bar-B-Q, begged on my behalf articles and books from the libraries of the nation.

After more than three years of compiling, refining, editing, and writing, I gave this book to Jim Fitzgerald who found a home for it. I am grateful to him. Andrea Schulz at Da Capo found ways to make this book more meaningful, useful, readable. I appreciate her contributions.

Thanks to Dawn Oberg and Kent Henderson of the Country Music Foundation Library and Archives in Nashville, and to Rick Tindall, Luther Perkins fan.

Two people gave me valuable editing assistance early in this collection's life: my wife Leslie Bailey Streissguth, without whom little is possible, and Ed Brown, believer.

Thanks also to Kelly Hancock at House of Cash; Nick Shaffran at Sony; Lou Robin, Cash's manager, who suggested articles; Alanna Nash for encouragement and permission to use her review of *The Mystery of Life*; Michael McCall for direction and permission to use his review of *American III: Solitary Man*; Steve Andreassi of the IUP Lodge and Convocation Center in Hoboken, New Jersey; Mark

James for extending his arm in Nashville; Len Mustazza of Penn State–Ogontz, co-editor of *The Frank Sinatra Reader*, for tips on dealing with this kind of book; Ma and Pa Bailey for babysitting and clippings; Dad for taking my brother and me to the Salvation Army to find singles and albums and Mom for letting us keep them.

Introduction

Johnstown, Pennsylvania, 1985. Johnny Cash fans had almost filled the dank War Memorial, an old arena wedged between the rusty downtown and a sharp bend in the crumbling U.S. Route 56. Men and women eased down aisles to their seats or sought out paper tubs of beer and popcorn, while I contemplated how I might get backstage. Just arrived from the nearby Indiana University of Pennsylvania, where Shakespeare, Tocqueville, and Freud were frequently drowned out in my dorm room by Cash, Presley, and Lewis, I kept playing in my mind "I Walk the Line" and "The Baron," Cash's corny yet catchy ballad about a long-in-the-tooth pool shark who meets his long-lost son. Would these songs take new meaning when I met the Man in Black? To find out, I shuffled through the crowd, passed the mildest kind of security, and entered the family-like atmosphere of Cash's backstage.

Unmistakable in the milling crowd of techies, musicians and fans and a few paces from a table of modest, untouched refreshments, the tall troubadour spoke with a group of admirers. He was draped in black, a few hot pink stripes on his shoulder the only concession to color. Trying to collect myself, I turned to pianist Earl Poole Ball for an autograph, but when I refocused on Cash, he and an old man were chatting like two farmers after a Grange meeting. Cash clasped this man's right hand, turning it palm-up in his own hand, considering its calluses and deep wrinkles. "These are working hands," he bellowed, "farm hands, chopping wood hands." The elderly fan, probably retired from the once-great steel mills of Johnstown or the coal mines outside town, glowed and regained a long-lost posture.

❁ ❁ ❁

I've lost the details of my one-on-one with Cash. An autograph on a program survives, but the memory of Cash and the old man lingers intensely. In retrospect, it underscores Cash's place in twentieth century country music. He is one of the last country music superstars rooted in the rural reality that birthed and sustained country music. His interest in the elderly gentleman and his calluses that night in western Pennsylvania sprang from his own Depression-era childhood on an Arkansas farm, a time and place defined, in part, by hard work.

Cash's direct connection to rural life and culture have filled his music from his debut in 1955 all the way through 2000, when his most recent album was released. When Johnny Cash sings about trains, you know he feels the rattle of long, dark convoys that passed his farmhouse, sees his father Ray jumping one when work took him far afield. Similarly, Cash knowingly ruminates on humping it in performances such as "Nine Pound Hammer" (1963) and "Sixteen Tons" (1987) because he picked cotton, lugged water pails for laborers, and chopped tall piles of logs. His life experiences contribute to the sum of Johnny Cash, and he's acutely in touch with them. "Life isn't just for living, it's for singing about," he wrote in the liner notes for his 1977 album *The Rambler*. "Loneliness is real, the pain of loss is real, the fulfillment of love is real, the thrill of adventure is real, and to put it in the song lyrics and sing about it—after all, isn't that what a country singer-writer is supposed to do, write and sing of reality?"

❁ ❁ ❁

Just as Cash is one of the last authentic voices in country music, he was also for many years country music's standard bearer, the name that first came to mind when many around the world thought of country music. Cash introduced himself to country in the 1950s when he recorded "Folsom Prison Blues," "I Walk the Line," "Guess Things Happen That Way," and other major country hits for Sam Phillips' Sun Records. And as he rolled into the 1960s with a new Columbia Records contract, superstardom danced in his headlights. Plying his broad country music base, his exploration of the folk scene and his old 1950s rock and roll association (which was cemented by his Sun Records credentials), Johnny Cash made himself known to a large and diverse group of individuals: the Alabama farmer who drove to the feed store with "Five Feet High and Rising" crackling on his radio; the Washington, D.C., office girl who grooved to "Ring of Fire"; the Village searcher who found inspiration in "Dark As a Dungeon."

The briskly bubbling enthusiasm for Cash boiled over in 1968 when he released a live LP recorded at Folsom Prison in California. The album's expression of solidarity with the down-trodden in a season of such expressions, and Cash's ferocious enthusiasm as he sang and goofed off in front of Folsom's prisoner-fans, spiked the nation's curiosity. A year later, when Columbia released the universally appealing single "A Boy Named Sue" (recorded at California's San Quentin prison), Cash's name and image caught fire. Serious journalists gathered to capture the Cash phenomenon in print, scholars weighed his influence, and the publishing, film, and television industries sought him.

From the late '60s to the mid–'70s, Johnny Cash outpaced his country peers in record sales and became the music's primary emissary to the world. He made country music appealing to a mass audience during the Age of Aquarius, when new musical sounds might have been expected to bury country music. And as the abundance of thoughtful journalistic pieces published at that time illustrates, Cash was one of the most talked-about entertainers in America.

In country music, he had become the most important figure since Hank Williams. Hank, of course, injected color and energy into country starting in the late 1940s with an infectious boogie-woogie style and seductive—often humorous—musings on love and ruin. His tone drifted into the work of virtually every country musician who followed him: If performers in Williams' afterglow didn't sample some aspect of his singing or instrumental presentation, they covered his songs or attempted to copy his songwriting style. In the years after Hank's 1953 death, he would become the quintessential country music figure. There would be no other—until Johnny Cash reached his own apogee. Memphis entertainment critic Robert Johnson wrote in early 1957 that Cash could be "the logical successor" to Williams, and forty years later author and music critic Alanna Nash upped the ante, suggesting that Cash would "be reckoned the single most important country-music figure of the postwar era."[1] No doubt, both were accurate.

Cash had for years appealed to pop audiences, but by the late 1960s, he was saturating the general entertainment market, not merely crossing over into it. Cash had his own ABC prime-time television show (1969–1971); he starred with Kirk Douglas in the well-received Hollywood film *A Gunfight* (1970); he and his wife June Carter were dissected by the national media from their 1968 marriage on; and he spawned numerous books and documentaries. When the White House wanted country music, it invited Cash to its stage; when ABC-TV sought to emulate the success of CBS-TV's country-based

---

[1] See page 47 to read more of the Robert Johnson piece; Alanna Nash appears on page 209.

Hee Haw and *The Glen Campbell Goodtime Hour*, it turned its cameras toward Cash. Advertisers, such as American Oil and Lionel Trains, invited Cash to pitch their products.

No country musician had ever enjoyed such attention; and just as the world knew Ali meant boxing and Elvis meant rock and roll, Cash meant country music. He became the face of the genre. "To cavil any longer over his position as the greatest country singer of our times," argued scholar Frederick Danker in 1969, "would seem pointless."

Johnny Cash's ascent, while obviously profitable for himself and the marketing of country music in general, also endorsed traditional country music. In the late 1960s when the songs of Eddy Arnold, Glen Campbell, Sonny James, and others whose performances were sweetened by strings, brass sections, and lush background vocals rivaled for commercial success the sparser performances of Merle Haggard, Loretta Lynn, and George Jones, Cash's following confirmed a ringing endorsement for the latter. He had coaxed flame from the dimming torch of Jimmie Rodgers and Hank Williams and, in doing so, kept vibrantly alive the uncomplicated instrumentation and rural-based images those men had so ably proffered. In Cash's music, listeners still found desperate men, pleas for salvation, trains, jailhouses, and cotton farms. Steering away from the simple cheating and loving ditties that had come to dominate country music, he breathed new life into the themes of rural and working-class culture. And he would continue to conjure such themes well after his halcyon days. As the world spiraled into the 1970s, into disco and Tanya Tucker in tight pants, critics rode Cash for dwelling on his olden themes, and the sales of his records diminished markedly. Nonetheless, Cash at his peak had given a thunderous jolt to the themes that, in the early twentieth century, first launched and popularized country music. In doing so, he reminded his vast audience of country music's roots, and he nourished those roots so they might occasionally thrive—as they did in 2001 in the wake of the *O Brother Where Art Thou?* soundtrack.

❁ ❁ ❁

Cash remained a figure symbolic of country music, but in the midst of the 1970s his influence and inventiveness began waning. The mass media—finding nothing new to rummage through or tired of Cash's rural-based themes, un-hip explorations of his religious faith and loud declarations of patriotism—directed their pens and microphones elsewhere. In his 1977 book *Country*, Nick Tosches directed his sharpened quill *at* him:

> Johnny Cash and his God are a particularly tedious act. The strongest drink Cash serves at his parties is non-alcoholic fruit punch. . . . In the first show of his "Johnny Cash" series, broadcast by CBS in August of 1976, Cash referred to his mother-in-law, Maybelle Carter, as "one of the most influential instrumentalists in country music." Mother Maybelle Carter's influence as a country-music instrumentalist is equal to that of, say, Rudy Vallee.[2] Each year, Johnny Cash's mind seems to grow more monomaniacal. His 1976 hit "Sold Out of Flagpoles" was an absurd mess of godly patriotism, a song berserk with blandness and as dumb as any in the 1975 film *Nashville*.

By the mid-1970s, Cash was clearly still fixed in the firmament of American stars, but he was no longer a red-hot media darling. On top of that, his recordings, which regularly had placed on the top five of

---

[2] *Editor's note*: Country music historian Charles Wolfe wrote in the Country Music Foundation's *Encyclopedia of Country Music* (1998) that "Maybelle Carter crafted the 'Carter lick' on the guitar and watched it become the best-known picking style in the genre."

the country charts and crossed over to the pop side, now struggled to find a place in country's top twenty. When "One Piece at a Time"—his 1976 novelty about a car built with a crazy mix of stolen parts—spent two weeks at number one, the country music press hailed the re-emergence of Cash. But "One Piece at a Time" proved not to be Cash's return train, only a special that had wandered out of the tunnel of lackluster chart performance.

It appeared that declining media attention, changing tastes, *and* a changing Cash were sapping his commercial viability. Throughout the later 1970s and straight on through the 1980s, self-parody, over-production, and sickly sweet sentimentality often marred his work. The music lacked the old growling Johnny Cash edge. To be sure, the shining performances still appeared occasionally: "The L&N Don't Stop Here Anymore" in 1979; his covers of Bruce Springsteen's "Highway Patrolman" in 1983 and Elvis Costello's "The Big Light" in 1987.

And it's not that the balance of his music was *bad*. It was enjoyable, hummable, occasionally poignant, produced with the best Nashville musicians and recording technology. But it lacked the authority, the desperation, the closeness to the earth that defined the music that Cash first offered to America in the 1950s. The new Cash relied heavily on other songwriters. Many of them used themes that Cash adored (such as in "The Cowboy Who Started A Fight" by Billy Joe Shaver, recorded in 1980; and "Paradise" by John Prine, recorded in 1980 and 1982). But these writers lacked Cash's style. Like Hemingway, Cash was direct and uncomplicated, quickly communicating deep despair or a circumstance of rural life. When Cash turned to ballads penned by others, often his telling of them sounded cumbersome. He worked best with his own material, plainly told and drawn from his own experiences and observations; yet from the late 1970s into the 1990s, few fresh Cash compositions sat in the hopper.

Outside the studio, Cash's concert schedule continued to fill as quickly as a pretty girl's dance card, and the networks frequently called on him to host specials, do guest spots or star in made-for-TV movies. But in the world where it mattered professionally, the recording world, Cash seemed to be failing (though, to be fair, so were other country music veterans). In the mid-1980s, Columbia Records, which had given him such a strong platform in the 1960s, unceremoniously jettisoned him, and a subsequent relationship with Mercury Records found Cash at odds with the recording industry's new youth movement. In a December 1992 *Rolling Stone* interview by Steve Pond, a desperate Cash railed against Mercury and its parent company PolyGram: "Nobody at that company is excited about my recording career," he complained. "If I hear 'demographics' one more time, I'm gonna puke right in their faces. I mean, I recorded songs that I think are really some of my best work, like the last album, *The Mystery of Life*, but I think they must have pressed a hundred copies and sent 'em out. I don't know. They're excited about Kathy Mattea and the other young PolyGram artists. Which is all right. I was there once. But they're gonna be old someday. And the thing is, if you got it, you *always* got it, you know?"

But Cash may not have "had it" in 1992. *The Mystery of Life* was far more okay than outstanding, prompting Alanna Nash to announce that he "rummaged through his attic and came up with an odd set of songs, several of which are so old they practically sport toupees." Such a dismissal of Cash's song selection had rarely been voiced and illustrated the rut in which Cash was limping during the early 1990s. Other figures—most notably Garth Brooks—had become the voices of country music to new generations of fans around the world.

❁ ❁ ❁

Enter Rick Rubin. Record producer and proprietor of the American Recordings label, Rubin had stalked onto the 1980s music scene by giving voice to the Beastie Boys, Slayer, DJ Kool, and other alternative rock acts and hip-hop artists, some of whom swelled with violent irreverence and, in the case of acts such as Sir Mix-A-Lot and comedian Andrew Dice Clay, misogyny.

The violent irreverence and misogyny lurking in Rubin's stable also dwelled in Cash's catalog and, with regard to the former, in Cash himself. In the old days, Cash had surely raged with haphazard irreverence—much of it drug-induced—throwing radio equipment out the window during his early 1950s Air Force stint and, later, in 1965, smashing every last footlight on the Grand Ole Opry stage. But Cash had also spewed fury with clear-eyed purpose, against oppressors of American Indians, in advocacy of imprisoned men and women, and in condemnation of the country and western establishment, which he saw as a threat to the dissemination of his music.

Cash had mellowed measurably when Rubin met him in the 1990s, singing for evangelist Billy Graham's crusades, championing religion and love of country, and living (for the most part) drug free. But never mind that. When Johnny Cash signed with American in 1993 and released the album *American Recordings* in 1994, the publicity machine fed the dark side of Johnny Cash into its processors. Old stories of his drug use and unfaithfulness secured his membership in the American clan and made him relevant again. The entertainment media ate it up. In an era when the music industry opened the gate to musical acts that frequently romanticized hatred and violence, there was no place—at least in a marketing sense—for the Cash who had recorded "Ragged Old Flag" or "Strawberry Cake" in the thick of the 1970s, or who turned recording sessions into family picnics by asking his son, daughters, sons-in-law, wife, and sisters-in-law along. Instead, it was the Cash who back in '56 had sung "I shot a man in Reno just to watch him die" in "Folsom Prison Blues" who lumbered into the *American Recordings* flak effort. Promo shots framed a grim, wild-eyed, and grizzled Cash. One wondered if he wielded a butcher's knife under the frock coat he was always pictured wearing. In a disturbing music video for the album cut "Delia's Gone," there was Cash, long shovel in hand, burying the pale model Kate Moss whom he had shot—à la his "Cocaine Blues" of yore—because she'd been a bad girl. *First time I shot her/Shot her in the side/Hard to watch to suffer/But with a second shot she died. Delia's gone/One more round/Delia's gone.*

And many shouted hallelujahs for the return of the old Cash. No more overproduction, no more Carter women moaning on his records, no more dressing up as cowboy with Waylon Jennings to sing sappy odes, no more *Muppet Show* appearances. Fans who had drifted away from Cash in the '70s and '80s rediscovered him, and new fans saw him as American Recordings had marketed him—as the godfather of metal and gangsta rap. Cash had become relevant again, not as the standard bearer of country music, but as the antecedent to the intense strains of music that Rick Rubin marketed. Young people flocked again to shows, and the national press began to write about him with vigor that recalled the late '60s and early '70s.

Back in the ring, Cash had another forum from which to remind his listeners of the roots of country music. The cuts on his American albums were country music imbued with the traditions of Jimmie Rodgers and his progeny, figures such as Ernest Tubb and Hank Williams. In fact, Cash's first album with Rubin was the closest any country singer had come to the spirit of Jimmie Rodgers and company in a long, long time.

Cash's new work was not specifically marketed toward the country audience, and country radio treated it like, ahem, a country cousin. But whether country music was listening or not, Cash was there to remind it from whence it came. At a time when mainstream country music was filled mostly with faux cowboys and clichés, there returned a voice harking back to the themes of sin and redemption and rural life that once were just as common as faux cowboys and clichés. In the mid-1990s, Nashville had flash; American had Cash.

However, the story soon changed. As the 1990s drew to a close, Cash was battling for his life. A Parkinson's-like nervous disorder had revealed itself late in 1997, and during the ensuing years the illness confined Cash to his homes in Tennessee and Jamaica. He ventured out for rare appearances and another Rick Rubin album, *American III: Solitary Man*, a recording that understandably failed to equal his earlier American work. Early in 2002 his cover of Hank Williams's "I Dreamed About Mama Last Night" captured a Grammy nomination, and his voice could be heard on TV ads promoting Ford trucks. Cash keeps adding to his legacy, but how vigorously he will continue to do so remains a mystery.

❁ ❁ ❁

So why a *Johnny Cash Reader*?

Simply put, it is long overdue.

Clearly, he is one of the most important names in twentieth-century popular music as well as the most-written-about name in country music. The extent to which that is true became strikingly apparent several years ago, when I was researching a Cash biography. I found many early biographies, book chapters, scholarly articles, and enough newspaper and magazine articles to fill a Pennsylvania Railroad porthole caboose. As I thumbed through this mass of prose, I decided that the Cash biography would have to wait: Many of these long out-of-print profiles, essays, reviews, and analyses deserved to be collected and reintroduced to the public.

Many articles I selected for the *Reader* reveal aspects of Cash's life and career that have been obscured by the recitation of tired anecdotes that have come to characterize much writing about Cash over the years. The writers I was drawn to tightly focused on Cash, catching him backstage on his first night on the Grand Ole Opry in 1956 or between breaks during a filming of his ABC prime-time show in the late 1960s. In 1959, a *Time* reporter observed Cash practicing his draw while his wife and children flitted about in the background, and in 1989, columnist Dan McCullough watched a heart-wrenching encounter between two disabled boys and their country music hero. Dorothy Gallagher—a memoirist and long-time magazine writer—engaged Cash in a discussion of social mores and religion in 1971. Veteran country music writer Patrick Carr led him through a series of conversations about songs he recorded in the mid–'70s—"Daughter of A Railroad Man" (1976) and "No Expectations" (1978), to name a couple—that would rarely be discussed again anywhere in print.

To understand two key aspects of Cash's past—his brother's death and his drug use—I selected chapters from his first autobiography, *Man in Black* (1975). It seemed to me that nobody could better recount those vital periods of his life. Furthermore, I believe that no collection of writing about Cash could be without Cash's own writing. Not only a songwriter, Cash has proven himself to be a capable writer of prose, penning numerous liner notes, a novel (*Man in White*, 1986), and two autobiographies.

These writers' observations, conclusions and musings, it seems to me, are maps that orient and reorient newcomers and long-time fans to Cash and his multifaceted life and career. Samples from the body of writing about Cash naturally lead us to a greater understanding of him. Furthermore, when so many writers consider a subject, they give us the benefit of multiple insights into the man's professional and personal development. We are so often confined to one or a handful of authors' perspectives on a subject; in a reader, each writer adds a new dimension. Certainly, this collection can never bring the unifying style and thematic continuity of a seamless biography, but it does promise a variety of perspectives formed at various way stations on Cash's journey. Journalistic accounts show us Cash changing: humble in the first blush of success, cocksure as he becomes an established entity in American entertainment, humble again after he permits God to guide him.

Not to say this approach to understanding Cash is without its flaws. The journalistic rush to meet deadlines and push on to the next story often leaves factual errors unchecked. You will find several in this collection. The articles containing such errors remain because the insight offered into Cash's life and career overshadows the misstep. When the mistake was flagrant and potentially misleading, I deleted it or added a note for clarification. Interestingly, Cash himself was often the source of the misinformation. Readers will note that many Cash chroniclers refer to his Cherokee background; he has no such background, but trotted out the dubious detail, he said later, to toy with reporters. Cash also proffered conflicting accounts of his early days on tour. In various publications printed in the 1960s and '70s, he claimed to have never played roadhouses or honky-tonks during his Sun Records days; however, by 1994, he was telling people about bloody buckets that he and Carl Perkins played in the '50s.

Despite the fibs and contradictions, Cash has been remarkably open about his highs and lows. Many of the articles are particularly engaging because of his candor and willingness to go beyond pat messages fed to him by some publicist.

I reviewed each article using three criteria: the extent to which it provided a unique glimpse of Cash's life and career; the quality of the writing; and the integrity of the information. The reader may note the repetition of certain biographical details; however, especially in the long profiles of Cash, they are important in setting up the writers' narratives. When it was clear to me that the repetition did not advance the narrative, I removed it. (Deletions are noted with bold ellipses.)

This collection includes the writing and observations of thirty journalists, many of whom are among America's finest music writers: Alanna Nash, biographer of Dolly Parton and Col. Tom Parker; Patrick Carr, close observer of Cash's career and collaborator on his second autobiography; Chris Dickinson, former editor of the *Journal of Country Music.* There are many unheralded, too, and here they assemble with their counterparts to reveal the varied colors of the Man in Black.

PART I
ARKANSAS TRAIN

His is the music of America. He sang the songs of the people he loved, of a young nation growing strong. His was an America of glistening rails, thundering boxcars, and rain-swept nights, of lonesome prairies, great mountains and a high blue sky. He sang of the bayous and the cotton fields, the wheated plains, of the little towns, the cities, and of the winding rivers of America.

—INSCRIPTION ON THE STATUE OF
JIMMIE RODGERS, MERIDIAN, MISSISSIPPI

When John Cash approached Sun Records in early 1955, the twenty-three-year-old believed he might make a decent gospel singer. He had already tried his luck at a Pontiac, Michigan, auto body plant and an Arkansas margarine factory, then served a stint from 1950 to 1954 as a radio interceptor in the U.S. Air Force. He had landed in Memphis, just fifty miles away from his hometown of Dyess, Arkansas, with his wife Vivian Liberto, whom he had met when he joined the air force and married just after his discharge. To establish a career that might support her and a new baby named Rosanne, he had attended radio broadcasting school and traversed the

Bluff City's neighborhoods selling used appliances. Neither promised much income or fulfillment.

A music career seemed far more appealing. After all, music had coursed deeply through his childhood and beyond. Cash had always been around music; his mother's songs, gospel in the church, country on the radio. In the air force, he had bought his first guitar and kicked out wobbly tributes to Ernest Tubb, the Carter Family, and Jimmie Rodgers with a bunch of comrades dubbed the Landsberg Barbarians. In Memphis, he dawdled on his sales route to absorb the city's blues and sifted through records on Beale Street at the Home of the Blues record shop. After hours, he jammed with Luther Perkins and Marshall Grant, two mechanics at the Automobile Sales Company. The trio played a handful of gigs in the area as well as a radio spot on KWEM, across the Mississippi in West Memphis, Arkansas. They were only one among dozens of aspiring bands in the Memphis area but they were also one of the most determined to break out. At least John was, and that's why he showed up at Sun Records, the home of rockabilly sensation Elvis Presley.

Cash first told proprietor Sam Phillips about his gospel aspirations, but Phillips didn't need gospel: it didn't sell. Did he have anything else? He did: "Hey Porter," a song he had written in the air force that, with enough steam, could keep up with the rockabilly rhythm shooting out of the Sun studio. It would be the B side of Cash's first release. With Perkins and Grant, Cash recorded another of his compositions a short time later: "Cry, Cry, Cry." It took the A side. On both sides, John Cash became Johnny Cash, a ploy to woo the teens. Perkins and Grant became the Tennessee Two.

In September 1955, "Cry, Cry, Cry" lurched onto the local charts. Phillips probably met the news with little more than his familiar tempered grin, for to him Cash was little more than a groomsman to Elvis Presley. But on November 22, 1955, RCA-Victor signed Presley after dropping $35,000 in Phillips's lap. Fittingly, Cash and "Cry, Cry, Cry" broke out nationally four days later, and although the song vanished from *Billboard*'s country and western chart after one week, the time had come for Phillips to open the floodgates on Johnny Cash.

Sam nudged Johnny through the touring and promotion doors that Elvis had opened: introducing him to Bob Neal, Elvis's first manager, and pointing him south to the ArkLaTex, where he appeared on radio's *Louisiana Hayride* and *Big D Jamboree* and in the dance halls and schoolhouses of music-mad Texas. Sam's efforts paid dividends. Cash's two releases after "Cry, Cry, Cry"—"So Doggone Lonesome" and "Folsom Prison Blues"—each spent about twenty weeks on the national country and western charts. In 1956, "I Walk the Line"—Cash's fourth Sun hit—camped for six weeks at number one and crossed over to the pop charts.

Phillips apparently saw a new Elvis in Cash, particularly when labelmate Carl Perkins failed to follow up on the early 1956 smash "Blue Suede Shoes." But Elvis, with his brilliant voice and style, followed his pop sensitivities, singing of hound dogs, teddy bears, and teen angst. Cash—his voice decidedly varicose in comparison—tapped his rural roots for lyrical themes. The Arkansas well from which Cash drew inspiration during his Sun years produced constant allusions to trains ("Hey Porter," "One More Ride"), the rural life ("Country Boy," "Pickin' Time"), and sorrow of the kind well beyond boy-girl heartbreak ("Give My Love to Rose," "I Still Miss Someone"). Cash's was serious music, the product of battling life with bare hands.

It is those early battles and rural experiences that the *Reader* first considers.

Excerpt from *Winners Got Scars Too: The Life of Johnny Cash*

by Christopher S. Wren (1971)

Cash was born February 26, 1932, in a dying farm community near Kingland, Arkansas. In 1935, Cash's father Ray, a World War I vet, shepherded wife Carrie, daughters Reba and Louise, and sons Roy, Jack, and J. R. (Johnny's given name) out of Kingsland to a U.S. government–sponsored agricultural cooperative near Dyess. It was there that Cash grew up and first saw the rigors and rewards of Depression-era farm life.

This excerpt from chapter three of Christopher Wren's biography Winners Got Scars Too *chronicles the Cash family's existence post-Kingsland. Wren's biography—which the singer has praised as generally accurate—grew from a Cash profile that Wren wrote for* Look *magazine in the 1960s.*

THE Federal Emergency Relief Administration, created by Franklin Delano Roosevelt in 1933, had turned to alleviating the poverty thrust upon farmers by the Depression. Much assistance went directly to farm owners, but the neediest were those farmers who didn't own their own land. They were being forced out to join the swelling tribes of migrants.

The FERA tried to relocate the most deserving of these landless families on what became forty-six experimental resettlement projects. The first was in Mississippi County, Arkansas, where the federal government purchased sixteen thousand acres of uncleared swampland for six dollars an acre.

Mississippi County sits in the northeast corner of Arkansas, bounded on the north by Missouri and on the east, across the Mississippi River, by Tennessee. The county's wealth was its land—a rich, black Mississippi River loam that ran up to several hundred feet deep and was perfect for a lucrative cash crop like cotton. In fact after the Civil War, one gentleman landowner, relieved of his slaves by the Emancipation Proclamation, journeyed clear up to New York and hauled back seventy-five Irish immigrant girls to chop and pick his cotton on contract for $20 a month and board. He cajoled them with hearty meals, six shots of whisky a day, and a Catholic priest imported to hear confessions. Even with such overhead, he cleared $45,000 on his cotton crop. After the Irish girls tired and went back north, he recruited fifty-five German immigrants, and, later, eighteen coolies newly arrived from China.

But into the twentieth century, Mississippi County remained a pocket frontier where travelers used to lean out of the train windows and pot-shoot at rattlesnakes sunning themselves. Work and play were equally rough-hewn. One local paper, the *Osceola* (Arkansas) *Times*, attended a picnic of the 1870s: "After eats, gander pulling was engaged in. Mr. W. P. Hale succeeded in pulling in twain the gander's breathing apparatus, after which dancing was resumed . . . "

When the FERA purchased the sixteen thousand acres of alluvial delta loam in 1934, 90 percent of Mississippi County's cultivation was in cotton. The growing season, which ran nearly eight months, encouraged such a long-money crop. The government land, though, only fifteen miles from the Mississippi River, was still a near impenetrable jungle of undergrowth. Lumber companies had cruised the swamp land for cypress and oak, but the trees left uncut had grown to enormous size and a tangle of second growth made logging difficult.

The FERA decided to open the land to homesteaders, who would have to clear each twenty-acre holding before it could be cultivated.

Bankrolled by some $3 million in federal aid, the Arkansas ERA administrator, W. R. Dyess, created what was first termed Colonization Project Number One. Construction began on May 22, 1934. About two thousand men, taken from the state relief rolls, were brought into Mississippi County to build roads and houses. Tools and equipment arrived from Evadale Junction on a new railroad spur laid on ties from oak trees felled and trimmed along the right-of-way. Other trees were chopped down and dragged by logging mules to six improvised sawmills, to become rough lumber for houses and barns.

The new colony was laid out French-fashion like a wagon wheel, with a village at the core, and farms stretching out along sixteen expanding circles of roads. Skilled construction crews, drawing prime wages of up to five dollars a day, worked fast on the 502 farmhouses, with their adjacent barns, privies and hencoops. Ten men could throw together a five-room house in sixteen hours. Ditches—ninety miles of them—were dug to drain the land. The resulting fill went to surface sixty miles of elevated roads with clay and gravel. Such improvements were only rudimentary. The project's colonists were expected to do the rest themselves.

Once Dyess began recruiting the 500 families, he ran into a surfeit of desperate applicants. The ERA could afford to select the best. Interviewers, equipped with a formidable six-page application form, went into each Arkansas county to evaluate the volunteers.

At the courthouse in Rison, Arkansas, Ray Cash stood patiently in line and waited his turn for an interview.

He wasted no time pleading his case: "I told them I wanted to make a home for my family and myself." Afterwards, he told his family he didn't know if he'd been selected. The panel had demanded answers to questions about his birthplace and education, his family, his crop experience and other work skills, even about his military service. They forwarded his answers along with their recommendation for the final selection.

Whatever self-doubts Ray Cash might have had, his reputation as a go-getter had preceded him to the interview. The Cash family was one of the five picked from Cleveland County. A letter notified Ray Cash to ready his family on twenty-four hours' notice for the move north.

On March 23, 1935, a hired ton-and-a-half pickup truck appeared to haul the Cashes with what furniture they had to the new home. The ride wasn't free; Ray Cash had been told the moving cost would be tacked onto the price of his homestead.

"We took everything we had that we considered worthwhile, which frankly wasn't a lot," remembered [son] Roy. Carrie Cash, holding baby Reba, and Louise squeezed in the front seat with the driver. Ray Cash, with Roy, Jack and young John, huddled under the tarpaulin in the back.

The trip over 250 miles of muddy roads was cold and wet. A stinging rain froze on the windshield and the tarpaulin as the truck lurched and sloshed from one ice crusted mudhole to the next. John Cash was just three years old, but the long truck ride became his first memory as, peering out the back, he saw icicles cracking off the swaying trees along the route northward.

The roads were so bad that the journey could not be finished in a day. Near Marion, Arkansas, the truck pulled over for the night. The Cash family dozed until dawn as best they could.

The singular memory that the Cashes retain of the trip was its bitter cold. They left Kingsland at nine in the morning. Just after noon on the next day, they arrived at the colony. The truck took them out along Road Number Three to their homestead, Number 266, a little more than two miles north of town. The Cashes climbed stiffly down from the truck and, in the rain, admired their new $1,340 home.

"It was a brand-new house," recalled Ray Cash. "The paint buckets were still on the floor. It was painted white and trimmed in green outside. We had two large bedrooms, a living room, a kitchen, a dining room, and the front and back porches. It was a nicer house than any we had ever lived in."

The yard was underwater and, according to Carrie Cash, "that black mud would stick to your feet like glue." They could not get the truck into the yard to unload; the underbrush was too thick and the mud too deep. So the children were dispatched to forage for firewood, while Mrs. Cash took the baby inside.

Ray Cash was hell-bent to walk all around his new twenty acres before it got dark. Much of it had been hidden by the heavy rains. He pulled on a pair of heavy rubber boots and made his way through the thickets. He stepped into a stump hole and fell into icy water up to his chest, but the mishap didn't deter him. He walked back into the new house dripping wet and announced to his family, "We have some fine land." That night they slept on the floor. No one seemed to mind.

Down at the colony center, Ray Cash drew a subsistence advance of $253.59 to tide the family over until the first crops could be planted, harvested and sold. The living expenses had been calculated to the penny. The yearly cost of clothes for Ray Cash would be $14.60, for his wife $11.05, for a child the age of John $6.55. The currency that first year was "doodlum," a local scrip in five, ten, twenty-five and fifty cents denominations that could be exchanged at the center for food, clothing and groceries. A small amount of surplus clothes and food was also available, but the Cashes were expected to pay their advance back. The new colony did not run on charity.

Nor did Ray Cash own his twenty acres outright. Like all the other colonists, he was a "licensee," working on probation. Three years later, when he had transformed his holding from swamp to fertile cotton fields, he signed the final contract that became his deed to house and land. But once he began working the land, he felt that it was his. "It gave our entire family a new start. We'd always been sharecropping on other people's land. We felt more free. So many of our neighbors were in the same category as we were—not destitute, because we were never destitute, but needy. It was the first land we owned, and we felt ourselves equal with everybody.

"They put down on the books everything we was issued. We agreed to pay what we could—so much each year."

With spring, the water began to recede. Ray Cash set out with his son Roy, not yet fourteen, and they began at the highest ground they could find, and pushed out. They worked together with double-bit axes, with a two-man crosscut saw, and with a Kaiser blade. Once they had taken the timber down, they chopped it into firewood or burned it outright. Many of the stumps had to be burned or blasted out later with dynamite.

Because the twenty acres were infested with poisonous snakes, Ray Cash sometimes packed along a hoe. With it he beat back or killed the cottonmouth moccasins and large rattlesnakes that he stumbled into.

They had been issued a flop-eared mule, which Ray Cash named Joe. With a turning plow, they opened the soil for the first time. While the younger children shouldered the regular farm chores, father and oldest son left before sunup and returned exhausted long past sundown. Like the labor that had preceded it, the plowing was tedious and slow. The roots were so numerous that they would snarl the plow and either break off the point or, if the plow broke through, fly back and knock the plowman sprawling. "It was about as rough going as a feller'd want," remarked a Cash neighbor, "Goat" Rogers.

Still, the Cashes managed to clear and plant three acres the first year. Ray Cash put two acres in cotton and got a fine yield of three bales. The money—$50 a bale—went to pay back the government what he had borrowed. The third acre was put into food for the family and corn for the animals.

Carrie Cash had problems of her own setting up a household. The day she arrived, she stocked up the wood stove and set some white beans on to boil for supper. The beans turned green. Though safe for drinking, the water was iron-hard. "If you tried to cook or make tea, the water would be black as ink. Or you'd put soap in that water and it would curdle just like buttermilk. It would be gummy and you just couldn't use it."

Her husband fetched a few barrels and some ten pound bags of lime from the colony center. He put two barrels below the eaves to catch soft rainwater. The children were taught to fill a third fifty-gallon barrel from the well pump and slack the water with a cup of lime. The iron would settle with the lime to the sides and bottom and every week one of the children would scrape away the hard green ring of sediment that had stuck to the barrel. The resulting water was soft enough for cooking and washing.

A government home economist issued each farmwife a twenty-two-quart pressure cooker and showed how to can the summer vegetables for the coming winter. Carrie Cash learned fast. "We grew everything the land would produce that we could eat. I canned enough in summer to keep us through the winter. When the vegetables got low, we made soup with what was left. We didn't waste anything."

Through the next winter, when the rain and cold again took over, Ray Cash got a job constructing the last houses and barns. "He worked at anything and everything he could to make an honest day's pay," said his son Roy of those first years at the colony. "We were never hungry. There might be beans twice a day and bread and gravy for breakfast, but there was always plenty."

The colony center and back was a four-and-a-half mile trip. Ray Cash first built himself a mule-drawn sled, but several trips over the rough roads wore down the runners. So he fashioned a cart from the building lumber that had been left around his house. He found two old iron wheels and fastened them under the cart. The mule-drawn vehicle was serviceable, if noisy. It lasted for several years until the family could afford a regular wagon.

The mule was kept with a part-Jersey milk cow and some Poland China pigs in the barn. The Cashes also bought a large flock of laying hens. In 1936, about cotton-picking time, Ray Cash began losing his hens. When he checked the hencoop in the morning, he would find another hen had been taken. A trail of feathers led into a nearby thicket.

One day, as he was working a new cotton patch, he saw a large wildcat heading for the chickens. He ran the huge cat off. That night, he staked a hen out in the thicket. Around it he set four traps. The next morning before daylight, he went out with his .22 rifle and an oil lantern, to find he had snared the wildcat. He shot the cat and dragged it out. The animal weighed twenty-seven pounds on a cotton scale, and after Ray Cash had skinned it, the pelt was so large that three Cash youngsters could stretch out across the hide.

Ray Cash was proud of such a pelt. One day, while he worked out in the fields, a fast-talking salesman came by the house selling subscriptions to the *Kansas City Star.* Carrie Cash was a woman who loved reading, and she was hungry for news outside the colony. She had no money, but she struck a bargain with the salesman—the wildcat skin for a newspaper subscription. Her husband came home for supper to find that his trophy was gone and that henceforth they would be receiving the *Kansas City Star.* Ray Cash "didn't like it much." Carrie Cash was terribly pleased.

W. R. Dyess, ERA administrator of Arkansas, never saw his work in Mississippi Colony completed; he died in a plane crash on January 14, 1936. The following month, his Colonization Project Number

One was incorporated as the Dyess Colony. Eleanor Roosevelt, who was building her amazing reputation for surfacing in remote places, showed up for a formal visit on June 9. The project was a significant one for her husband's administration. Mrs. Roosevelt appeared in a limousine trailing dust, with four state troopers bouncing along on motorcycles. Despite the heat, virtually the entire colony turned out in its Sunday best. Mrs. Roosevelt shouted a short speech from the front porch of the white administration building, then gamely stepped down and shook her way through every outstretched hand in Dyess center. It took several hours. At last, she adjourned for supper at the Dyess café, which prided itself on its homemade pies. The colonists peered in through the windows as they discussed her handshaking feat—something they would reminisce about years later.

Other official big-wigs—among them Agriculture Secretary Henry A. Wallace and Presidential assistant Harry Hopkins—dropped in to inspect the colony and give pep talks to whatever colonists could be spared from the fields. Colonel Lawrence Westbrook, who as Hopkins' deputy ran the resettlement programs from Washington, predicted Dyess would become the most prosperous community in Arkansas. He assured its new residents:

"You may have to draw in your belt and do without some things you would like to have, but never again need you be assailed by the terrible fear that you and your family will have no roof over your heads, nor that stark hunger will overcome you. There is more real security here in the little homes that you live in than there is in the finest mansions in the most fashionable and arrogant residential sections of Memphis."

Johnny Cash, with some perspective, was later to quip of his boyhood at the Dyess Colony: "I grew up under socialism." Certainly the Dyess Colony, as a social instrument, was far ahead of its time. Many southern landowners professed to see in the new colony a threat to the sharecropper tradition that underpinned the agricultural economy of the South. For Dyess was envisioned as "one large community cooperative" of ex-sharecroppers, with its roots more in the cooperatives of Scandinavia than in anything from Arkansas. The Roosevelt administration knew how radical its experiment was. Colonel Westbrook was candid enough with the colonists.

"I wonder if I need to tell you that these things we are trying to do here are going to cause violent and bitter criticism from some quarters as we get under way. It is already so—some gentlemen already have said that this is a mad, socialistic scheme, doomed to failure from the start. . . . They say in effect that you are better citizens when you are so far in debt to them that you cannot even call your soul your own. . . . Now listen to me, some of these boys have already declared war on this idea. Why shouldn't they? They are the ones whose profits will be gone if this thing works. And if it works, they might even have to get behind a plow themselves, and they don't like to think about that."

What ensured the survival of the Dyess Colony in the frightened South of the 1930s was the one defect in the dream: though Mississippi County was 40 percent black, the colony existed for whites only. Yet as new an experiment as the Dyess Colony, in such a place and at such a time, couldn't have been formed differently without inviting its own destruction.

By now, the Cashes were old-timers. "We knew practically all the others in our part of the colony," remembered Ray Cash. "Lots of times, we'd all work together clearing land. We'd cut down the trees and have 'log rollings'—pile up the logs and burn them. The women would get together for projects like quilting or stuffing mattresses with ginned cotton.

"We made up our minds to make a home out of it when we moved there. Times were pretty rough, but we didn't get disheartened.

"The land we had worked near Kingsland was old land. It had been cultivated for years. The land we got in Dyess was full of roots and stumps, but it was very rich bottomland and it produced so much that we liked it."

The colony expanded. At the beginning of 1936, 139 families, the Cashes among them, had homesteaded. Another 354 moved in during the year, but sixty-six families, mostly hill people uncomfortable with flatland living, gave up and left. The farm families that remained were large ones, and the colony's population approached three thousand.

The community center took on the dimension of a farm town. Besides the store and café, it now had a service station and garage (though hardly any colonists owned a car or truck), harness shop, feedmill, blacksmith, printing shop, ice house, sorghum mill and cotton gin. A factory was set up to turn out furniture, and a canning factory put up garden produce.

With help from the state of Arkansas, the colonists started a library. By the end of 1936, Dyess even had a twenty-bed hospital, with two doctors and three nurses. Sometimes, five babies a day would be born there. Such news of births, deaths, crop yields and other goings-on ("Ray Cash was in Lepanto Saturday") appeared first monthly, then later every Friday, in the *Colony Herald*, a mimeographed newspaper.

The new land yielded enough food crops so that the colony administrators didn't have to purchase outside foodstuffs to tide the colonists over the coming winter, as was first expected. A two-day fair was held in the community center that September. By now, the colony had organized Boy Scouts, Girl Scouts and a Home Demonstration Club for the farm wives, whose get-togethers were detailed at length in the *Colony Herald*. The colonists boasted that their new 4-H Club, from the standpoint of membership, was the largest in the world. This was probably true, since nearly a thousand of the colonists were of school age. The social fabric of Dyess was taking shape.

Prosperity of a sort took over the colony as "doodlum" gave way to hard currency. Each family grew its own food, but staples traded briskly at the cooperative store: ten pounds of sugar for fifty-five cents, a quart of peanut butter for twenty-five cents, ten bars of soap for twenty-five cents, forty-eight pounds of Red Top flour for $1.85. Men's broadcloth shirts sold for seventy-nine cents, ladies' organdy dresses for ninety-five cents, and dressy Tom Sawyer suits for boys cost $1.25. Ladies who wanted to make their own could get "the latest New York patterns" for fifteen cents apiece.

The Dyess café served up a complete dinner for thirty-five cents, or a fancy Sunday chicken dinner for two, for seventy-five cents. A beauty salon working out of the back of the new barber shop offered customers a shampoo and finger-wave for a half-dollar.

"I remember riding to town in our two-wheeler car," says Johnny Cash. "We'd go to the store on Saturday. We had a shopping list—flour, tobacco, sugar, salt, coal oil, matches. We used doodlum, and with it I could get a nickel's worth of candy. The counter was on the right, and the sugar and stick candy were in big glass jars, but the man that ran the store would always give us more than a nickel's worth.

"They had a clothing section in the store. I had one good Tom Sawyer suit, but I usually wore denim jeans. I'd walk through the section looking at all the clothes. When you know you can't have things, you don't want for them. I always got something to eat when I was hungry and the rest didn't bother me."

The Cashes, like most of the other colonists, remained country-frugal. They hadn't forgotten the Depression years. In 1936 they made one concession. Carrie Cash wrote off to Sears Roebuck and bought the family an upright battery radio.

The year 1937 at the Dyess Colony began with a cold drizzle that turned into a downpour and wouldn't stop. It rained for twenty-one days and nights. Sometimes the rain would slack a little, and the water would freeze; then it would sleet, and as the day warmed, the rain would again take over.

The Cash family watched as the water rose in their front yard up to just under their porch. Three of the four front steps were submerged. What concerned Ray and Carrie Cash was not the condition of their yard, but the news on the big battery radio. The Mississippi River, barely contained behind levees some fifteen miles to the east, was up forty-nine feet. That was fifteen feet above flood level, and teams were working around the clock piling sandbags on the levees to contain the water. Ray Cash knew: "The Mississippi was full and it didn't have anywhere to go and then it froze over. When the Mississippi gets full, she's dangerous, I'll tell you."

The word spread through Dyess that if the Mississippi's levees broke, the colony would disappear under fifteen feet of water. Still, the rain kept falling. The Tennessee River, which fed into the Mississippi, was flooding, but the biggest worry was the wind, blowing hard out of the east. Unless the wind changed, the levees would collapse under the battering of wind and water.

Ray Cash's friend Frank Huff went out and put up a measuring stake at the community center. The water was at least three feet deep. Out at Ray Cash's, the water was even deeper. By mid-January, the colony officials decided that Dyess would have to be evacuated.

The colonists prepared to leave. The families nearer town were loaded with their possessions into boxcars and hauled out by freight to Wilson, where they could be transferred to waiting passenger trains. The rest, like the Cashes, were to be taken out by whatever trucks and buses could be requisitioned. On January 18, Ray Cash said good-bye to his wife and four of his children. He decided to stay with his land as long as he could. His oldest son Roy stayed with him. They carried the children—Louise, Jack, John, and Reba—piggyback from their homemade boat to the waiting bus. Ray Cash passed up their things to his wife and watched the bus with his family churn down the road. The way from Dyess to Wilson, which was under water, was staked out with markers so that the bus would not topple off the road. Several small bridges were floating. The dozen miles to Wilson seemed to last forever.

Many families with no place to go were taken to Camp Pike in Little Rock, to be crowded together in army tents and fed in soup lines. Carrie Cash decided instead to push on down to her people in Kingsland. Her husband told her he would try to join her there if he could.

Young John R. Cash—family had nicknamed him "Shoo-doo"—was five weeks shy of his fifth birthday, but his recollection of the trip is indelible:

"It was late at night, and everybody on the train was sleeping. My mother, I remember, had dressed me in my new suit. I kept running up and down the aisles.

"Down near Stuttgart, Arkansas, we weren't moving over five miles an hour, because the water was clear over the tracks. They were afraid they might hit a big log across the tracks if they went faster. I remember a lot of the women and children were crying because they were so worried and upset."

The flood of 1937 was to become the earliest experience that Johnny Cash as a singer would reach back to in one of his autobiographical songs:

How high is the water, Mama? Five feet high and rising.
How high is the water, Papa? She said it's five feet high and rising. . . .

Father and son back at the flooded farm began to prepare their home in case the levees broke. They propped the front and back doors open, so when the water flowed in, it would carry the mud out again. They fetched the chickens in from the henhouse and stuck them in the living room. They propped open the corn crib in the barn so that the pregnant Poland China sow could eat.

The family dog, a large brown rabbit hound, was left in the house. Ray Cash, not knowing when he'd be back, took a precious fifty-pound ham and cut it into chunks on the floor for the dog. Other farm dogs abandoned by their owners were already collecting into wild packs and, starving, would eventually turn on each other.

Finally, on January 24, Ray and Roy Cash dragged the cow and mule from the barn and, with a last look back at their home, sloshed two and a quarter miles through water to the big mule barn in Dyess center, where the colonists' stock was being collected. Then, with the last of the other farmers, they caught a ride over to Wilson. Only one family refused to evacuate. As the men left, boatloads of armed deputies sent by the State of Arkansas floated in to patrol the colony against looting. A week after saying good-bye, Ray Cash and his son joined their family in Kingsland.

On the Mississippi, the wind from the east shifted and the levees held. The exhausted sandbag crews relaxed. The rains stopped and the water began to recede. The Cashes loaded on the train bound north to Dyess. On February 16, nearly a month after they had left, they arrived home.

Most of the land was again dry, but there was still enough to worry over. The dog packs were running wild. Cottonmouth moccasins and rattlesnakes had slithered to high ground and, sluggish from the cold, had collected into balls in the houses and barns. Ray Cash had to beat a good two dozen cottonmouth moccasins off the barn rafters. But he also found that his brood sow in the barn had given birth to "five of the prettiest spotted Poland China pigs you ever saw."

The chickens in the house had laid eggs all over the living room sofa. The children collected the eggs and carried the chickens back to the coop. The flood had done little but dirty the house, and the family began cleaning up. Because of Ray Cash's precautions, they had lost nothing.

Other families were hit harder. Some colonists caught pneumonia or flu; at least one died. Families, their homes full of mud, had nothing to eat, and the colony officials appealed to the Red Cross for help. The administration paid out $11,262 in transportation alone to evacuate the residents, as well as $7,407 to feed the temporary refugees and still more outlays for medical supplies, emergency clothing, even lumber for makeshift boats. The flood of 1937 sunk the colony $47,095 in debt.

Ray Cash dragged the driftwood off his cotton fields. The heavy silt dumped by the water only left his soil richer. He planted eight acres in cotton the following month. The next year, the Cash family picked the best crop they would ever have—two bales of cotton to the acre and a large crop of soybeans and corn.

On February 5, 1938, Ray Cash was at last given ownership of his twenty-acre farm. The property had been valued originally at $2,684.90, but he had put such work into it—by 1938 he had completely cleared and planted the land—that the purchase price was depreciated to $2,183.60. It was a considerable sum for a poor Arkansas farmer, but it was converted to a mortgage which he could pay off at $111.41, or 6 percent, a year. The Cashes would plant, chop and harvest eighteen crops on their Dyess farm.

With the deed to his farm, Ray Cash got a share in the Dyess Colony cooperative. The seed was bought and the cotton ginned and sold through the cooperative, to keep up quality and give the farmer the best profit. Ray Cash earned enough to discard his rattling cart with the iron wheels for a real Shay farm wagon which he used to haul his crops. There was even money left for his wife to locate a second-hand upright piano for thirty-seven dollars and install it in the living room.

The colony had recovered from the 1937 flood and, the following year, there were 637 homesteads. Now Dyess had a post office and a drug store and later on a movie theater that was open Saturday afternoons and evenings and a bank. Ray Cash went down and deposited twenty-five dollars in the bank and thought he'd "really done something." Money was scant enough in the colony that the bank folded shortly thereafter. But Roy Cash, then fifteen, and a friend managed to wrest away a .32 revolver one morning from another teenager who had planned to hold up the bank and use the loot to run away from Dyess. Not knowing what to do with the pistol, they went over to the local library and surrendered it to Mrs. Holland, the librarian.

Trouble in Dyess Colony was sufficiently rare as to be gossiped over for years afterwards. Two idlers matching half-dollars on the café porch one rainy day exchanged some heated words. One went for his jackknife. The other began hitting him so hard and fast that he never got it open. Jimmy Bass and Sam Richards, the sheriff's deputies, broke up the fight before anyone was really hurt.

A year later, the man with the knife (who had become known around Dyess as something of a bully) got into a car accident and tried to batter the other man with a hammer. His opponent pulled a jackknife and cut him up so badly that a bystander recalls, "he like to killed him with it." Still, Dyess was a quiet place. Brawls were more frequent up at the beer joint in what was the old center three miles north of town, and now conveniently off colony property.

Troublemakers didn't last long, for the colony took its work seriously. "Some of them—pretty trashy stuff—didn't make it and were asked to leave," says Ray Cash. "And some came and decided they didn't like it and left when times got better."

The suffusion of old-time virtues, drilled into Johnny Cash as he grew up, was essential to the welfare of the colony. Industriousness, thrift, honesty, religious zeal so flourished that they were bound to constrict, breeding within Cash a latent restlessness that would erupt into rebellion years later.

By the end of 1939 Dyess had dropped back to about 400 families. Those who stayed sunk roots. Some of the colonists joined together and built their own churches—Baptist and Methodist—in the community center and invited in pastors. The two churches provided a popular family meeting place. The Cashes, whom neighbors knew as "good Christian people," joined the Baptist church, which met regularly on Sunday morning, Sunday night and Wednesday night.

In 1939, the Dyess Colony became trapped in a political feud between Floyd Sharp, the colony's president, who now ran the state Works Progress Administration, and Arkansas' governor, Carl E. Bailey. The colony was then under the WPA, which had assumed responsibility for its corporate shares. Governor Bailey issued a proclamation revoking the Dyess Colony's charter on the pretext that the colony hadn't paid a corporate franchise tax of eleven dollars. The federal government stepped in and, with a bureaucratic sleight-of-hand, removed the colony from the WPA and gave it to the Farm Security Administration. The colony was incorporated anew in December 1939 as the Dyess Farms, not that any of the residents seemed to notice or care. For years afterwards, they still called their home the Dyess Colony.

It's called just Dyess now, a desiccated little cotton town that seems as eternal as the vast, flat bottomland that surrounds it. The ramshackle two-story building from which the colony's affairs were once administered has been cut up into apartments. The café and movie theater closed long ago. Dyess has progressed, of course. It has about forty street lights, paid for with the five-dollar blue and gold windshield stickers on the cars haphazardly parked around the weathered Dyess monument. When Dyess was finally incorporated as a town in

1964, its population had dwindled to 409. It may be 500 now—not much more.

The Dyess Colony was a brave, even outrageous experiment in the Depression years, but a stopgap nonetheless, and it carried within it the seeds of its eventual demise. Once unshackled from a cycle of rural poverty, a colonist learned to expect better than the sharecropper's lot. His children were educated to hope, but could not find room for their ambitions within the physical and emotional confines of the colony. Johnny Cash himself would inevitably have to push out to find a fuller life.

"When we grew up," remarks Cash, "it was second nature that we wouldn't live in Dyess when we were grown. It was the aim of every person to get a better job. But if I hadn't grown up there, I wouldn't be what I am now. It was the foundation for what I became." . . .

"Fork in the Road" from *Man in Black*

by Johnny Cash (1975)

Dyess proved to young J. R. and his family that hope and faith could lead to greener grass or, in the Cashes' case, thicker cotton. Hope that one's world could improve, that life could be better, continued to drive Cash long after he left the family farm. But it was in Dyess that Cash first saw hope and faith in God conquer life's hardships. The Mississippi River flood of 1937, for example, branded Cash's psyche: informing him of the power of nature and the reality that to survive man must sometimes press on with only faith in his back pocket. That faith, he saw, helped the family overcome the flood's scourge. Later, faith would sustain him during the difficult years that accompanied his fame.

The death of his brother Jack was similarly demonstrative of faith's potency—and immensely meaningful to Cash. "Jack and I were close," Cash told Dotson Rader of Parade Magazine *in 1995. "When he died, I was 12, he was 14. I was really skinny and weak, and he was my big, strong protector. Maybe I idolized him too much. He became my life."*

Although reconciled in faith that Jack had gone on to glory, Cash was nonetheless haunted by his brother's death. Guilt and anger became a more acute part of Cash's range of emotions. As Cash tells it, he felt that he had not tried hard enough to divert Jack from going to the job where he was mortally injured. One might point to Cash's loss and the accompanying torment to understand the recklessness, inattention to relationships, and lack of self-esteem that characterized aspects of his adult life.

Writers have told the story of Jack's end over and over. Here we see Johnny Cash's own version as told in chapter four of his first autobiography, published in 1975. Readers should note that in 1995 Cash revealed to writer Nick Tosches that he believed Jack was murdered (see page 233). This statement, both confounding and unproved, ran counter to anything he had said elsewhere on the matter. Perhaps further scrutiny will uncover the truth.

I HAVE no opinion on premonitions. There are those who say they experience, from time to time, the feeling that "something's going to happen." What that sensation is, I really don't know. But I think my brother Jack did.

On May 12, 1944, a Saturday morning, Jack was going to work at the school workshop. I was going fishing in one of the larger drainage ditches that ran through Dyess, a ditch which was more like a river. I had asked Jack to go with me.

It was hard times. The family financial situation was bad. Jack was making three dollars for a Saturday's work at the workshop cutting fence posts and cleaning up the bushes and the weeds around the agriculture shop. Daddy was plowing in the cotton fields from sunup to sundown, six days a week.

Before we left home that morning, I remember Jack stood in the middle of the living room floor with his hands on a kitchen chair and spun it around and around and around. I was out on the front porch waiting for him with my fishing pole and crayfish bait I'd raked out of the ditch. I kept calling inside, "Why don't you come go fishing with me?"

It was a beautiful, warm May morning in Arkansas. The lush black dirt was growing not only good cotton we would be hoeing, plowing, and picking, but a few watermelons we might sell out at the mailbox to make enough money to go to the movies on Saturday night.

Jack and I had been to the movies together many times at the Dyess Theater which then was at the school theater. Often Jack and I had roasted peanuts and taken them to the theater, hoping to sell enough to the people going in so that we might go in, too. Sometimes we did, and sometimes we didn't.

But this morning I wanted Jack to go fishing with me.

"No, I've got to go to work today because three dollars will help a lot," he answered, spinning the chair.

I said, "Well, why don't you come on then, and I'll walk part of the way with you? It's a mile before I turn off for where I'm going fishing."

And he said, "I don't know. I just don't feel like I should go to work today."

"Well why don't you go fishing with me then?"

"Because I need to make that three dollars."

Mama interrupted. "Why don't you feel like you should go, son?"

He said, "Well, I feel like something is going to happen, and I don't know what it is."

And she said, "Then please don't go."

"Mama, I've gotta go," he said. "We need the money I can make."

He started out the door, but turned around and went back into the room. He took that chair again and spun it around like a top. Killing time. Fooling around. I knew we were late if he was going to work, and I was anxious to get going myself. But he kept on killing time.

He put the chair down and walked back through the house, then into his bedroom. He sat down and read his Bible. A moment later he came back into the living room, grabbed the chair, and started kidding with me.

At the time, Warner Brothers' cartoons were very popular. He started imitating Bugs Bunny while he spun that chair around, saying "What's up, doc? What's up, doc?

I kept trying to get him out of the house. "Come on and let's go fishing."

He finally did leave with me, and for the entire mile we walked together, I kept begging him not to go to work but to come on fishing. I had the feeling something wasn't right, too, because it was a forced kind of thing he was doing—the imitation of all the cartoon characters. It wasn't like Jack to clown around. I'd never seen him like that before in my life.

So I kept after him. "Jack, why don't you please go fishing with me?"

He'd say, "What's up, doc?"

We got to the fork in the road where I had to turn off. I went left, and he walked straight ahead toward the school. As long as I could see him, which was for about half a mile, he was yelling at me imitating Bugs Bunny and Porky Pig, waving his hands. When he got to where we couldn't hear each other, he still was walking backwards down the road waving his arms at me.

I don't think I got even one bite that day. About noon I came back from the ditch, walking up the road with my fishing pole in my hand. It was hot and humid. Heading for home, I reached the place where I had left Jack about two hours earlier. And coming down the road in an A-model Ford came our preacher and my daddy. When I saw Daddy, I knew something was wrong. The preacher pulled over and stopped the car.

"Throw away your fishing pole and get in," Daddy said.

I didn't even ask what was the matter, but I knew it concerned Jack, for they were coming from town.

Finally my daddy managed to say, "Jack's been hurt awfully bad."

The preacher never said a word. And I didn't ask another question. I knew it was terrible. I'd never seen Daddy like that.

We stopped at the house, got out of the car, and daddy took a brown paper sack—it was soaked in blood—out of the back seat and said, "Come out to the smokehouse, J.R. I want to show you."

We went out back. I still hadn't said a word, and he didn't say anything else. He took Jack's pants and shirt and laid them on the floor of the smokehouse.

I remember the smell of hickory smoke out there that day. We smoked and sometimes sugar-cured the hams, bacon, and pork shoulders from hogs we'd kill in the winter. Just a little pile of hickory chips smoldering in a pan for a few days in the smokehouse and the bacon would be hickory-flavored.

Dad laid my brother's khaki pants out on the floor with his belt and khaki shirt and a pair of brown shoes. The pants and shirt were cut from the bottom of the rib cage down to the pelvis, and the belt was sliced in two.

"He was cutting fence posts, and one got tangled up in the swinging saw and pulled him into it—jerked him in. He fell across the big table saw."

It was the first time and the only time I've ever seen my daddy cry. "We're gonna lose him, J.R.," he said.

I remember stumbling out of the smokehouse, weak and trembling. I sank down on the woodpile; I couldn't stand. I knew Jack would die.

The preacher took us back down to Dyess Center but I don't remember anything he said. I'm sure he must have tried to give some word of consolation, but there was nothing that could have been said at that particular time.

There was a well-equipped, thirty-two-bed hospital in town with a fine doctor named Dr. Hollingsworth. He had a little gray at his temples, wore rimless glasses, and hummed all the time. The thing I remember most about Dr. Hollingsworth was the way he hummed. He didn't hum anything in particular; he just hummed.

The preacher stopped the A-model Ford in front of the hospital, and my daddy said, "I know you won't be able to see him or talk with him now because he's still unconscious."

The doctor estimated it would be a six-to-eight-hour operation with all there was to do—if Jack stayed alive that long. The internal damage was beyond repair. When the surgery was over, Dr. Hollingsworth told us, "Well, I just have to give it to you straight. There's no chance for him. None whatsoever."

He didn't expect Jack to live through the day. But the next morning Jack was alive and feeling better. Though there was a little rise of hope, everybody knew it was a false hope.

We all went to Sunday church the next morning. It seemed like an eternity had passed since noon the day before. Everybody in the family had been up all night.

Word had gone out to my brother Roy to come home, and to my sister Louise who was living at Osceola, Arkansas, at the time. They were told that Jack couldn't last.

The church had a special prayer for Jack, and the place was packed. Many who'd never been were there that day. Even Mr. Steele was there. All those people Jack had delivered papers to had loved him so, and they knew it was his church. What the service was all about that day was prayer for Jack Cash.

I had gone into his hospital room before church that morning and tried to talk to him. But that joking Jack I'd left at the fork in the road the morning before was nowhere in sight. He didn't even look at me when I walked in. And as the years went by, that was one thing I never could understand—why Jack didn't look at me, and why he didn't have anything to say to me that Sunday morning in his hospital room. He was sitting there talking to my mother, and I don't remember anything they said except my mama showed me his hands and said, "They worked so hard on the operation on his stomach that they've neglected to bandage up his fingers, and two of his fingers were badly cut." Mama had just bandaged them herself.

Jack was wide awake and apparently wasn't feeling any pain. I didn't know it then, but they had him on morphine.

That was one of the two times I remember Jack being conscious during the next week. The other time was later on in the week when I went into his room. I think it was Wednesday. He was reading a letter from Mrs. Williams, a schoolteacher who had been at Dyess and later left there. He also had a letter from a girl he had been "going steady" with. Those two were talking like they were twenty-one years old. I mean, he was going to be a preacher, and she wanted to be a preacher's wife. They were both so sure. She was strong in her faith like he was and was trying to encourage him and was reminding him that if he had to go, he was a child of God and everything was going to be all right. But Jack seemed not the least bit concerned about his own condition.

He still didn't have anything to say to me. He knew he didn't need to. It was like he was saying by *not* talking to me, "There's no need telling you about what's going to happen because you know I'm going. Anytime now you're going to learn to live without me, so start learning now."

At Wednesday night prayer meeting—a special prayer meeting for Jack called by a Baptist preacher who lived down on Road Fifteen—the whole community turned out again for special prayer. His condition had wavered—it had gone up and down. He had times when he felt strong, and mama said he'd lie in bed and laugh about things that had happened in the past. Then he'd have times when he'd lapse into a coma.

Saturday night the doctor told us that Jack had blood poisoning. Gangrene had set in and Dr. Hollingsworth said Jack could go any hour. So the family gathered around his bed, and I remember there was a lot of crying and a lot of praying. Jack was still in a coma. He didn't know any of us were there.

Along about midnight he started hallucinating and talking to my daddy. He mentioned the crops and the fields of cotton and that we had to get the weeds out of the cotton. "If it keeps on raining, we won't get back in the fields, daddy. We must get the crab grass out if we're gonna raise any cotton this year, if we're gonna have anything this winter."

And then he'd lapse back into a coma for awhile, then go back into hallucinating. He'd be plowing with the mules and yelling at them. They were plowing up the cotton. He'd shout, "Open the gate! Open the gate!" And then he'd be quiet for awhile.

At about 4:00 Sunday morning I went into an empty room there in the hospital to go to sleep. At 6:00 I heard somebody praying, and it woke me up. It was my daddy on his knees at the bed across the room from me, praying and asking God for the life of his son. I knew the time had come. I could hear it in my daddy's prayer.

I sat up on the side of the bed and I think it was the first time my daddy realized I was in the room. "J. R.," he said, "you better come on in Jack's room. He's dying."

I went in there, and my mother was sitting on his bed holding his hand. Dr. Hollingsworth wasn't humming. This unemotional doctor, who had seen hundreds of people come and go, was kneeling on the floor beside the bed, praying, "Lord, I've done everything a doctor can do. Only you, the Great Physician, can save him. It's out of my hands."

Jack's stomach was horribly swollen. He was laid back on his pillow, his face gray and ashen, and he was gasping for breath.

I remember standing in line to tell him good-by. He was still unconscious. I bent over his bed and put my cheek against his and said, "Good-bye, Jack." That's all I could get out.

My mother and daddy were on their knees.

At 6:30 A.M. he woke up. He opened his eyes and looked around and said, "Why is everybody crying over me? Mama, don't cry over me. Did you see the river?"

And she said, "No, I didn't, son."

"Well, I thought I was going toward the fire, but I'm headed in the other direction now, mama. I was going down a river, and there was fire on one side and heaven on the other. I was crying, 'God, I'm supposed to go to heaven. Don't you remember? Don't take me to the fire.' All of a sudden I turned, and now, mama, can you hear the angels singing?"

She said, "No, son, I can't hear it."

And he squeezed her hand and shook her arm, saying, "But mama, you've got to hear it." Tears started rolling off his cheeks and he said, "Mama, listen to the angels. I'm going there, mama."

We listened with astonishment.

"What a beautiful city," he said. "And the angels singing. Oh, mama, I wish you could hear the angels singing."

Those were his last words. And he died.

It was like a burden had been lifted from all of us, and it wasn't just the eight-day burden of fighting for Jack's life. Rather, we watched him die in such bliss and glory that it was like we were almost happy because of the way we saw him go. We saw in our mind's eye what he was seeing—a vision of heaven.

Jack's body was brought home to rest in our living room for Monday and Tuesday until the funeral. There were prayer meetings from time to time during the two days, and people knelt by his casket. I recall people thanking God for the influence Jack's life had brought into their lives. Somebody from over on Road Fourteen, someone we'd never seen but Jack had known, came by. Jack had delivered their papers and always had a good word for them, like, "Hope the Lord lets it rain so your cotton will grow."

At his funeral the sermon was John 14, which is preached at many funerals. Of course it has special meaning for me every time I hear it.

> Let not your heart be troubled: ye believe in God, believe also in me. In my Father's house are many mansions: if it were not so, I would have told you. I go to prepare a place for you. And if I go and prepare a place for you, I will come again, and receive you unto myself; that where I am, there ye may be also. (1–3)

Then the songs began, like "I Am Bound for the Promised Land" and "Shall We Gather at the River."

The memory of Jack's death, his vision of heaven, the effect his life had on the lives of others, and the image of Christ he projected have been more of an inspiration to me, I suppose, than anything else that has ever come to me through any man.

"Johnny Cash: The Sun Sound"

by Hank Davis (1985)

The connection between Cash's music and aspects of his boyhood was undeniable during the Sun years. Early releases such as "Folsom Prison Blues," "Big River," and "Give My Love to Rose" communicated pain far more profound than that of most country songs, which sniffed about nothing more serious than broken barroom romances. Cash's was the stuff of unadulterated tragedy brought on by death, disaster, or loss of freedom. It harked back to the dark songs and themes of Vernon Dalhart and Jimmie Rodgers and contrasted sharply with the "Why don't you love me anymore?" verse of many Cash contemporaries.

And Cash's voice augmented his lyrics. Anchored by the "boom-chicka-boom" rhythm of the Tennessee Two, it was a desperate and mysterious bass baritone, and although it ran in the vein of country pioneers Rodgers, Ernest Tubb, and Hank Williams, it expressed an authority and seriousness rarely if ever heard in country music.

In the following article, which first appeared in Goldmine, *Hank Davis, who has written extensively on Sun and Sun artists, dissects the musical engine that produced the Johnny Cash sound. He demonstrates that the sound is best understood by analyzing its hodgepodge components: Johnny's guitar and voice, Luther Perkins's electric guitar, and Marshall Grant's bass. Cash and his Tennessee Two did not produce technically perfect music, Davis writes, but they did uncork an effect uniquely their own.*

According to label owner Sam Phillips, when Johnny Cash arrived for his audition at Sun Records, the first thing he did was apologize for his band. From a technically purist point of view, Cash had a lot of reason to apologize. But far more importantly, as Sam Phillips knew almost immediately, Cash and his band produced a very special, totally unique sound. It epitomized the sparse productions Sun specialized in during its golden years and it presented the best of Sun's primitive recording technique.

The sound of Johnny Cash's early Sun records has some precedent, although it is essentially a unique development in the history of country music. Historically, there are traces of Cash's sound in the recordings of Jimmie Skinner and Ernest Tubb. Both men were limited but effective vocalists who were confined by nature to the baritone range. Their recordings, especially those of Jimmie Skinner, often featured very limited instrumental support. There is also a similarity between Cash's early Sun sound and the muted electric guitar sound behind Hank Williams' recordings. The difference is that Williams also worked with a fiddle and steel guitar. His rhythm section, featuring Zeb Turner's muted guitar, was simply there for support. In Cash's case it was everything.

If one shines the severest critical light on each of the elements of Cash's early Sun records, they appear woefully inadequate and barely survive scrutiny. Marshall Grant played a competent string bass and Cash's rhythm guitar was adequate. That's the good news. The rest of the story is that Luther Perkins was a remarkably limited musician. The term "lead guitarist" doesn't really fit. But if Perkins' playing was limited, it met its match in Cash's singing. Cash's voice was deep and lonesome sounding, but it's hard to find a more restricted range in any singer of Cash's stature.

So much for each of the elements. Fortunately, if ever there was a case of the whole being greater than the sum of the parts it's Johnny

Cash and the Tennessee Two. Together they produced an utterly compelling, often spectacular and innovative country sound. Of course, it didn't hurt that Cash wrote some of the finest country material of his day; songs that were uniquely geared to his own vocal style and range.

It also didn't hurt that Phillips' use of tape delay or "slapback" echo was nowhere better suited than on Cash's records. His stark baritone became even more lonesome sounding when fed through Sun echo. The "chigga-ching chigga-ching" rhythm that Cash made famous (and vice versa) became even more "sticky" and impenetrable when fed through slapback echo. Sam Phillips used Sun echo to "fatten up" the limited instrumentation on Cash's records as he had on records by Elvis Presley and Jerry Lee Lewis.

Phillips also had Cash insert a piece of paper between the strings on the neck of his guitar. When Cash strummed it simulated the sound produced by brushes on a snare drum. Finally, to his credit, Phillips never considered fleshing out Cash's sound with fiddle or steel guitar. As he later mused, "Can you hear 'I Walk The Line' with a steel guitar added to it?"

Like Presley's work at Sun, Cash's records are the artistic high point of his career. Each was dramatic, unpretentious and unadorned. Not a bad side in the six releases. What followed was often good as well. But the stark and lonesome side of Cash, so clearly present on both sides of his first six records, was often reserved for the flipsides of later releases ("Big River," "Come In Stranger").

Through it all, Luther Perkins never made any bones about the limitations of his playing. His solos were so constrained that they seemed to be an extension of Cash's vocals. Ernest Tubb once explained his own popularity by pointing to the limits of his voice. "Any guy sitting in a bar who heard my voice on a jukebox could say 'I can sing that good.'" If that logic has any merit, it certainly applied to

Luther Perkins' playing as well. How many guitarists did Luther Perkins inspire? It was instant gratification. Even a slow learner could play like Luther in a matter of weeks, if not days or minutes. Merle Haggard recalls being an inmate at San Quentin when Johnny Cash gave a concert in January 1958. "There were about 40 guys in the joint who played guitar and the day after the show every one of them was trying to pick like Luther."

Perhaps Luther's most famous work came early in his career. His solo on "Folsom Prison Blues" is one of the few times Luther ventured off the bass strings. It remains totally memorable and, in the ultimate gesture of respect, is often repeated note for note by technically superior musicians.

At some point, Sun (largely in the person of Jack Clement) felt it was necessary to augment Cash's sound. The first step was the addition of a drum. This was arguably excess baggage since it's hard to imagine a tighter, fuller rhythm section than on Cash's early recordings. In fact, the entire band was nothing more than a rhythm section on these records. But this change crept in, to the extent that Cash eventually began using drummer W. S. Holland on his personal appearances as well. Thus, the Tennessee Two grew to become the Tennessee Three.

But drums were the least of the change. Soon came the piano and choral embellishment. Clearly, producer Jack Clement was influenced by country-pop hits such as "Gone," "White Sport Coat" and "Young Love." He realized that his boy Cash could do as well given the right sound and material. And he proceeded to provide both.

On "Guess Things Happen That Way," Luther's simple bass note runs between chords were overdubbed with a bass singer singing the same notes in unison with Luther! At least you could still hear Luther's playing. Eventually, records like "Down The Street To 301" and "You're The Nearest Thing To Heaven" were awash with choral embellishment. Sadly, they bore little similarity to the stark simplicity of Cash's earliest recordings like "Train of Love."

As the liner notes to Cash's second Sun LP tellingly noted, "Almost reluctantly, Johnny evolved a pop-country style in arrangement and instrumentation to supply the demand for Cash records by fans of both types of music." Just how "reluctant" Johnny Cash was is anybody's guess, but it is worth noting that Cash's music returned to vintage form as soon as he switched label allegiance to Columbia in 1958 and regained artistic freedom. This marked one of the few times that Sun competed directly with a major label and offered the less affecting, more highly produced product.

"Johnny Cash Achieves 'Life's Ambition,' Wins Opry Hearts"

by Ben A. Green (1956)

❋ ❋ ❋

"It Looks as if Elvis Has a Rival—from Arkansas"

by Ralph J. Gleason (1956)

❋ ❋ ❋

"Gleason Signs Cash for 10 Guest Spots"

by Robert Johnson (1957)

The following three articles spotlight Cash in his first two years of country stardom: 1956 and 1957. His name stretched across the banners of country music's most heralded broadcasts—the Louisiana Hayride *and, later, the* Grand Ole Opry*—and soon he would appear on the national television stages of Ed Sullivan, Jackie Gleason, and Dick Clark. By 1958, he would move his family from Memphis to Los Angeles to further immerse himself in the media outlets—movies and TV, primarily—that could amplify his name and music.*

In the era of Cash's initial ascent, publicists and their press releases drove music journalism, even more so than today. The result was often fawning, uncritical articles, such as the following three. The pampering of Cash notwithstanding, these articles do have the merit of speaking to us from the beginning of the Cash phenomenon. The coverage—particularly that of the established music writer and cofounder of Rolling Stone *Ralph J. Gleason, which appeared in the* San Francisco Chronicle, *and of Memphis reporter Robert Johnson—confirms the buzz that encircled Cash during these times.*

Perhaps the most intriguing article of this trio is Ben Green's, which appeared on July 16, 1956, in the Nashville Banner. *The piece memorialized Cash's first appearance on the* Grand Ole Opry, *but far more interesting is its illustration of the Nashville establishment's eagerness to lock Cash in a stable away from Elvis and rock and roll. It wanted to take the Memphis out of the boy. Undoubtedly, the radio show, which debuted on WSM in 1927 and later enjoyed an NBC network hookup, could amplify Cash's performances like no other country music radio show, but, despite its power, Cash never cozied to it. Later, it would become clear that Cash resented the* Opry, *a resentment still burning in a 1992 conversation with Steve Pond of* Rolling Stone *about his first appearance: "A lotta people supported me coming to Nashville: Ernest Tubb, Hank Snow, Minnie Pearl. . . . And then there were some who would make it a point to let me hear the remarks they were saying as I walked by. It was the same thing they were calling Elvis: 'white nigger.' And you know, when I left that night, I said: 'I don't wanna go back to this place anymore. I don't have to put up with this crap.'" Of course, Johnny would return, even joining the* Opry *cast in 1957, but it was clear that there was little that Nashville and its* Grand Ole Opry *could do for him that the music and media industry outside Nashville hadn't done already.*

I

"Johnny Cash Achieves 'Life's Ambition,' Wins Opry Hearts"

by Ben A. Green (1956)

TENSION gripped the big Ryman Auditorium stage as young Johnny Cash stepped forward to "achieve his life's ambition" and sing on the Grand Ole Opry.

You could feel the charged atmosphere—some folks in the wings held their breath. All the Opry people were pulling for this newest member of their family to score big with those 3,800 folks looking on and folks listening to the network show from coast to coast.

Minnie Pearl put it into words: "Look at that handsome Johnny. He's scared to death. Wish I could get stage fright again. You do better when you have it, but I got over that after the first five years." Then she broke the tension with: "If I was 30 years younger and 30 pounds lighter, we'd be courtin' tonight." (Later she said the same thing to the audience.)

Carl Smith, veteran Opry star and emcee, swept into his introduction, calling Johnny "the brightest rising star in country music of America." (A proved fact, incidentally.) The crowd applauded experimentally, then Johnny began to sing.

He had a quiver in his voice, but it wasn't stage fright. The haunting words of "I Walk The Line" began to swell through the building. And a veritable tornado of applause rolled back. The boy had struck home, where the heart is, with his song that is No. 2 in the nation today.

As his last words filtered into the farthermost corners, many in the crowd were on their feet, cheering and clapping. They too had taken a new member into the family.

One of America's foremost authorities on country music told us:

"He'll be every bit as good as Elvis Presley. Probably better, and he'll last a whole lot longer. He has sincerity, he has bombast, he has tone, and he carries to the rafters, the top row hears him.

"He'll be better than Presley because Johnny's a true country singer, and Presley isn't and never has been. Presley's a rock and roller and has sung only once at the Opry and that time as a visitor."

Johnny Cash, just 11 months on stage, is one of the youngest stars ever to reach a Grand Ole Opry feature role on a network show. What was his reaction?

"I am grateful, happy and humble," he said. "It's the ambition of every hillbilly singer to reach the Opry in his lifetime. It's the top for us. I feel mighty lucky to be here tonight . . . and I thank everyone, especially those fine Opry stars who recommended me to the officials in charge. The crowd was mighty kind . . . all of them, the nicest kind of folks."

Bob Neal, president of Stars, Inc., . . . and manager of Johnny Cash was equally grateful.

"Naturally we are proud of Johnny's wonderful success in such a short time," added Neal. "He is a fine character, a devoted husband, and father of two of the most beautiful little girls you could want to meet. All of us at Stars, Inc., are grateful to the Opry people for their help to Johnny." Neal's office is in the Sterick Building, Memphis.

Johnny says he has admired Opry stars for years, and used to try to "imitate Hank Snow and Ernest Tubb" while carrying on as an entertainer in the U.S. Army.[1] While in service he met Vivian, his wife, in San Antonio, Texas.

---

[1] *Editor's note:* Cash actually served in the U.S. Air Force.

When Johnny had his first show date 11 months ago he was working in Memphis as an appliance salesman, and attending radio school.

His three records out so far for Sun Records have all been within Billboard's "first ten" on the charts, and his "I Walk the Line" this week ranks second on two charts and forth on one.

Johnny has already travelled all over the South and out to Denver on show dates. His bookings for the next few weeks carry him to Canada and other points far from Dixieland.

He is usually accompanied by the Tennessee Two, Marshall Grant and Luther Perkins. Jack Stapp, WSM–Grand Ole Opry program director says the twosome is the smallest musical group at the Opry. Grant plays bass and Perkins the take-off guitar.

They developed their style while practicing for the first Sun record by Johnny.

Johnny, Marshall and Luther are a "fishing threesome" and carry complete equipment for the sport in their car. They stop at every chance to "wet a line."

Johnny says he is 100 per cent a country music artist, and never intends to be anything else. "The fact some of the songs have definite rhythm beat does not make them rock and roll songs," he says.

He says he has written some rock and roll songs, but does not intend to sing them. His "Rock and Roll Ruby" was recorded by Warren Smith on Sun, by Rusty Draper on Mercury and by Lawrence Welk on Coral. He may try a parody sometimes on stage.

Johnny writes "mournful, lonesome" ballads. He doesn't know music as such, and has his tunes set out in musical score by other trained persons.

"Nothing unusual about that," a veteran Opry official said. "Most of these natural singers do not know how to read and write music—

but they sing it from the heart—and that's where it reaches the listener. Johnny did that tonight. He's one of us."

II

"It Looks as if Elvis Has a Rival—from Arkansas"

by Ralph J. Gleason (1956)

ELVIS Presley is the number one attraction in the popular record field all right, but there's a 23-year-old Arkansas lad who is going to give him competition, a number of observers believe.

He is Johnny Cash whose disc, "I Walk the Line," is a substantial hit even though it is on the relatively unknown label, Sun, on which Presley's first records appeared.

During the past week, Cash has been playing one-nighters in California (he was in Vallejo the middle of the week and last night was set for Niles) and if the reaction of the crowd at the performances is any indication, Presley has a rival.

Like Elvis, Johnny Cash sings and strums a guitar, but unlike Presley there are no bumps and grinds in his routine. He is a fair-to-middling country guitar player himself and composed the words and music to the first four tunes he recorded.

Cash, at 23, is the father of two baby daughters and lives in Memphis, which is the Times Square for country and Western singers these days, it seems. He has appeared on numerous radio and TV shows including the *Grand Ole Opry* and *Louisiana Hayride* and earlier this year made a tour with the Opry group.

Although Cash has had only one big hit disc—"I Walk the Line"—that has broken out of the country and Western field to the popular record market, he is already accumulating the usual fan clubs. In the first three months of his recording career, Cash had only four fan clubs but in the past six months clubs have sprouted up like weeds all over the country.

Although he has made considerable money in personal appearances and in record royalties this year, Cash so far has continued to live calmly and resisted the impulse to buy Cadillacs by the gross. Perhaps the reason for this is a simple one—fishing. It seems that every chance he gets Cash slips away from work and goes fishing. His press agent even claims he writes his best songs while angling for a catfish.

III

"Gleason Signs Cash for 10 Guest Spots"

by Robert Johnson (1957)

THE magic door swings open for still another young Memphis singer!

Johnny Cash gets a chance at the glory road via a contract for 10 appearances on the *Jackie Gleason Show*, beginning Saturday night, Jan. 19, it was announced today by Bob Neal, his personal manager, and Sam Phillips, for whose Sun Records Johnny has become a major artist.

It was Gleason Enterprises which gave the big push to national prominence for Elvis Presley, when he made five appearances on the Gleason-produced *Stage Show* with the Dorsey Brothers.

Johnny goes on the Gleason show under approximately the same terms that Elvis had, but for twice as many contracted appearances.

That's easy to figure: Gleason and his associates helped build Elvis, but everyone cashed in on his flash success except Gleason's own shows—Berle, Steve Allen and then Ed Sullivan. They're taking no chances with Johnny. They figure he'll hit and they want to be the ones to realize on it.

Johnny, 23, is originally from Dyess, Ark., where he grew up on a farm. He spent four years in the Air Force, three in Germany as a staff sergeant, and came to Memphis to study broadcasting at Keegan's School.

He is married to a former San Antonio girl, and they have two babies and a new home out at 4492 Sandy Cove, in the Berclair Section.

Johnny had sung all his life, with Ernest Tubb and Hank Snow as his particular favorites. He asked Sam Phillips to listen to him, and Sam liked what he heard.

Johnny's first record, "Cry, Cry, Cry," backed by "Hey Porter," hit right away. "Cry, Cry, Cry" is now seemingly on its way to a lasting popularity, may well become a standard. It has been picked up by many other singers.

He followed up with "So Doggone Lonesome" and "Folsom Prison Blues," then hit big with "I Walk the Line" and "Get Rhythm."

"I Walk the Line" has been the biggest so far, selling about 750,000 copies, phenomenal in the country music field. It spread over into the pop record charts, bridging the gap from country music, and has been getting a big play from pop deejays in the East. In fact, Johnny's name was mentioned as one of the guesses on *What's My Line* last night.

"I Walk the Line" was the second biggest hit in the country music field last year, was in No. 1 spot on the charts for many weeks. At one time he had four records in the Top Fifteen.

Johnny has come a long way in a year-and-a-half, but Gleason does not exactly get an unknown. Johnny has already had considerable success, was signed last June by Grand Ole Opry, is one of the biggest names thru the South, particularly in Texas, where Elvis got big so fast.

The thing which sets him apart is not only his own vocal style—he has a voice which I once described as being big and lonely—but also the fact that he writes all his own recorded songs, and they're marked by originality and imagination of lyrics.

In Memphis' growing professional music colony, he has been marked as "the man to watch," and there are those who see him as the logical successor to the tremendous popularity of the late Hank Williams.

His latest record, "There You Go" and "Train of Love," has already hit high in the country music charts and has made the Top Fifty in the pop field.

Johnny gave Carl Perkins the original idea for "Blue Suede Shoes," and he also wrote "Rock 'n' Roll Ruby," which Warren Smith recorded. Hoagie Carmichael "covered" "I Walk the Line" with a record of his own, and that's a compliment coming from Carmichael.

A quiet, pleasant and observant man who doesn't mix much in crowds, Johnny is described by his friends as being a cheerful, jolly person when he is with those he knows. Luther Perkins of Memphis is his electric guitarist and Marshall Grant of North Carolina plays bass.

"Johnny, Luther and Marshall are not the play-around type you find often among musicians," said Neal. "Their interests lie more in the outdoors. When they go on a tour, they take their guns and fishing equipment with them, frequently stop on some back road to use them. I remember once Marshall spent two weeks building a bomb. We stopped in a lonely field out in West Texas and set it off, and all the boys got a big kick out of it.

"When they travel they don't usually stop at restaurants, but will go into a grocery and buy some crackers, bologna, cheese and milk and have an old-fashioned lunch. It makes my nervous stomach tremble, but they like it."

Neal has already turned down three offers for Johnny to make appearances in "one-shot" pictures featuring a lot of entertainers doing their specialties, but picture plans are in the making. Neal envisions Johnny in the sort of roles which John Wayne and Gary Cooper played—the rugged, silent type.

While details of the contract are not disclosed, it is certain that Johnny will make from his Gleason appearances in one year the equivalent of three or four average salaries—not to mention the impetus it will give his career, both in records and public appearances.

"Write Is Wrong"

from *Time* (1959)

Mainstream periodicals such as Time *and* Newsweek *often are slow to detect pulses outside the mainstream.* Time, *queasy about attending to the rock and roll and the country genres, ignored Cash until 1959, three years after his records had begun selling at an eye-popping rate. When the publication finally remarked on Cash, it offered a validation of sorts, confirming his nationwide popularity. But the article also illustrates* Time's *unwillingness to write seriously about country music. Cash's world is likened to a hillbilly's shack, full of kissin' cousins and livestock.*

By Hollywood standards, Johnny Cash's $50,000 ranch house, the single Cadillac and the li'l old Ford Thunderbird are unspectacular. But by anybody's standards, the Cash household is unhinged. Around the swimming pool, by day, a trio of little girls (ages 3½, 2½ and ½) raise continual riot. A yellow parrot named Jethroe screeches, whistles and squawks "There's a girl" whenever Mama glides past in skintight velvet pants. A hefty brother-in-law lounges around listening to a recording of rock 'n' roll music that he composes himself. Through it all, Johnny Cash, head of the household, relaxes in pointy Italian-leather loafers and practices a fast draw with his Colt .45.

Even in Hollywood, though, somebody has to pay for the groceries, so last week Daddy Johnny Cash put away his .45, unlimbered his guitar, and hit the road to rustle up some cash. In Saskatoon, Duluth, Hawaii or Australia, wherever tall (6 ft. 1 in., 195 lbs.) Johnny sounds off with his own "country" ballads in his deep, twanging baritone, the tour is sure to pay off. For these days the jukebox set is again on a crying jag: hangings, murders, deaths, burials and blighted loves are the subjects they want a man to sing about. And ever since Johnny Cash came out of the Arkansas delta, he has been singing about sorrow with spectacular success. In four years, half a hundred Cash-composed songs have sold more than 6,000,000 records. The biggest Cash hit, "I Walk the Line," passed the million mark with ease; the latest, "Don't Take Your Guns to Town," is well on its way to repeating that performance.

As a youngster, Johnny had something to cry about. Born near Kingsland, Ark. ("just a wide place in the road"), he grew up on a hardscrabble farm. Johnny's Baptist family were mainly hymn singers, but his mother reckoned that it was all right to teach the boys how to strum her battered old guitar. At twelve, Johnny was writing poems, songs and gory stories. At 22, after a tour in the Air Force, he was married, making a poor living as an appliance salesman in the poorer sections of Memphis.

But he and two friends—billed Johnny Cash and the Tennessee Two—were also working at church socials. Four years ago they got a singing tryout with Sun Records (the outfit that discovered Elvis Presley and Jerry Lee Lewis), and their first song was Johnny's "Cry, Cry, Cry." And Johnny had it made.

"Cry" sold 100,000 copies in the South alone. "Folsom Prison Blues," "Ballad of a Teen-Age Queen"—everything he composed came easily. "I write songs in the back of the car," Johnny explains, "or in hotel rooms, in planes." But "write" is the wrong word. He cannot read a note. Johnny simply picks out the tunes that arrange themselves in his head, plays them over and over till the boys know them well and can record them on tape.

Now that Johnny has hit the big time, he has switched to Columbia Records, and he is incorporated six ways from Sunday. He has two managers—one to mind the store in Los Angeles and the other to travel with the boys on the road—plus a personal press-agent and a paid president for his national fan club. He has his own song-publishing company, a syndicated television show in the offing, and some movie roles on tap.

Somehow he has remained a country boy, a little concerned because he can't keep his elbow away from his side after his fast draw but much too sensible to ape the rock-'n'-rollin' musical delinquents. "I'm trying to sell authentic folk music," says Johnny, as he goes right on composing the saddest kind he can:

At my door the leaves are fallin'; the cold, wild wind will come.
Sweethearts walk by together, and I still miss someone . . .

"Johnny Cash"

by Peter La Farge (1965)

By 1958, Cash and Sun Records were flipping songs to the upper reaches of the charts as quickly and methodically as a jukebox drops discs on its turntable. Coming off "Ballad of a Teenage Queen" (a bubble-gummy effort aimed at the kids), which spent ten weeks on the country chart's highest rung, and "Guess Things Happen That Way," which spent eight weeks in the same spot, there seemed to be no stopping the Johnny Cash juggernaut.

But Cash had grown impatient with his Sun environs. Although the production decisions of Phillips and Sun producer Jack Clement were integral in fueling Cash's record sales, the young singer often disagreed with them and wished to assert himself more in the studio. "There were also some business matters that we didn't see eye to eye on," Cash revealed to Robert Hilburn of Rolling Stone *in 1973. "He had me on a beginner's rate after three years and I didn't feel right about it. But mainly I knew that I could do different kinds of things with a larger label. I could record an album of hymns for Columbia for instance, and that was important to me at the time."*

So with some acrimony in the air—ignited by Cash lying to Phillips, telling him he wasn't negotiating with Columbia Records—the singer abandoned Sun and signed with the giant New York–based label. He began working with Don Law, the pioneering producer who had documented volumes of American roots music, including that of the fabled bluesman Robert Johnson and (with A&R man Art Satherly) Western swing daddy Bob Wills. Law had more recently been supervising the work of Columbia stars such as Marty Robbins, Carl Smith, and Lefty Frizzell. Among those stars, he was generally praised for his laissez-faire producing. Accordingly, Law allowed Cash to follow his interests and inclinations.

And Cash responded. Invoking the simplicity that characterized his early Sun recordings, he indulged his love for gospel, Americana, and reminisces of old country days. Some of his first hits for Columbia, such as "Don't Take Your Guns to Town," "Frankie's Man, Johnny," and "The Rebel—Johnny Yuma," traded on American folklore and images of the frontier, themes that in the late 1950s were as popular in country music as Fess Parker's Davy Crockett was on TV.

In 1959, not long after signing with Columbia, Cash told Time *magazine that he was trying to sell "authentic folk music"; he would hold tight that goal throughout the 1960s, recording concept albums such as* Blood, Sweat and Tears *(1963) that recognized the workers' role in American history and* Bitter Tears *(1964) that remembered American Indians. These subjects resonated with Cash's established fan base and attracted new interest from those who explored the burgeoning folk scene of the early to mid-1960s.*

Peter La Farge, a formidable composer and performer on the folk music scene, celebrated Johnny Cash's folk orientation in the following piece. The fact that the essay appeared in Sing Out!*—the almost-official organ of the folk music movement—and that the respected La Farge wrote it gave credence to Cash's place in the group of singers and artists who celebrated America's folk roots and the common man.*

In this highly impressionistic essay, La Farge suggested that Cash came to the folk scene looking for "depth and truth" and that life began for Cash when he recorded La Farge's "Ballad of Ira Hayes," about the Pima Indian who raised the flag over Iwo Jima only to later descend into alcoholism (which appeared, with four other La Farge pieces, on Cash's Bitter Tears: Ballads of the American Indian *album in 1964). But Cash had long made startling, socially important music, and probably had influenced the folk movement far more than it influenced him. In a 1973 interview with*

Rolling Stone, *Cash placed in perspective the influence that writers such as La Farge and Bob Dylan had on him. "There was a time I guess they influenced me quite a bit. Of course, Dylan is going to influence anybody that is close to him, I think, as a writer some way or another. He's a powerful talent. But the influences in my life come and go and there's always something fresh coming along. There's always a change taking place. I don't know what the influences might be right now." Whatever Dylan's influence may have been, the two recorded and appeared on television together in the late 1960s; their relationship stemmed from a mid-'60s exchange of letters and continued with some intensity into the early 1970s.*

JOHNNY Cash, ungrateful to his legend, a-crawl with nerves, charred by his own poetry, leaving a mighty wake and singing down great storms of beauty, has lain in too many lonely hotel beds. Fame makes bitter eating when you doubt the worth of what you've done. Staggered by an image he became but could not be, at the highest reach of country-and-Western music, Johnny Cash appeared on the folk scene, trailing his majesty down the steps to the Gaslight coffeehouse of MacDougal Street, beside Ed McCurdy. The hillbilly minstrel who'd walked too many lines next to the man who wrote "Strangest Dream." It was a valid passport. "That's Johnny Cash." . . . "What's he doing here?" . . . "What does he want?" the murmur went. He wasn't looking for much, just himself.

Driven, complicated, and expert, Johnny is a great American voice. He's hated himself for success he earned. He hasn't sung just trash, witness "Five Feet High and Rising," his flood song, or the songs he's sung, "Folsom Prison Blues" and, as a matter of fact, "I Walk the Line." But Johnny wanted more than the hillbilly jangle; he was hungry for the depth and truth heard only in the folk field. (Until Johnny Cash came along, anyway.)

The secret is simple: Johnny has the heart of a folksinger in the purest sense, and he has a very lovely soul. He is capable of anything he puts his soul and his band-aid heart to, and he is capable of being a folksinger in the very essence of folk truth. He would love to be out from under that heavy legend that binds him to Hillbilly Heaven. But Johnny didn't break into using folk material by picking a catchy love song. That would be too easy for Cash. He decided to do a song a friend of his, Gene Ferguson, had played for him over the telephone. A protest song about some drunken Indian.

Johnny made "Ira Hayes" into a national hillbilly hit, but when he appeared at Newport among all those folksingers, he didn't have to change a note to make it fit. He "bridged the gap," Bob Shelton, writing in the *New York Times*, said—and it was a gap Johnny needed badly to bridge.

Johnny at work in a recording studio is amazing. He and the Carter Family and his hand-picked musicians work in a kind of magic spontaneity, somewhat agonized at times on Johnny's part. I was with him in Nashville when he cut the *Bitter Tears* album, and take after take was perfect. *Bitter Tears* grew out of that protest song he sang at Newport, "Ira Hayes," and is an album of Indian protest songs, on which Johnny does some of his proudest writing. If "Ira Hayes" was a gamble, *Bitter Tears* must have been more of a one, but Cash sang and Columbia recorded. When he sings they usually do. The record was a fantastic winner in the hillbilly and Western field, then jumped to the popular charts. And a beautiful thing happened: Johnny's records were suddenly recognized by record dealers across the nations, and are now sold as such. Johnny has recently recorded a Bobby Dylan tune, "It Ain't Me Babe," and may be expected to stick pretty close to the minstrel set from now on.

But Johnny still often walks the dark side of the road. "Catastrophe" Cash I call him; he's my blood brother, and I love him. He cares too damn much. He hates the lie of publicity and the selfish grabbing of the crowd. Look at him, everyone, he's different, Johnny Cash cares. . . .

"Seven One Night Stands" from *Man in Black*

by Johnny Cash (1975)

Through the 1960s, as Cash built an increasingly diverse fan base, his fame multiplied with every year and almost every new song. To go with his pioneering concept albums, he recorded singles that became country favorites, singles such as the deadly serious "Ring of Fire" (1963), the playful "Understand Your Man" (1964), and the joyful "Happy to Be with You" (1965).

Puzzlingly, it was at this same time that Cash started down the path of self-destruction. It would seem logical that his self-destructive streak would have threatened his steadily increasing fame. But Cash's career thrived in spite of his self-inflicted abuse—abuse that, if left unchecked, could have killed him.

He had begun taking pills for sustenance on his arduous road trips, and so enjoyed their energizing and enervating effects (depending on the pill) that he developed an addiction. It warped his moods and disrupted his judgment. His drug-induced selfishness broke up his first marriage, and his crazy stunts (like blindly tearing down a mountainside in a jeep) tempted death. "I think it was the miserable streak in me," Cash told Christopher Wren in his biography. "Maybe I was afraid to face reality then. I wasn't very happy then. Maybe I was trying to find a spiritual satisfaction in drugs."

In October 1965, he found himself in jail because of drugs. Federal authorities in El Paso, Texas, seized him after a resupply mission into Mexico. A picture of Cash in handcuffs, his pompadour perched over a pair of overly large sunglasses, rolled out across the pages of American newspapers. It was an embarrassment, but far from a conversion. After paying his fines, he defiantly resumed his pill consumption and railed at anybody who derided him or his habits. "I claim to be nothing but me, whatever that is, and for whatever that's worth," declared the singer to Music City News *reporter Dixie Deen in January 1966, not long after the arrest. In Deen's story, Cash hammered out his defense: "I don't pretend to be anything I'm not. I've seen the horrible pictures of me in the papers within the last couple of months, and I don't even read what it says, because I know exactly what the papers want to do. . . . They want to make it sensational and prove that they are heroes by tearing down an image, or an image which they think has been built up. I am guilty of as many sins as the average person, but I don't say that I am guilty of any more than the average person. I may have a few different ones, but certainly no more."*

June Carter, her sisters Helen and Anita, and her mother Maybelle—an original Carter Family member—had joined Johnny Cash's touring show in the early 1960s. When Cash finally decided to face his drug addiction in the late 1960s, he called June—with whom he had long before fallen in love—to help him climb out of his cave. "Without June, he couldn't have done it," said Cash's bass man Marshall Grant in a 1970 Playboy *interview with Saul Braun. "He wouldn't be alive today." She and Cash married in 1968.*

Cash has described his drug ordeal many times but never as fully as in this chapter from his 1975 autobiography.

I HAD to get a work permit to perform at the Hilton Hotel in Las Vegas. It doesn't matter if you're a guitar player or what, everybody has to have one. So during our first booking at the Hilton in 1971 they came backstage with these personal information forms. There were several specific questions to answer, and then at the bottom of the page were five spaces—if you needed that many—that said, "Have you ever been arrested? Where? When? For what?"

I didn't know until I started writing that five spaces wouldn't be enough. I had to turn the paper over and put some answers on the back. Because for the first time I realized it was seven times I'd been in jail. Seven different times, seven different places. And for five of the seven I couldn't tell them what I had been busted for; I never did really know.

The seven arrests were over a seven-year period. Seven steps down, an average of once a year. Filling out that form backstage at the Hilton, I began to reflect on those episodes.

There was that time in Nashville in 1959, which was the first time I was in jail. I know that one was for public drunkenness, and I deserved to be in jail. I was trying to break down a door and get in a club that had already closed.

Another time, I was out after our concert drinking beer in Starkville, Mississippi. It was reported that when they stopped me I was picking flowers in someone's yard at 2:00 A.M. Actually I was wandering down the sidewalk to find a service station open where I could buy some cigarettes. The police picked me up and took me to jail. I went into a rage—screaming, cussing, and kicking at the cell door all night long until I finally broke my big toe. At 8:00 the next morning they let me out when they knew I was sober.

Other times I was in overnight in Nevada, Texas, and California. The police found me wandering around on pills and alcohol and put me in jail with the rest of the drunks till I slept it off.

There were some hairy experiences in those jails. Like the big, burly lumberjack in Carson City, Nevada, who sat on the bunk opposite mine, crying. His mood would keep changing. He'd get angry, and he'd stand up and pound his chest and yell like Tarzan. He'd show me his powerful arms and tell me he could break my neck like a twig. And I knew he could.

I did some fast talking, complimenting his muscles, saying, "I know you can! I know you can!" I was very sober by then. An arm the size of a mule's leg went around my neck, and I started singing. He stopped for a moment. I sang "Folsom Prison Blues" and "I Walk the Line," and he sat down, trying to figure me out.

Finally he said, "You sound like Johnny Cash."

With a sigh of relief, I said, "I *am* Johnny Cash."

And that made him angry. "You're a liar," he said, and he stood up to challenge my remark.

Now I was not only sober, but really praying.

"Sing," he commanded.

I sang one of the songs I had recorded in an album of hymns, during some of my better days, "When He Reached Down His Hand for Me." . . .

The big lumberjack had tears in his eyes now. "Sing another one," he said, and I sang another one. After that one he said, crying, "Me and you are a couple of drunks, but you sure sound like Johnny Cash. Sing another one."

He laid down and closed his eyes, and I sang until I knew he was asleep. Soon it was morning and they let me go.

By 1965, I was taking more pills than I could find doctors to supply. In Nashville, as in California, I easily found illegal sources; a friend, for example, would know someone who worked in a drugstore. That friend would get me hundreds of pills at a time through altering order blanks from distributors. Or, in a couple of instances, I was supplied through drugstores where, because of large demands for pills from people like me, large quantities were brought in illegally from Mexico or from fly-by-night manufacturers.

On a stopover from Dallas to L.A., I decided to cross the border myself at El Paso to obtain a supply. I had run out of pills or had lost those I had, so I hired a cab and asked the driver to get me all he could.

I was nervous and a little afraid as I sat waiting a short time later in Juarez while the driver got out of the car and went into a bar to get the amphetamines and barbiturates. I felt like the outlaw I had become, sitting in a taxicab on a hot, dirty back street behind a bar in Mexico waiting impatiently for the pusher to fill my order. I slid down a little lower in the back seat each time someone looked my way. I had never done it this way before, but I'd been told by a pill-head in Nashville I could get all I wanted in Mexico.

He was right. The taxi driver soon returned with several hundred of both kinds of pills, and we headed back across the border and to my hotel in El Paso.

When I got back to the room, I popped three or four and soon started rambling. I ended up in downtown El Paso where I bought an antique pistol in a pawn shop. It was a nineteenth-century cap and ball type and was in perfect working order.

As I walked out of the shop, a man stopped me. I found out later he'd been following me since I'd come back across the border.

"Hello, Johnny Cash. I'm a fan of yours," said the plainclothesman.

I knew instantly he was a policeman, though it did not occur to me that he knew of my trip across the line into Mexico. I assumed he was watching me because of the gun.

"I collect antique pistols," I said, showing him the relic.

"It's a nice one," he said in a friendly manner. "Do you have a show in El Paso?"

"No—just passing through on my way to L.A." I answered, turning to walk away.

"I've got all your records," he said, walking beside me.

"Thank you," I said. Does he know I'm on the pills I wondered.

"When are you leaving El Paso?" he asked.

"Tonight at 9:00," I said. And I got in a cab and returned to the hotel.

I tied up the pills in two socks and put one of them inside my guitar and the other in the lining of my suitcase. A little wariness came over me about leaving at 9:00 since I had announced my departure time to that policeman.

But the gun was legal—an antique. Besides, he'd seen it. The pills? They were well-hidden—except for dozen or so I had in my pocket.

I reached the airport a bit early and checked my suitcase and guitar in at the ticket counter. I got on board the plane as soon as they would let me and took my seat with my briefcase containing the pistol on my lap.

The plane door was about to be closed when I heard a man tell the stewardess, "Wait a minute—we've got to take a man off here."

"Who?" she asked.

"Johnny Cash," the voice said. "Where's he sitting?"

He stepped inside, and I recognized him immediately as the man I'd seen and talked with outside the pawn shop.

"I'm right here," I said quietly, embarrassed. "What do you want?"

"Do you have a gun?" he asked.

By now, everyone on the plane was watching and listening. He was sweating, nervous, out of breath, as if he'd been running.

"You know I do," I answered. "I showed it to you this afternoon. What about it?"

"Come on, let's go," said another man who had just appeared in sight. By now I was glad to get off the plane and away from all those passengers who had witnessed my arrest.

They took me inside the terminal to an empty room. Empty, except for my guitar and suitcase. That was what the rush had been about. They had barely managed to get my bags and me off the plane before it took off.

They shook me down, found the pills in my pocket, opened my suitcase and began a systematic search of every piece of clothing in it. Then, they found the pills in the lining.

"Do you have any more?" one of them asked.

"No," I said.

He opened the guitar case, removed the guitar, and shook it.

"Do you want to loosen the strings so you can get them out, or do you want us to break the guitar to get them?"

I didn't answer. I took the guitar, loosened the strings, reached my hand inside and brought out the rest of the pills.

They poured them all out in a big ashtray and looked at them. They examined the guitar case again, and then both men sat down and looked at me.

"Where is the H?" one asked.

"The what?" I said.

"The H, the horse, the heroin?" he demanded.

I had been calm, quiet, and submissive to their search and seizure up to this time, but now I saw their real reason for it and became angry.

"Is that why you arrested me? Because you thought I had heroin?" I asked.

They didn't reply.

"I don't have heroin," I said. "I've never touched heroin."

"What are you on?" one asked.

"Dexedrine," I answered. "You've got it all there in the ashtray."

After a moment, one of them looked at the other and asked, as if I weren't even there, "Do you believe him?"

"I think I do," came the response.

"You see, Cash," one of them continued, "We apprehended you because your cab driver made your purchase from a known heroin pusher. We thought sure the contact was for heroin."

I began to breathe easier, thinking maybe they weren't going to hold me.

"These are amphetamines and barbiturates," I said. "You can get them from most any doctor on prescription. I just wanted enough to last me for awhile."

"But you got them illegally," they said. "We'll have to book you."

My cell in the El Paso jail hadn't been cleaned since its last occupant. The plumbing didn't work. There was no mattress, no pillow—just a dirty blanket over the springs.

The light stayed on all night. I watched the roaches crawl across the floor. Some of the other inmates were laughing and cursing each other. I heard a boy crying and another one praying. I tried to pray and couldn't.

The pills wore off about sunup, and I finally slept. At noon they brought me a bowl of black-eyed peas and a piece of bread, which I ate.

"You have a phone call," said the man with the keys who unlocked my cell door.

"Who is it?" I asked.

"How do I know?" he said. "Come on."

"John, this is Sam," said the voice on the other end. "Is there anything I can do?"

"Sam who?" I asked, trembling.

"Sam Phillips," he said. "What do you want me to do? Should I come down there? Can I send my lawyer? What can I do?"

I wanted to ask him how he'd found out, but I was afraid he'd tell me he'd heard it on the news. I hadn't seen Sam in two years, and at a time when I figured nobody cared much for me, here he was on the phone.

"I'll be all right. Thank you anyway."

I choked up and couldn't say anything else, so I hung up.

Back in the cell a few minutes later, the same man returned. "You have a phone call, Cash," he said.

It was Neal Merritt, songwriter and disc jockey on El Paso's country music station.

"Sorry to hear about your trouble, John," he said. "Can I do anything?"

"How did you hear about it, Neal?" I asked.

"It came over the Teletype," he answered.

"Oh, no," I said. "My mother, father, my wife, my children—they all know about it by now."

I didn't think I'd have the strength to make it back to the cell. Then another call. This time it was Don Law, my record producer at the time from Columbia. How many times I had failed to show up at recording sessions because I knew I wouldn't be able to sing. How many times Don had sat at the control booth all night long, hoping I'd get in the mood to cut a record. And he'd never complained, never criticized. He even turned his apartment over to me at times when I was unable to face the world. Now here he was, on the phone with me, encouraging me, telling me he'd help.

I was numb when I hung up. "I don't want any more calls," I told the man with the keys as I walked on wobbling legs back to my cell. And fell down on the bunk.

"I don't ever want out of this cell again," I said silently to myself. "I just want to stay here alone and pray that God will forgive me and then let me die. Because I'm too weak to face everyone I'll have to face. Knowing my family is heartbroken, knowing my friends, and fans are hurt and disappointed—it's more than I can reconcile with them."

I could see my family crying. I could hear them ask, "Why, Daddy?" "Why, John?" "Why, Son?"

And I cried. I wanted to pray, but I could only cry.

"You have a phone call, Cash," the man said again.

"Leave me alone," I said. And he left.

A few minutes later he was back, opening the door, tapping me on the shoulder.

"Come on," he said.

At the front desk, a lawyer, Woodrow Bean, and two policemen stood waiting.

"Marshall Grant called me," said the lawyer. "Know him?"

"Yes," I said.

"Bond is being posted, and we have to go over to the courthouse to get you released," he stated. "Put on these sunglasses."

"Why" I asked.

"Because you have to wear *these*," said one of the policemen, as he put handcuffs on me. "Sorry, but it's the law."

"This will soon be over with, Mr. Cash," said Lawyer Bean. "When we go out the door, stay right with me and walk fast."

"Why?" I asked again. By now I was dazed, scared, ashamed. *Handcuffed.* How could I drop so low?

"Because," said Mr. Bean, "there are several press photographers waiting for you to come outside."

The pictures in the newspapers across the country the next morning, including the Memphis *Press-Scimitar*, were a public documentation of the low point of my entire career. I faced the shame from it sober for the next six weeks. But as humbling and defacing as it all was, the memory of embarrassment faded into the heightening schedule of demanding tours. And I returned once again to my shadows of death—the pills.

My last time in jail was one night in October 1967 at Lafayette, Georgia. And that was the turning point of it all.

The following morning at 8:00, Sheriff Ralph Jones came in and wakened me. I got up with that old familiar sick, sober, and sorry feeling.

He said, "Come on up to the desk, Mr. Cash."

I walked up to his desk and stood there waiting to be reprimanded and admonished like they usually did. Sheriff Jones opened up a drawer in his desk and took out my money and a handful of pills. He held them in his hand and looked up at me and said, "I'm going to give you your money and your dope back because you know better than most people that God gave you a free will to do with yourself whatever you want to do. Here's your money and your pills. Now you can throw the pills away or you can take them and go ahead and kill yourself. Whichever one you want to do, Mr. Cash, will be all right with me."

I stood looking at him a long time before I could answer.

"But I don't understand why you're giving me the dope back. It's illegal."

He said, "Right, it's illegal. It would be a sin and a crime for you to kill yourself, too. And that's exactly what those pills are doing to you.

"I've followed your career for over ten years," he continued. "My wife and I have every record you've ever made. We love you. We've always loved you. We've watched for you on television, listened for you on the radio. We've got your album of hymns. We're probably the best two fans you've ever had.

"It broke my heart when they brought you in here last night. I left the jail and went home to my wife and told her I had Johnny Cash locked up. I almost wanted to resign and just walk out because it was such a heartbreaking thing for me."

And he slapped the pills down on the desk and said, "Go on. Take 'em and get out of here."

And I picked them up and said, "Sheriff, you won't be sorry that you let me go like this."

He said, "Do with your life whatever you want to. Just remember, you've got the free will to either kill yourself or save your life."

I put the money in my pocket and walked out of jail. Just three or four dollars was all I had left. I threw the pills on the ground. A friend of mine, Richard McGibony, was waiting in his car. He'd found out I'd been picked up and had come there to wait, hoping they'd let me out the next morning.

I got in the car and said, "Richard, I'm going back home to Nashville. You'll never see me high on dope any more."

"I hope you mean it," he replied.

"That sheriff back there is something else," I said. "God sent him to me, or sent me to him. He made me know, he made me realize I really was about to kill myself. He also made me remember that I really can live."

So I went back home to Nashville, and I called June.

"I'm home," I said.

"How are you John?" she asked.

"I'm all right. But I wish you would call [Dr.] Nat Winston [who was then Tennessee commissioner of mental health] and see if he can come out and talk to me, because I need help. See if he can give me some pointers on how to fight the terrors from the devil who's busy crawling up my back."

She called back later and said, "Nat is gone all day long everyday, way into the night. But he said if you will see him, he'll be out tomorrow night when he gets in from East Tennessee."

I made it through the night. But the next day I found a bottle of amphetamines I had hidden in the bathroom. And having been off them only two days, I swallowed a handful.

I don't remember what I did the rest of the day. But just about dark, I decided to get my tractor out of the shed and drive along the cliff overlooking the lake to see how close I could get to the edge without going over. It was then late October and already very cold. I had on a long leather topcoat and the rest of the pills in my pocket.

I moved along the edge of the cliff overlooking the lake. Suddenly the earth gave way underneath me. The next thing I knew I hit the lake, the tractor coming down from above. It turned over and barely missed me.

I tried to crawl up out of the ice-cold water onto the bank, but I was stiff from the cold. A moment later, almost from out of nowhere,

Braxton Dixon came running down to the water and reached out his hand to me. Right behind him were June and Nat Winston. I was so cold I couldn't talk, and they took me in the house. I didn't want them to get my coat because I knew the rest of the pills were in that pocket. But they managed to get the coat off and away from me, and they found the pills and got rid of them. I went to bed and finally went to sleep from exhaustion.

About four in the morning I woke up, and sitting in the chair beside my bed was Nat. I really didn't know him too well at that time.

He said, "How are you feeling, John?"

I sat up immediately, thinking about my pills, trying to remember where I'd put them, and said, "Oh, great, great, Nat. I feel great." ("If I could just have a few pills to kind of taper off on," I thought.)

"You look hellish," he said.

That put my head back down on the pillow, because I knew from then on there'd be no fooling Nat Winston. I knew if I tried to slip a pill with Nat around, it would never work.

He said, "I wanted to be sure and be here when you woke up. When you called me, I figured you wouldn't have done it if you hadn't really intended to get your life straightened out."

"I never meant anything more sincerely," I said, "But I see I need some advice on how to fight the problem from somebody like you."

"John," Nat said, "I'm a doctor, I'm a psychiatrist, and I've seen a lot of people in the shape you're in. And frankly, I don't think there is much chance for you. I've never known of anyone as far gone as you are to really whip it. Only you can do it, and it would be a lot easier if you let God help you."

I knew he was right. God had been waiting all this time for me to come back. Now that he knew I was finally serious. He was beginning to surround me with His people to fight with me—Nat Winston, June, her parents, my parents, Braxton Dixon, and others. But mainly it was my fight. Only I could do it, and I had to lean on God—like he'd knew I'd have to.

"I'll do it, Nat," I said.

"Get set for the fight of your life," he said. "I'll be back tomorrow night, and we'll see how you're doing."

He left me alone, and I faced the truth that I had long known: there could be no tapering off; I had to get off them—or die. One pill would call for another, and another, and . . .

There would be no fooling anyone. Especially myself.

PART II

APOGEE

What do you think a man does who has one hundred sheep and one of them gets lost? He will leave the other ninety-nine grazing on the hillside and go and look for the lost sheep. When he finds it, I tell you, he feels happier over this one sheep than over the ninety-nine that did not get lost.

—MATTHEW 26:12–13

Nineteen-sixty-nine would stamp American politics and culture with an impression still visible in the early twenty-first century. Woodstock, Richard Nixon, the *Apollo* moon landing, each became lasting symbols in the American consciousness. Johnny Cash would ascend, too. Straddling his "Daddy Sang Bass" and "A Boy Named Sue," he spent eleven weeks at number one on *Billboard*'s country music charts in 1969, more weeks than any other performer that year. In addition, "A Boy Named Sue"—a crazy ballad about a reunited father and son written by Shel Silverstein—became one of the biggest pop hits ever by a country-based performer: consider the song one of the primary factors in Cash's late 1960s climb. Network television, an infatuated press, and other popular songs such as "Blistered" (1969), "What Is Truth" (1970), and "Sunday Morning Coming Down"

(1970) turned ascent into sustained dominance in the country music field. Cash had become the face of the genre.

One important measure of just how significant Cash had become is the amount of mass media attention he garnered. From 1968 to 1973, there was far more than I could include in this *Reader*. Media coverage shapes perceptions and sets the public's agenda, popularizes, and, for many, legitimizes art in America. The fact that the media recognized Cash's greatness helped build and sustain the impression among those inside and outside his fandom that Cash was . . . great.

In the late 1960s, when America's establishment mass media began its celebration of Johnny Cash, it could no longer ignore the voices and symbols of the youth and antiestablishment cultures. To some degree Cash had been such a voice and symbol since the 1950s, but the respected organs of journalism only began to consider him as such fifteen years into his career. Jazz and folk styles had long attracted thoughtful press, but up until the late 1960s, rock and country often were deemed simply fodder for fanzines and gossip columns. Cash was among the first country musicians to receive serious attention from the general mainstream media.

The Cash story was appealing to the media for reasons beyond his obvious knack for delivering a song. His music and philosophy advocated the viewpoint of the oppressed, a popular sentiment of the day, and his childhood and coming of age contained drama only found in the theater. The crawl back from drugs as well as his love affair with second wife June Carter Cash only added spice to the story.

But it was the prison concerts that made him the kind of antiestablishment figure the press could adore. Johnny Cash had visited and performed at prisons since the late 1950s, but few knew until Columbia released the *Live at Folsom Prison* LP. No country or rock or folk artist had walked among the marginalized with tape rolling and expressed such exuberant solidarity with them. One cut from the album—his old "Folsom Prison Blues"—locked up the number one spot for four weeks in 1968. Another popular prison album—*Live at San Quentin*—followed in 1969.

The concerts are more remarkable for Cash's animal-like bravado than for the songs he reeled off. He sounded like a caged tiger pacing, taunting his captors and inciting his fellow captured to tear down the place. The power he felt in front of the prisoners, he later confessed to music writer Bill Flanagan, inflamed and intoxicated him:

> The guards were scared to death. All the convicts were standing up on the dining tables. They were out of control, really. During the second rendition of that song ["San Quentin"] all I would have had to do was say "*Break!*" and they were gone, man. They were ready! I've got a book called *Extraordinary Popular Delusions and the Madness of Crowds* that I've studied for years. I knew I had that prison audience where all I had to do was say, "Take over! Break!" and they would have. Those guards knew it, too. I was tempted. But I thought about June and the Carter Family—they were there with me, too—and I controlled myself. 'Cause I was really ready for some excitement. (*Musician*, May 1988)

His disdain for Folsom and San Quentin sprayed from the recordings, and in the wake of the concerts, his hatred often boiled in conversations with reporters. "You can't be in prison without being a prisoner," Cash observed in 1969 about Folsom to Michael Lydon in the *New York Times*. "They had guards all around with riot guns. Before and after, we were kept in the kitchen. None of the boys were allowed to talk to us. One kid broke regulations. A guard stepped between us, but I said it was O.K. so the guard let him have one question. 'You know so-'n'-so back in Arkansas?' 'Never heard the name,' I said. 'He said he knew you,' the kid said, and the guard pushed him back. He broke the rules just trying to make an old country boy connection."

He became vocal on the subject of prisons, maybe because he realized that but for God and good lawyers he could be among the men in faded blue. Perhaps the prisoners provoked him to think about what he shared with them: enslavement, faltering, struggle, drifting, loneliness, and redemption.

Through his interest in the incarcerated, whatever the root of it was, he became inescapably associated with prisons. Even years later, when he played prisons less often and rarely referred to them in interviews, the connection remained, becoming so strong in the public's eye that many believed Cash had done hard time in prison. He hadn't. He had only entered the pens to ease their residents' lives.

"When Johnny Cash Visited Leavenworth"

by Albert Nussbaum (1973)

In Johnny Cash's 1997 autobiography—the second one—he called the Folsom Prison concert a major stepping stone in his career. Any objective accounting would agree. In 1968, Time, *almost ten years after running its last item on Cash, called the* Folsom Prison *release "one of the most original and compelling pop albums of the year." The following passage from the* Sunday Gazette Mail *of Charleston, West Virginia, sketches Cash's appearance at Leavenworth in the early 1970s. Inmate Albert Nussbaum, once among the FBI's ten most wanted men (for bank robbery) and later a popular mystery writer, described Cash's effect on those prisoners whose minds he tried so hard to ease through his music and rebellious outbursts.*

BURT "Cosmopolitan Centerfold" Reynolds, Dinah Shore, Jonathan Winters, and Merle Haggard and his orchestra supplemented by talented federal prisoners recently taped a segment of "The Late Burt Reynolds Show" inside the U.S. Penitentiary, Leavenworth, Kansas. But as unusual as this is, it isn't the first time a top star has brought a show to Leavenworth.

It was there a couple of years ago when, without advance publicity, fanfare, recording, taping, or filming, Johnny Cash brought his entire road show to Leavenworth. Nearly every Leavenworth prisoner knew who Johnny Cash was. If we hadn't seen him on TV, we had heard his records. To some he was "the greatest"; to a few he was "just another hillbilly," but the name was familiar.

Country music is popular at Leavenworth. Many of the men come from Texas, Oklahoma, Cash's home state of Arkansas, and all the other places where music without a guitar just isn't considered music. Most of the Easterners also have a taste—or a tolerance—for country music. Mine can be traced back to blaring barracks radios while I was in the service, and to early-morning cross-country auto trips with only a "country" disc jockey for company.

So, when the notice appeared on cellhouse bulletin boards—and even before when rumors started to circulate—a tension began to build. Cash was going to arrive on Friday afternoon. The prison factory was going to close. Anyone wanting to see the show—could. For once, the making of shoes and furniture wasn't the most important thing.

There was a rainstorm on Thursday and tornado warnings were posted for parts of Kansas. We all grumbled, cursing our bad luck. If the weather didn't break before the next afternoon, the show would be in the prison auditorium. In that case, instead of the one long show we hoped for, the entertainment would have to be split into two short ones because the auditorium couldn't accommodate the entire prison population at one time.

Friday morning was bleak and unseasonably cold. It rained during the early hours and that water plus the previous day's deluge turned parts of the exercise yard into a quagmire. The section hardest hit was the skinned-back area of the baseball diamond directly in front of the bleachers where a flat-bed trailer had been parked as a stage for the performers. The ground around it had the consistency of chocolate pudding, but hopes were high that the water would drain away as quickly as it usually did.

I had a job assignment that gave me a chance to sneak away and see what was going on. All morning the men assigned to the prison recreation department worked under the threatening sky to make the truck trailer a suitable stage. They sawed and hammered on a temporary tar paper construction despite the howling wind.

As they worked, more men ventured from the cellhouses and took seats beside me on the damp wooden bleachers. It was barely 10 A.M. Cash wasn't expected much before 2:00 P.M.; but the rush was on and we were joined by other men who didn't have jobs somewhere. Hours before anyone could hope to see a show the bleachers were almost full.

At last, two square-bodied trucks were backed up to the trailer to serve as dressing rooms. Then, at 2:15 P.M., a group of technicians drove through the prison's east gate and pulled up behind the makeshift stage. They checked the set-up and went to work, hooking up microphones and sound equipment. It was warmer now, the ground more firm. Breaks in the clouds were allowing the sun to shine through with greater frequency; but sudden gusts of wind continued to sweep over the west wall. The bleachers were filled to capacity and chairs had been set up between them and the stage, but there were still at least a couple of hundred standees at both ends of the platform.

A few minutes later, Johnny Cash and his beautiful wife, June Carter, came strolling arm in arm from the direction of the prison administration building. A roar of welcome went up to greet them. We didn't know it at the time, but, though Leavenworth was the first federal penitentiary where Johnny Cash had been allowed to perform, it was the third institution his group visited that day. They had already stopped at the Kansas State Prison and the Kansas Women's Industrial Reformatory.

"We've been to most of the good prisons—most of 'em," June Carter said at one point, catching her breath between songs. An old convict called back, "So've I!"

The show consisted of the fast-paced, highly polished acts of the Statler Brothers; Carl "Blue Suede Shoes" Perkins; June and the

Carter Family and Johnny Cash—all backed up by Johnny's band the Tennessee Three. It was an impressive display of talent and skill, but it was Cash we cheered the loudest.

"This is the same show we took to the President a few weeks ago," Cash said, and we all grinned at him like a bunch of happy high school kids. Then his tone grew deeper and more serious.

"We came because we care," he said. "We care. We really do. If there's ever anything I can do for you all, let me know somehow, and I'll do it."

The guy in front of me turned to his buddy and whispered.

"Do you think he means it?"

The second man looked at Cash, studying him for a moment from hooded eyes. He nodded slowly. "Yeah. I think he does," he answered.

Cash is a big man. He has the huge shoulders of a weight lifter or professional fighter, and he has a boxer's narrow hips. At Leavenworth, he wore a black Lincolnesque coat over a turquoise sport shirt. His dark hair was combed straight back in a pompadour and hung down over his collar. Narrow-legged black trousers made it seem that most of his weight was centered high up in his V-shaped torso. His shiny black, high-buttoned shoes with western heels raised him far over six feet in height.

But it wasn't his size or his costume that captured and held everyone's attention—it was the look on his face and the sound of his voice. Cash is real. He has a bad cough and smokes too much. So did most of us who had come to see him. He has a look of suffering caused by a hard life and years of one-night stands in forgettable places. We all had pasts we didn't like to think about either.

Cash is a man's man. The songs he sings are a man's songs, full of life's sad and unkind moments. Even his hit song, "A Boy Named Sue," has a humor he is uniquely qualified to exploit.

Cash is no Andres Segovia. He doesn't pretend to be a guitar virtuoso, but only Cash could stand in front of that audience strumming the neck of his guitar like a music student waiting for his first lesson and not get laughed off the stage. And only Cash could handle a guitar as though it were a weapon—slinging it out of sight across his back when he had no use for it—without appearing slightly ridiculous. With him, such gestures were as natural and unaffected as his smile and way of speaking.

When he sang "Folsom Prison Blues," a song he wrote, he substituted the word Leavenworth for Folsom. And when he reached the words—"I ain't seen the sunshine since I don't know when . . . "—we who hadn't seen the horizon in years were able to identify with the tone and mood or the song. It captured our own feelings so exactly that our roar of approval completely drowned out the music and the amplified sound of his deep bass voice.

He sang several numbers, both solo and with his wife. They were all received with loud ovations, but his version of "The Prisoner's Song," the one that goes, "If I had the wings of an angel . . ." was almost a show stopper. It's said that the man who originally recorded that song earned over a million dollars from it, but that earlier version couldn't possibly have been sung with more feeling and sincerity than Johnny Cash's. Johnny has an empathy, a sympathy and understanding for prisoners that would be difficult to counterfeit.

Not that all of his Leavenworth fans were prisoners. Several prison officials asked for and received his autograph before and after the show. Many guards hadn't left the prison when their shifts ended earlier in the day, and others come to work hours before their shifts began so they could see the show. It was the largest turnout anyone could remember for a show on the prison's exercise yard.

When the show was over, we were told to remain seated until the performers had packed and left. I could see Cash behind the platform, talking to one of his group and waiting for the signal that they were all ready to leave together.

"Come over here, Johnny!" someone near me called. The guards won't let us roam over there.

Cash's head jerked around and he circled the parked trucks, coming toward us with long strides. His black coat was open and his forehead was shiny from the effort he had put into his songs. He spent the next ten minutes shaking hands, getting his back slapped and signing autographs on matchbook covers and small scraps of paper. When it was time to go, he hung back a bit; he seemed genuinely sorry he had to leave so soon.

"I think it was a fine, unselfish thing for him to come here," one of the guards said as we were filing back to our cells for the late afternoon count. "He can command a lot of money for his time, and if he wasn't here, he could be somewhere else being well paid."

That pretty well sums up Johnny Cash's visit to Leavenworth—he didn't earn a nickel, but he made a lot of friends.

Excerpt from *The Nashville Sound: Bright Lights and Country Music*

by Paul Hemphill (1970)

Paul Hemphill has traced the South for more than forty years, enticing readers with stories, both real and imagined, set in the minor leagues, on the NASCAR circuit, and in racially torn Birmingham, Alabama. The former baseball player and Nieman Fellow at Harvard University took a peek behind country music's curtains in the late 1960s and wrote a book that engagingly revealed its backstage story. In this excerpt, he sits for a spell with Johnny Cash and collects his thoughts on prisons, Dylan, and foreign policy.

. . . ALL 13 of the one-hour segments of *The Johnny Cash Show*, scheduled as a summer replacement for *Hollywood Palace* over ABC-TV on Saturday nights, were being pre-taped during late spring of 1969 at the Grand Ole Opry House, leaving little time for Cash and the rest of the cast to even eat at home. Writers had been shuttling in and out of Nashville for more than a month now, visiting the Cashes at their lake house and writing about the taping of the show and interviewing Cash on everything from why he prefers to wear black to what he thinks of Bob Dylan, and by the end of May he should have been climbing the walls of the Opry House. But Cash seems to have become immune to fatigue, after all these years of having to pick himself up one more time, and with two more shows to put in the can he was in relatively good spirits as he and June grabbed a late-afternoon meal in the Ramada Inn coffee shop before hustling downstairs for a read-through. A week later they would fly off to the Virgin Islands for a two-week vacation, once the taping was finished, and they planned to come back home and stay for a month before hitting the road again.

"Some diet, isn't it?" June was saying to a young songwriter named Mickey Newbury, seated at the table with them.

"Ummph," Cash mumbled, his mouth full of fried potatoes.

"See, when you go on one together, you can quit together."

"Ummph-hummph," said Cash, ripping apart a fried trout, laughing at something somebody said at the next table where some of the other members of the cast were drinking coffee, then returning to his plate. The conversation had moved around to causes and crusades, and more specifically to Cash's preoccupation with prisons and the American Indian, and Cash was saying, "I didn't go into it thinking about it as a 'crusade.' I mean, I just don't think prisons do any good. They put 'em in there and just make 'em worse, if they were ever bad in the first place, and then when they let 'em out they're just better at whatever put 'em in there in the first place. Nothing good ever came out of a prison. That's all I'm trying to say. If I can get some good done by writing and singing songs about prisons, it's a bonus."

June said, "At Cummins, now, John . . . "

"Where?" somebody said.

"Cummins, in Arkansas."

"The place where they dug up all those skeletons?"

"Yeah, that's the one," Cash said. He had stopped off at the prison to play a benefit, en route to Hollywood to guest on the Glen Campbell show. The prison had made the papers a year or so earlier when news leaked that several skeletons had been dug up on the grounds, touching off an investigation by Governor Winthrop Rockefeller. "Well see, I said some things during the show, like, here you are wearing old ragged clothes, and everybody's only got one suit to wear, and why don't they take some of that money the state's got and do some things here . . . "

"The Governor was there for the show," June said.

"Governor—"

"Rockefeller, isn't it?"

"Winthrop Rockefeller," somebody said.

"Yeah, well," Cash said, "anyway, after the show the Governor came up to me and said, 'I want to thank you for saying things I cannot say.' It got in the papers, because they had a lot of reporters there covering the show, and I heard later they got some things done. That's what I mean. I mean, I'm a musician. But if I can help out a little, well, it's a bonus."

Charley Pride, the only Negro star in country music, came in. He was going to be on the show they were working on. Cash reached across the table and shook hands, then went back to eating. He was asked about his friendship with Bob Dylan (Cash had written the album liner for Dylan's recent album, *Nashville Skyline*, which leads off with a Dylan-Cash duet recorded in Nashville, and Cash had once given his guitar to Dylan at Newport). "A lot of writers have just tried to make something out of it," Cash said. "I like him. That's all. He's a friend of mine. He's a good performer, and I like him, and I don't care what he stands for. Some of these writers have said stuff about how it didn't fit, that Dylan's for one thing and I'm for another. . . . "

"How *do* you feel about, say, Vietnam?"

"We're over there."

"Do you support it?"

"I support our Government's foreign policy," Cash said, wiping his hands on a napkin and pushing his plate out of the way now. "I don't know that much about the war. We were over there, and I'll tell you one thing, when you see our boys being brought back in helicopters and their guts spilling out it makes you a little mad about some of these folks back home. The way I feel about it, the only good thing that ever came from a war is a song and that's a hell of a way to have to get your songs. I don't know how patriotic I'd be if I was poor and hungry, though."

It was time to get downstairs and go over the script. The others were getting up and stopping by the cash register to sign for their checks. Cash, wearing a powder-blue one-piece flight suit with his name over the left breast, forever fidgeting, was anxious to get moving. In a playful mood, he began to sing softly to "I Walk the Line" words he had made up the afternoon before during a break in taping at the Opry House. *I keep my pants up with a piece of twine . . .*

"*John*," his wife gasped.

"Yes, love," Cash said, getting up and strolling out of the coffee shop, a little-boy grin on his face. *Just say you're mine, and pull the twine.*

"Something Rude Showing"

by Richard Goldstein (1969)

❁ ❁ ❁

"First Angry Man Of Country Singers"

by Tom Dearmore (1969)

Network television schedules had never been as full of country music as they were in the late 1960s and early 1970s. The Jimmy Dean Show, *the* Ozark Jubilee, *the* Midwestern Hayride, *and other programs featuring country music had appeared here and there on the big three networks, but in 1969, viewers could find three popular programs built around country music and country performers: The* Glen Campbell Good-Time Hour, Hee Haw, *and the* Johnny Cash Show.

For Cash, the ABC-TV show was an opportunity to introduce new material, feature guests whom he believed were important to the American music landscape, and promote the age-old country themes he held so dear. However, the new television star adapted uneasily to the medium, tolerating it only because he knew it was good for his career. "I never liked television," he confessed to the National Observer *during his show's run. "But now I have decided I am going to like it. I mean, if I'm going to do it every day, I might as well enjoy it. I don't like being so confined, but I like my guests, and it's my show, and it has to be good."*

The following articles sketch the singer during the late summer and autumn of 1969 and into 1970. In a piece of impressionism for Vogue *akin to*

Peter La Farge's essay in Sing Out!, *Richard Goldstein renders Cash from the rest of pop music's milk, declaring him, not Dylan, the true messenger of the 1960s. It is an appropriate introduction to the* New York Times Magazine *profile by Tom Dearmore, which echos the "messenger" theme. It was one of the most extensive considerations of Cash to date, and although Dearmore erroneously crowned Elvis Presley the spokesperson of the underclass (and, victimized by Cash's deception, refers to Cash's imagined Cherokee heritage), he captured the diverse composition of Cash's audience. At Cash's concerts, observed Dearmore, the rural Cash faithful opened their lawn chairs right next to the "suburban types" and "collegians."*

The very fact that the Times, Vogue, *and other urban-based, urban-oriented publications featured Cash illustrated the changes that were afoot. Certainly urban audiences were coming to him because of his association with folk music and the recent Man-in-Black press storm that Folsom Prison whipped up. But in addition, those who had first come to him—the country folk—were urbanizing. Over the previous thirty years, rural people in ever increasing numbers had been abandoning the farms of America for the wage work of the city, many seeing their incomes rise and their children go to college. But the prospering migrants also harbored nostalgia for their old country homes. Many who had grown up in the country listening to Cash looked to him to conjure the old days and the old ways. Cash—with his traditional country themes—was their memory.*

I

"Something Rude Showing"

by Richard Goldstein (1969)

THING about Johnny Cash is, you can't pin him down between margins, in quotes and metaphors, like nearly every other pop species. He defies classification by sound, scene, or sensibility. You can't call his music acid-placid. He doesn't come on with his fists clenched, either. You don't acquire his kind of chic seeing and sunning in the obscure Antilles. Even when he dresses the fop—in Edwardian waistcoat and ruffled shirts—there's always something rude showing. Like his neck or his expression.

It won't do to talk about Cash as down-home fascist country pie. Not with his "Ballad of Ira Hayes." Not with those best-selling albums recorded live behind bars (and not the kind that close on Sunday). He's into hymns, but they aren't excuses to knock the Supreme Court and bigcity sin. When Johnny Cash sings a hymn, you get this very solitary search for grace. And it's that same quality of struggle resolved, or deferred, or verging on agony that transforms just about everything he sings into what you feel when you're alone in a new room.

That's a kind of aloneness The Beatles never touch. It's something Bob Dylan is reaching for now, in the guise of simplicity. To Johnny Cash it's right out there, like a goddamn scar.

Like, if he were French, you wouldn't catch him singing about Springtime on the Seine.

And it's unnerving to see that on summertime television where you'd expect to find Mr. and Mrs. Young America and their Goodtime Freakout. Instead, on comes this big bulky warehouse of a guy, without a trace of the Whip 'n Chill mentality you need to make it as an M.C. in prime time. He isn't very quick on the comic draw. When he reads those cue cards, you know he's reading. His show is taped in Nashville. The sets look like old calendars, and his guests are a wilder assemblage than Braniff ads. Start with someone homey and franchised, like Minnie Pearl; then add the darling of Laurel Canyon, Joni Mitchell; and end with a gap-toothed Cajun fiddler who insists on smiling.

And even Bob Dylan. An old acquaintance. Once, you thought Cash would come around to Dylan's vision, and maybe start singing about hard women and tooth decay. But it's Dylan who's come over instead. His latest album, *Nashville Skyline*, has a duet with Johnny Cash. They sing "Girl from the North Country," an early Dylan composition, and it's an eerie experience for any long-ago folkie, because here's that song you once thought exclusively yours, opened wide again by a low-slung easy voice, with Dylan just tagging along in there. Watching that duet on television is even weirder than hearing it, because Dylan seems to be following the sag in Cash's face and retracing the cracks in his voice.

The Opry audience gives Dylan a polite ovation. His is not exactly their cup of mountain dew. But then Johnny Cash pulls his guitar up hip high and gets into something low and mangy—like "I shot a man in Reno, just to see him die"—and the crowd goes wild. They *always* love that line down home.

It's hard to believe there's someone left around here who can plug me and the people of Nashville into the same socket. But if anyone can bring us together, it's Johnny Cash and not that other Man.

II

"First Angry Man Of Country Singers"

by Tom Dearmore (1969)

WHY on the threshold of the nineteen-seventies, is the United States reverting to its rurigenous music of the nineteen-thirties? To some observers it is almost a comic anomaly that country-Western music, the backwoods balm of the Great Depression, should in this time of affluence, technological dominance and blasé youth suddenly gain millions of converts among those who once were repelled by it.

Indeed the country seems to have gone "country"-crazy: *The Beverly Hillbillies* goes on and on, *Hee Haw* is a Sunday prime-time prize of C.B.S.'s and "country" singers have now "made the networks" with their own shows and are recorded with the Boston Pops.

Country-Western string music was the cultural adrenalin of the thirties and forties in all the little Dullsvilles of the South, suffocating in the humid heat of Saturday nights when the bawling jukebox voices drifted out of slot-in-the-wall honky-tonks. It told of the slovenly, busted boozer, the flawless sweetheart, the fast trains that held some mystic promise, the hobo's death, the cowboy's loneliness. Twangy gospel pieces mapping the road to salvation (a railroad to the pearly gates in more than one instance) were on the same Wurlitzers with low-down music-to-swill-beer-by and tearjerkers about home and mother. The form appeared in the twenties among the hillbillies and cotton pickers of the poor South—an amalgam of ancient folk balladry, Negro spirituals, fundamentalist gospel pep music and Prohibition jazz. It flowered in the early thirties when the farmers got their battery radios and heard songs both mournful and rousing from WSM in Nashville, wept as Jimmie Rodgers, "The Singing Brakeman," related how Hobo Bill died alone but smiling in a frigid freight car.

Many Americans despised it as the banal evocation of a tawdriness of life unworthy of notice, as a nasal cacophony, as ignorance put to music. But it now is not only rising in popularity at home, it is, as John Greenway points out in *The American West* (the magazine of the Western History Association), making headway abroad—it has devotees all over Western Europe; there is a *Tokyo Grand Ole Opry* on the air, featuring bands like Jimmy Tokita and His Mountain Playboys. American country singers have packed the London Palladium and drawn cheers in Hobart, Tasmania, equal to those in Nashville, Tenn., the capital of country music.

At the sizzling apogee of the country music market is Johnny Cash, a cotton-field hand turned millionaire singer, returnee from the depths of drug-use dissolution—a tall, heavy man who looks like an outlaw Indian, smiles a crooked smile and plays an ornate Martin guitar. Since his career's start in the middle-fifties in the hog-and-hominy belt of the South, where his medium was centralized, he has gained an audience whose size and diversity are astounding. This year he topped the field with a Columbia album recorded at California's Folsom Prison and in June he opened his own network television program (he and Glen Campbell are the only two country-Western balladeers with their own nationwide shows, but Campbell is more Western and Cash is more country). Cash sells more records and draws larger and wider crowds than any other country singer; in August he sang to about 100,000 in four shows at the Wisconsin State Fair. On Saturday he is assured of a sell-out crowd at the Hollywood Bowl when he presents a program marking the 10th anniversary of the bowl's pop season. On a Sunday last May at a Detroit stadium he drew a capacity crowd of 26,000 and the gross was more than $80,000—the largest in the history of country music performances. Recorded on more than 13 million records (including 42 albums) and about a million tapes, his voice is the hottest-seller in the country spectrum, and the *Folsom Prison* album, enriched with profane impromptu commentaries and the approving howls of inmates, has been a major recent propellant. "It's sold one million already," he says with no trace of pride. "That's about $5-million, and it's only been out a little over a year." Country-Western music's volume is figured at more than $100-million this year and Cash's slice will be several million—no one is estimating closely because no one knows how fast he will be accelerated by his television show.

As the first angry man of the country songsters—the first grim and gutsy pusher of social causes—he has broken the mold of Nashville Grand Ole Opry–type country-Western and is pounding out his own folk form, trying to entertain while moving away from the rackety, say-nothing song types that have prevented many people from taking his field seriously. Unlike the comical, cowboy-hatted, spangle-decorated country warblers of early fame, he comes to his mission with a fierce and looming personality and black attire. And down deep in this John R. Cash (the R stands for nothing; Cash is an old English settler name that is on the tax books in about every Southern county) is a boiling grudge against certain injustices.

The Cash bass-baritone voice resists description and comparison, but it is at its best something like smooth and mellow thunder. Cash is sometimes like Paul Robeson toned down and countrified, sometimes like what Dean Martin might be if he were melancholy, but he really is unlike either, or anybody else on records. The voice is earthy-deep, ominous sometimes, resonant, virile, untrained, unconventional. It can be lonely and haunting, coming out as practically a dirge, and the next minute be booming happily on a jumping rock piece.

Cash has a blue tonality, does not sustain his notes, does not sing by the scale or sing sharps, and he slides into his flats. "He is constantly bending the tone," an academic observer says. "He is singing what's inside of him, searching in a haunting way for a note that isn't there. He decorates his melody according to his own interpretation." Some of his songs are akin to the old field cries of the Southern slaves, some are interspersed with bass talk. More than singing, his current hit, which is above the million-record level, "A Boy Named Sue," is story-telling to guitar accompaniment—a bawdy, swinging poem ("I tell ya, life ain't easy for a boy named Sue").

And the accent, strangely, is not of the Mississippi River delta from which he came, but of the Southern highlands. No honey-mouthed drawl from him, but the harder coarseness of the Appalachians ("Wonted man in Tinnosee," he sings, not "wawnted" as a flatlander might pronounce it). The speaking voice reminds one strongly of John Wayne, although it is a rough farmer's voice, and there is a parallel, too, in the manliness and disenthralled individualism.

On a searing afternoon in July he was headed for the county fair at Arthur, Ill., he had just sung at the annual Newport Jazz and Folk Festival, and the covered stadium at the fairgrounds was filling several hours before evening arrival. The sun stood high above the prairies—and perspiring on a seat directly in front of the plank stage was a starry-eyed waitress, approaching middle age, who had driven 60 miles from Shelbyville.

Cash has been her jukebox hero for years and now she is about to see him, almost close enough to touch. She is more articulate than most of the early arrivers about why she is willing to broil for hours for a hard first-row seat. "The common people and the poor people just have a feeling for him. You just feel like he's one of you. He's just common, that's all. I told my husband if I had to walk and see him, I'd do it. . . . I have a 17-year-old son who just hates country-Western music, but he's crazy about Johnny Cash. He says Johnny Cash is cool."

Almost two hours before the first of two Cash performances, at 7:15 P.M., the 5,000-seat stadium is packed. Colorful umbrellas sprout up here and there against the sun, and some women moan because that's what they forgot. Seated beside the waitress is a mod young slacks-clad woman with her husband, a tanned heavy-machinery operator not long out of the Air Force. "I think Cash is ugly, but I like him," the young wife says. "I like 'Folsom Prison Blues.'" The waitress scoffs—"He's not ugly at all."

Workingmen in sport shirts and collegians in Bermudas fan vainly, some with records brought to be autographed, as the sun lowers, and then a brief breeze brings the special aroma of country fairs, a pungent essence of dust, hamburgers, animal sweat, beer, manure, watermelon rinds and alfalfa. A woman tells an uninitiated friend of Cash's power: "He just melts you down." Menfolk make the torturous trip to the midway, while wives hold their seats, to fetch foot-long hot dogs, with or without chili, and giant orangeades. A handful of town police and sheriff's deputies look from the stage with unbelief upon the sea of hyperenergized humanity—more than 12,000, inside and outside the stadium—through which Cash must be escorted.

They have come from half of Illinois. Even here, in a remote and somnolent little cornland town, is seen the astonishing cross section that finds Cash irresistible. American Gothics in bib overalls and dirty-footed hippies are jammed together, along with mechanics, cab drivers, factory girls, red-faced tractor hands, students from the University of Illinois at Urbana and a smattering of fashionable suburban types. There are innocent-eyed, gospel-singing folk from the back country and husky T-shirted fellows who are well fortified with beer. And there are even a few of the locality's Amish, with their beards and flat-brimmed hats. This is Republican country, but a town leader avowed that President Nixon wouldn't have drawn such a crowd to Arthur on a hot summer afternoon.

There is uneasiness, though, because of Cash's failure to appear at the fair in 1967, when he was near physical ruin because of pep pills and was missing many engagements. The fair association booked him for $4,200 then, and the Saturday night crowd was surly. "He skipped three in a row that week," said entertainment chairman Sherman E.

(Red) Robinson, a jolly Arthur casket salesman. "We caught him in Monticello (Ill.) and sued him. This appearance is a compromise settlement in that suit. . . . We couldn't really afford him this year, but when we booked him two years ago he wasn't nearly so high. It would be my guess that to buy his show today, it would cost $17,000."

"I see him, I see him," screamed a woman 30 minutes before showtime as Cash and his troupe slipped into a trailer dressing room near the edge of the grounds, and the collective excitement neared hysteria. But Johnny saved himself for the first 35 minutes of his show, sending out his three singing groups—the Tennessee Three, the Carter Family and the Statler Brothers. One member of the country-prestigious Carter Family—a mother and three daughters—is Cash's comely and shapely wife, June. She is expecting their first baby in March or early April, but that hasn't affected her comic liveliness onstage as the emcee of the Carters. "This is the sex part of the show," she shrills, flouncing her filmy blue skirt, showing adequate pantaloons underneath and chiding boys sitting beneath the stage ("You with that Brownie Hawkeye . . . ") that ogling will be fruitless. Beyond the stand in front of her there is a crack as a tree limb breaks and a boy clutches among the leaves, barely saving himself from plummeting. "Don't fall out," June yells. "Are you going into orbit? Say hello to Armstrong and all them up there." (It was the night before the moon landing.) The quartet—girls with guitars and Mother Maybelle with an Autoharp—pours out the favorites that Carters of one generation or another have been singing on the air for many years—"Wildwood Flower," "Wabash Cannonball," "If I Could Be a Child Again" and "I'll Be All Smiles Tonight."

Then Cash walks onto the platform, having entered from the rear behind a wedge of police. The roar is like nothing ever heard in Arthur.

The crowd is on its feet. Husbands and wives clutch, middle-aged women raise their arms in rapture. Everett Dirksen never received an ovation like that in Illinois, and possibly not even Adlai Stevenson when he received the Democratic nomination in 1952.

Cash's guitar tears into the soggy night with "Big River," the lament of a fellow who followed a fickle woman to no avail through towns along the Mississippi River:

Now I taught the weepin' willow how to cry, cry, cry,
And I showed the clouds how to cover up a clear, blue sky.

His short patent-leather boots with red heels and soles twist in a little dance as his big frame wheels. He pulls the guitar high up on his chest, crimps his right arm lightly over the top of it, runs his fingers far out on the neck of the instrument and back to the other end.

Creeks of perspiration lace his cheeks; this is hard work for him. ("Gene Autry once said if it weren't so hard everybody would be doing it," he recalls.) Before another number, he lowers his guitar and tells a story, his eyes turning about the faces to the southwest, toward Arkansas. "I remember when I was a kid about 5 years old one mornin' in 1937—the winter of 1937. The rain had been fallin' day and night, and all the old folks kept sayin' yes, if that river keeps risin' it's goin' to break that levee and come right over that cotton land.

"One mornin' the Mississippi River broke the levee at Wilson, Arkansas, and I woke up and that black, muddy Mississippi River water was right up to the front door, and I heard my daddy holler and ask my momma, 'How high's the water, momma?' 'Two feet high and risin',' she answered." This sends him into one his songs (he has written more than 300 of various kinds) about his poor small-farm boyhood—"Five Feet High and Risin'." . . .

Johnny deals early on the program with railroads, one of his three hangups (convicts and mistreated Indians are the other two). He has been enthralled by the rails since the nineteen-thirties, when his father hopped Rock Island freights to seek work in far-off places because the little farm would not support the family. A locomotive whistle across the cotton fields on a frosty midnight might mean that Ray Cash was coming home with a few dollars, or it might mean nothing. "In Virginia, back in the early days," he tells the crowd, "there was an old farmer sittin' up on the side of a hill, and he saw Old 97 comin' down the line, and he hollered and he said, 'Hey Etter, Old 97 is burnin' up the rails and she'll never make it around the bend.' Well, the thing he saw that day he wrote, and he later wrote a song about it, and put it to the tune of 'The Ship That Never Returned,' and it was the story about that train that wrecked down at the bottom of the valley"—"The Wreck of Ole 97."

Wild applause follows his announcement that it appears his A.B.C. television show will be extended through next winter. Hundreds of autograph seekers charge him as he leaves the stage, but he is saved by a wedge of six burly policemen. "No autographs will be given," the loudspeaker advises. "We will not be permitted to let Johnny Cash out of the house trailer until everyone is out of the arena." A tearful girl squeals, "I'll never listen to him again, never in a million years."

Noting that the audience was being forced to miss the Johnny Cash show on television, he had said almost apologetically, "We've been able to have some of our friends on the show. The network actually told us in so many words that we had to have this or that guest on. We were proud to have some of them on—we've had some beautiful people on, like Joni Mitchell, Doug Kershaw, Bob Dylan and some of them." But some of Cash's friends believe the expensive show, filmed in the Grand Ole Opry Building at Nashville, has too many guests, too much variety, too much slapstick comedy that blurs the image of the star and leaves the production without definition. And Johnny was irritated because some of his friends were not approved. “I want them to call me and tell me why Pete Seeger can’t be on my show,” he sternly told director Bill Carruthers in a Nashville hotel room in May. “Pete Seeger is a great American; he’s sold the Appalachian Mountains in Asia. Why can’t I have my friends on this show?” The network smiled on Bob Dylan, an embodiment of protest whom Cash calls “probably the greatest poet of our times,” but no nod came for Seeger, whose banjo and voice have damned the Vietnam war. “I tried, but they wouldn’t have him on it,” Johnny said following the Arthur program. “I think Pete Seeger is a good American as I’ve ever met,” he said.

Many hippies are drawn to Cash because of his affection for the rural poor and the incarcerated, because his profanity-studded language and strange attire place him outside the establishment, but they and other war-resisters and assorted demonstrators are not esteemed by him. He holds the rural South’s stubborn belief that U.S. foreign policy should be supported, that it is a man’s duty to bear arms. “I think everybody should serve their time for their country,” he says. “I did. It’s not up to every man to decide when it’s time to go defend our country. We elect men to decide that for us.” (He and June have sung for servicemen in Vietnam.)

Why do hippies tumble for him? “God, I don’t know. They say they’re searchin’ for truth, and maybe they find it in my songs. It’s nothing new to be searchin’ for truth. Pontius Pilate was after it hot and heavy.” As he and bluff Dan Blocker (Hoss Cartwright) were horsing around in a television show “talk-through” at Nashville this spring, someone spoke jestingly about adding the national anthem. “‘The Star-Spangled Banner’ is a warlike song,” Blocker said. “All that about rocket’s red glare, bombs bursting in air. We’re supposed to be a peace-loving country." Johnny turned away without comment, strumming his guitar.

Johnny is content, though, with "his thing" on the show—the "Ride-This-Train" segment announced by the roar and whistle or a steam locomotive. Cash sits by the tracks beside a dimly lit station, dispensing folklore illustrated with film clips, strumming as he talks, mainly singing about brave and simple folk, about the Depression-broken wanderers and how life was borne in that era. "I'm real pleased with that part of the show," he says. "This is what I'm trying to get across."

Cash, who has the face and stature of his Cherokee forebears, seems transposed from another time. When he sings in Nashville's Grand Ole Opry hall with his shaggy dark hair hanging over the back of his shirt collar, it is not difficult to imagine that he is a frontiersman who took a wrong turn on a trail 160 years ago and has just now delivered his pelts to Fort Nashborough. The face is a map with many miles on it and there is a powerful solemnity in the dark brown eyes, but no hardness. Bowing his body, kicking his shiny boots, he struts and turns, stroking deep guitar tones, and the smooth and virile baritone rolls out. And the clothes like the man fit no pattern, because he designed them himself—a copious, square-cut black "preacher's coat" reminiscent of the frontier, a dandy's low-cut vest; tight striped trousers; a high-collared white shirt with ruffles to the throat and ruffled cuffs.

There is a faint flavor of menace in his cheek scar and the facial twist as he sings out of the right side of his mouth. He could be a truck driver, a steel hustler dressed up, a card-dealing riverboat man, the marshal of Deadwood. The style is indefinable, but it gets results.

And how sweet is success to Johnny Cash, who made about $2-million last year? He is like a 6-foot–2 coil of high-voltage wires, never seated more than a few minutes, ever walking and twisting under the pressure of a cruel schedule, apparently relaxed in public only when he is singing. "Success is having to worry about every damn thing in the world except money," Cash said during the grueling creating of his television show. "I still don't know understand it. If you don't have any time for yourself, any time to hunt or fish, that's success."

But he sees his TV series as an advance for his kind of music, although he cannot define the genre. Stiffening at the use of the common terminology in his presence, he says, "My music is not country-Western. I am a country boy, and a lot of my music has a country sound to it." Well, what kind of music is it? "I don't think I'm the one to say, because I'm not all that dyed in the wool. I've only written two Western songs, out of the 300 I've recorded. I don't see trying to put something in a bag and keep it there. . . . My music—I just call it Johnny Cash–type music. I don't imitate anybody."

And why have his songs gripped so many people? "The honesty, the realism—telling it like it is." He takes satisfaction in what a newsman told him after he sang to the Folsom inmates: "You just sold your music to those guys, and you don't fool those guys about anything."

Cash has sung at Folsom four times and wanted to make an album there, with clanging steel doors and other prison sounds in the background. "And after six years of talking, I finally found the man who would listen at Columbia Records. Bob Johnston believed me when I told him that a prison would be the place to record an album live." He writes of the dehumanizing effect of lonely imprisonment, derides the efforts at rehabilitation in the context of the typical prison. "Can it work? 'Hell no,' you say. How could this torment possibly do anybody any good. . . . You sit on your cold steel mattressless bunk and watch a cockroach crawl out from under the filthy commode, and you don't kill it. You envy the roach as you watch it crawl out under the cell door." The writing is directed to the inmates, but he adjures his listeners, "Hear the sounds of the men, the convicts—all brothers of mine—with the 'Folsom Prison Blues.'"

"I speak partly from experience," he says. "I have been behind bars a few times—sometimes of my own volition, sometimes involuntarily. Each time, I felt the same feeling of kinship with my fellow prisoners." He likes to see convicts laugh because "I know how lonely they feel, how lonely they are." He has also sung for inmates in state prisons in Texas, Kansas, Tennessee and Arkansas, and his specialty is scrawling down a song for the particular prison just before he arrives. At Arkansas's Cummins Prison Farm, the scene of barbaric practices in the recent past and still no model of penology, he lectured the State Legislature in song on a brilliant afternoon last April. "There's a lot of things that need changin', Mr. Legislator Man," he belted out, eyeing a group of lawmakers who sat with scrubbed and whooping inmates on the ball field. His voice rolled across the table-flat cottonfields:

. . .
You say you're trying to rehabilitate us,
Then show us you are.

The appearance was being televised and Cash implored the "fat, rich Arkansas farmer" in the audience to give liberally to the fund to build a prison chapel. He said he was giving $5,000 to the fund and Gov. Winthrop Rockefeller had given $10,000, "but he can afford it." (Cash has since accepted the chairmanship of the campaign.) Tears welled in inmates' eyes when he and June sang old religious numbers, but the "yahoos" rose when the pair belted out the ultimate in hoedown, "Jackson"—about passion and passion spent.

Near the end of the musicale, Prisons Commissioner Robert Sarver came onstage and said that Cash had said "some things I've been afraid to say" in the Cummins song. "That's all right," Cash told Sarver. "I had nothing to lose." After receiving an honorary "life sentence," he mounted a wobbly mule-drawn prison wagon with Rockefeller and they drove it around the farm to the hoots of the convicts. Three weeks later the legislature gave Rockefeller the prison appropriation he had been seeking—the first tax money that had ever been allocated for that purpose.

Never has Johnny received an ovation like the one at San Quentin in February. He had the wavelength, he had the anger, and the inmates were on the chairs and tables in the mess hall before he finished a song he said he'd written the previous afternoon to convey "some of the things I feel about San Quentin." The record people are hopeful that his new San Quentin album will follow *Folsom Prison Blues* into the millions.

Ecstasy seizes inmates when he tells about his own misadventures with small-town bullies, and especially when he leans on Starkville, Miss. "You wouldn't believe it, but one night I got in jail in Starkville, Mississippi, for pickin' flowers," he told the San Quentinites. "I was walking down the street, you know, goin' to get me some cigarettes or sumpin's, about 2 o'clock in the mornin' after the show, I think it was. Anyway, I reached down and picked a dandelion here and a daisy there as I went along, and this car pulls up—AAARRRR—and says, 'Get in here, boy what're you doin'?' I said, 'I'se just pickin' flowers.' Well, $36 for pickin' flowers and a night in jail—you can't hardly win, can you? No tellin' what they'd do if you'd pull an apple or sumpin'."

Johnny's protest is not wide ranging, and he does not adhere to any politics. A private man, he does not like to bare his inner self through conversational philosophizing, but now and then a line he has written gives a glimpse: "I'd sing more about more of this land, but all God's children ain't free." And he has never sung in the campaign of any politician except pro–civil rights Governor Rockefeller of Arkansas who paid him and his troupe about $20,000 for singing at seven rallies last year, and Cash lured people from the countryside by the tens of thousands and magnetized them long enough for the ineloquent Rockefeller to get the political message across.

Cash has sung without charge at benefit events for Indians and recorded an album, *Bitter Tears*, dealing with their troubles. Indians in South Dakota and Oklahoma have heard him on their home grounds, and he helped the Senecas fight the damming of the Allegheny River. "I understood the Senecas' feelings about the flood waters flooding their ancient burial grounds," he said.

Compassion is Cash's main motive force. Drives against illness draw heavy donations from him; his special passion is a campaign to establish a $2-million burn-treatment center at Vanderbilt University.

Two years ago Cash seemed down for the count, after a seven-year struggle with drugs. Never a consumer of the more notorious drugs, he slipped into the pep pill–and-tranquilizer habit and as in the case of his eating (he consumes a steak, it seems, in about four breaths), he took them on voraciously. High on stimulants, he acted zanily, found himself in assorted municipal lockups, in 1965 was arrested and jailed briefly at El Paso, Tex., for bringing 1,143 pills into the United States from Mexico. That encounter caused his friends deep worry, even though the drugs turned out to be unstartling.

He missed appearances, his fortunes sank. "He was a wild S.O.B. around here," one of his Nashville friends says. The shock of waking up one day in a Georgia jail and not remembering how he got there (a policeman had found him wandering aimlessly) brought him out of the spin.

Johnny does not share credit with anyone for his comeback from the abyss. "I give myself credit for that," he said in May. "It was a tough fight, and nobody else can whip it. It's only been about 18 months ago that I quit pills. Eighteen months ago, I was walking death. I used to take up to 100 pills a day. I don't know why in the world they didn't kill me. Any doctor would tell you it would. I would play one against the other—pep pills to pep me up, tranquilizers to calm me down." No liquor was added to the mix though—"I never did drink badly; a beer now and then, but I don't like it. It burns up my energy, makes me sleepy."

On March 1, 1968, he and June Carter drove to nearby Franklin, Ky., and said the nuptial vows. It was his second marriage and her third; she had sung irregularly on the Cash show for seven years. Radiant, with long reddish hair and a face out of an Appalachian ballad, she came from the Blue Ridge foothills of Virginia with a guitar in her hands as a tot. Despite two years of dramatic training in New York, she retains more of the country intonations than her deep-voiced husband. If anyone understands Johnny Cash, she does, and their marriage seems idyllic. Rising before sunup, she cooks a farm breakfast of hot biscuits, ham and eggs for his mammoth appetite. She plies him with hot-dog lunches in paper plates as he rehearses in Nashville, and he hands her bill-paying money from a crumpled wad of greenbacks in his coveralls pocket. Her two daughters by a previous marriage—Carlene, 13, and Rose, 10—live with them, and his four daughters by the other marriage are with their mother in California.

The Cashes live in the hilly woods, beside Old Hickory Lake, in the fashionable suburb of Hendersonville, 20 miles north of Nashville, and their home is surely one of the most remarkable in the world. It is 10,000 square feet of Johnny Cash architecture, set in solid limestone and crooking around a bluff. Part of the roof is sod, with grass growing in it; inside, the beams and the stairways winding to turret-like round bedrooms are square-hewn logs from pioneer barns in the Cumberlands.

Outside, behind a rock dam and fed by a stream gurgling down a ravine, is the swimming pool, and below in a small inlet is a dock at which fishing boats are tied. Johnny fishes often, with Bob Dylan and other guests and with his father, mindful that the Cumberland River was the highway of the westering leatherstockings. It is here that he writes most of his songs—in a large oval living room above the lake. "I generally get an idea for a song every time I'm fishin' or out in the woods," he says. "That's generally when songs come to me. I write 'em down after I come home." And the vegetable garden (almost an acre) on a hilltop about the house is where he works off his nervousness, releases the pressures of success. "I can work in that garden all morning and I'm ready to come in here and make the show in the afternoon," he said during an exhausting rehearsal. The curious who drive past see him in blue coveralls, furiously swinging his hoe, a towering figure against a backdrop of sparkling lake. Across the road live his parents, Ray and Carrie Cash, in a spacious brick home he bought for them last spring.

Up from sharecropping—the Southern economic cellar—is the story of the Cashes. Everybody picked cotton (Johnny could gather 350 pounds a day as a boy). When Johnny graduated from Dyess (Ark.) High School, he traveled to Pontiac, Mich., to accept a beginner's job in the Fisher Body Company plant. Two weeks later, he was back home. "I hated up there," he says. He almost starved, he says, because others in his boarding house were faster at devouring food. At 18, on a July day in 1950, he laid down the traces on a mule-drawn plow, went to Memphis and was in the Air Force by nightfall. Trained as a radio intercept operator, he was sent to Germany and spent four years in the service, progressing to staff sergeant. He was able to buy his first guitar in Germany, and he "fooled around the barracks with it," kicking up Nashville tunes. "I was lonely in the Air Force," he says, in a still-lonely tone.

Discharged, he headed back to Memphis and took a course in radio announcing, hoping that would get him into studios. Soon he was introduced to two Memphis musicians-on-the-rise—Luther Perkins and Marshall Grant, "Tennessee Two." They liked Johnny's guitar and voice and it became "The Tennessee Three."

Suddenly, in 1955, the rainbow: Johnny was recorded for the first time, singing two songs he had written—"Hey Porter" and "Cry, Cry, Cry"—and Sun Records had a red-hot product on the first try, after having kept Johnny waiting for several months for an audition. He began pouring out new lyrics as the recorders waited eagerly, and he lodged in the big time with "I Walk the Line," the rhythmic testimony of a faithful lover: "Because you're mine, I walk the line." His hit records proliferated—"Ballad of a Teen-Age Queen," "Don't Take Your Guns to Town," "Orange Blossom Special," "I Got Stripes," "Ring of Fire." (His wife, June, won a Grammy for writing the last one. Cash himself has won about 75 awards, including four Grammys.)

Few of the songs Cash has written are superlative, except when sung by Cash, and a very few ("Flushed From the Bathroom of My Heart," for example) are notoriously bad. The Cash voice, the Cash style are essential to the success of most of the Cash lyrics.

Cash's most serious shortcoming is that he leans excessively on the Depression, which is fast becoming ancient history. He sings about the poor of yesterday, but not about the poor of today (with the exception of convicts and Indians, who are a tiny fragment of the whole). He sings movingly of Hobo Bill, but when Jimmie Rodgers sang that he was describing his own time, and that was the reason for the brakeman's greatness. There are few hobos today, but there is plenty of misery for Cash to interpret outside the prisons and the reservations. The poor in this period of richness are more controversial because they are raising a commotion and are disproportionately black. It has fallen to Elvis Presley to tell their story with Scott Davis's jumping ballad, "In the Ghetto," also sung hauntingly by Dolly Parton of country beginnings. Cash will not talk much of the contemporary poor, of civil rights and civil wrongs, of black people and Chicanos. Perhaps many of the down-South country folk who buy his platters would rather not hear about these subjects (prison reform has never been their strong suit either), but possibly in Cash there are recondite sympathies that will someday surface in song.

"Johnny Cash: 'I'm Growing, I'm Changing, I'm Becoming'"

by Dorothy Gallagher (1971)

❁ ❁ ❁

"Cash's 'Gospel Road' Film Is Renaissance for Him"

by George Vecsey (1973)

The Carter Family wrote its name into music history in the late 1920s, selling records so briskly that the Family helped start country music on the road to commercial viability. Its early recordings for Victor Records, done in Bristol, Virginia, in 1927, were among the first in country music, and they influenced the sound of future performers. However, the Carters' importance to country music didn't end in the 1920s. Forty years later they helped save Johnny Cash. Over the years they spent on the road together, the Carter Family's steadfast faith in and support of Cash helped him negotiate from his drug-filled life to a drug-free one. The Carters accepted him and nurtured him when it might have been have been easier to cast him off and find work elsewhere; they also kept the message of the gospel in J.R.'s ears. June Carter (by 1968 June Carter Cash), her mother Maybelle, and Maybelle's husband Ezra all took part in Cash's recovery.

As Cash regained the keenness of his senses—senses that had been dulled by drugs for so many years—he began to make his faith a part of his life again. Surely, he had never stopped believing in or acknowledging God; he had just ejected Him from the driver's seat. Slowly, he accepted God's presence into his life and began to acknowledge his faith more frequently in interviews with the press.

In 1971, he released the album The Holy Land, *a set of songs inspired by a pilgrimage to Israel. Then, in 1973, came* The Gospel Road, *a film he produced in the Holy Land based on his perception of the life of Jesus. The recovery from drugs, his revitalized faith and his surge in popularity made the project possible. He had the freedom to follow his desires. Cash called the movie his most important work yet, and the press followed along, not certain how to handle the story of this one-time pill worshiper who now had picked up the cross.*

The articles below, Dorothy Gallagher's from Redbook *and George Vecsey's from the* New York Times, *attempt to document the extent to which God and June Carter were influencing his life and work.*

I

"Johnny Cash: 'I'm Growing, I'm Changing, I'm Becoming'"

by Dorothy Gallagher (1971)

There is, first of all, nothing "country" about a country-music tour. There is the limousine, the airport, the plane, the limousine, the motel, the auditorium. On tour Johnny Cash goes through a plastic America. It is as though he is standing still while a stage backdrop revolves behind him, creating with different details the illusion of movement. Motel rooms vary only from fake Spanish to fake French Provincial. Auditorium decor changes only from pink and green to turquoise and orange. The tour gives Johnny Cash no sense of the country from which his country music came.

Waiting to go on stage in the dressing room of a Mobile, Alabama, auditorium, Cash seems irritable. This is to be the first of a three-day personal-appearance tour. Tomorrow he will be in Jacksonville, Florida; the next day, in West Palm Beach. Tonight he is surrounded by people and he looks as though he wishes they would go away. June, his wife, says something to him and he answers with a slight edge: "Aw, honey, what do you want to do like that for?" A young man is introduced to him as "Larry, the boy you sent the records to in Vietnam." He shakes hands with Larry, unsmiling. I am introduced as "the young woman who's doing the article," and he shakes my hand, again without a smile.

His reserve is disconcerting. Watching Johnny Cash on television, I have had the same sense of his reserve. Unlike most public personalities, he doesn't project a clear "image" to me, and that makes him a mystery.

He is a mystery also because to me the people and the part of the country he comes from are mythic. Johnny Cash's face is interchangeable with those of poor Southern whites photographed in the now-famous documentary studies of the Depression—closed, wary, prideful. They are the *real* Americans, and someone brought up like me in Eastern cities may never quite understand them.

So at the beginning of this three-day tour that I am about to make with Cash and his troupe I have few preconceptions about what I will discover.

Before leaving New York I had asked a long-haired 23-year-old what he thought about Cash. "I really dig him," he said. "He started out all gung-ho American—my country right or wrong, God will fix everything. But he's into what's happening now—kids and drugs and war. His head is changing, but he's still real, you know?"

At his Mobile concert, though, I watched a predominantly middle-aged audience file into the auditorium. The women wore print or "dressy" dresses, unhip rimless glasses and permanent waves. The men wore crew cuts, sports shirts; some wore bright-colored coats. Whatever it was they like about Cash, it wasn't primarily his sympathy for kids and drugs and war protesters. I wondered how it was possible for a man to maintain constituencies in the widely separated countries of Bob Dylan and Billy Graham.

The audience in Mobile was polite but reserved. The first half of the show was a warm-up; as in boxing matches, the main event is last. The Tennessee Three, Carl Perkins, the Statler Brothers, the Carter Family—to which June Carter Cash belongs—sang and did comedy bits. Intermission, and then from a backstage microphone comes the deep voice—"Hello, I'm Johnny Cash"—and he bounds on stage, guitar slung behind his back. "I'm glad to be doing a personal appearance back in the *South*," he says, and gets the first enthusiastic response of the evening.

Once he begins singing, he holds the audience in a world of nostalgia: songs of floods and failed cotton crops, of God who works miracles, of the longing for lost love, of midnight train whistles that promise better places and times, of men who do violence in desperation and pay for it because that's the way life is.

The world he sings about may no longer exist, but there are many in his audience who remember it very well. This much I already know about Cash: that is the world into which he was born—the rural South in the midst of the Depression. He was raised among people who suffered from poverty but believed that if a man had faith in the Lord, the love of a good woman and the willingness to work hard, he would overcome. Those people continue to believe that, and it is the source of their strength and righteousness.

Country music grew out of the Depression, and it reflects these beliefs. It is a mixture of gospel, folk, and jazz, to which the backwoods poor added their own experiences of poverty and helplessness. It is the music Cash sang as a boy on an Arkansas cotton farm, the music he wrote as a teenager and began to sing professionally in Memphis in the early 1950s. In the early '60s his popularity crossed the Southern boundary. The grind of one-night stands, an unhappy marriage and probably other things led him into the pep-pill-tranquilizer cycle. He was what is now known as a "speed freak."

By 1968, he had kicked the pills. He had divorced his first wife, who now lives in California with their four daughters, and married June Carter, by whom he has a baby son. He also in the past few years has branched out of traditional country songs to include themes of cruelties done to prisoners, to Indians. (Recently he appeared in an unusual film, *A Gunfight*, financed by the Jicarilla Apache Indian tribe of New Mexico.) And he has concerned himself with the predicaments of the young: " . . . And the lonely voice of youth cries: 'What is Truth?' . . . "

That is not one of the songs he sang on this Southern tour, maybe because no long-haired young were in his audiences.

After the Mobile concert, rather than take a plane the next day with the rest of the troupe, I hitched a ride to Jacksonville with the sound truck. There was a time when Cash traveled from one appearance to the next by mobile home bus. It must have been exhausting.

During the ten-hour drive across Alabama and northern Florida I talked to one of the sound crew, a kid from Dallas, about the performance we had just seen. Holding hands, smiling into each other's eyes, John and June Cash had sung love songs to each other. . . .

"June takes my breath when she goes," John had said to the audience when his wife left the stage.

"Do you think all that was for real?" I asked the sound man.

"I've seen a lot of people do that kind of thing," he said. "And when people don't like each other, they can't really look at each other. Those two look."

In Jacksonville the next night I talked to June for a few minutes. Watching her perform in Mobile, I had thought she was too good to be true. Too radiant, too gracious, too serene. But now she completely charmed me. I hadn't told anyone I would be riding the sound truck instead of the plane to Florida, and when I appeared backstage June rushed over.

"Oh honey, we were so worried about you," she said in her warm, throaty drawl. She had noticed my absence and made me a gift of her concern. It was too flattering not to believe.

The Jacksonville audience, more responsive than the one in Mobile, made a difference in Cash's performance. He moved around the stage more, let more energy out.

Afterward I asked Carl Perkins, who has toured with Cash for almost five years, if he could explain the difference between audiences. He couldn't really, except to say that "Mobile always was pretty dead." And he added: "John hates tours except once in a while when he can let go on stage. He started to holler tonight and I knew he was having a good time. That's one of his freedoms, when he lets go that way. John's restless, hates to be in one place. He gets nervous trapped in hotels and airports. He's always been like that; he'd rather get off by himself in the woods."

On the flight to West Palm Beach the next day the woman who handled public relations for the Cashes sat next to me and raved. John and June were marvelous, wonderful, so in love, so good to each other, so concerned for the friends. "You should see them with that baby," she said. "John Carter is his daddy's whole life."

Ten-month-old John Carter doesn't look much like either of his parents. He is a handsome, sturdily built boy, with red hair and dark eyes. When I saw him having lunch with his father and mother in the West Palm Beach hotel restaurant, he was elegantly dressed in white short pants, matching jacket and beret. He always goes along on their tours.

"I promised I would nurse him for a year," June said. "He's no trouble at all on tour. Look. Watch this." She applauded as John Carter succeeded in getting mashed potatoes on his spoon, and the baby giggled. "He's a real ham."

"Eat, John Carter, eat," his father told him. "Eat, Son. It's good."

June would talk to me, she said, when the baby took his nap.

In the days before Women's Liberation made me think twice about definitions of women, I would have described June Carter Cash as the essence of femininity. She is physically lush, with a full, voluptuous figure, fuller than usual now because she is nursing her son. She seems open and warm and she glows with a contentment that she says is due entirely to a man.

"I'm so happy," she said when we were sitting beside the pool. "I feel as though God has given us so much that sometimes—I know it's silly, but when we're on stage together, sometimes I can hardly keep from crying."

I knew there was a time when things were not so good for her, and I asked if she would talk about the years when John was on drugs.

"I don't mind to talk about it. I wasn't around when John first got on pills. I found out about it when I was hired to work his show; and then I just couldn't stand to do a show with someone who might be tipsy from pills. So when we were on tour I would find where he hid them and flush them down the commode.

"I wasn't emotionally involved with him then," she said. "But somehow, he took it from me. None of the boys who worked with him would have got rid of his pills, but I knew if *somebody* didn't do it, we wouldn't get through the tour. So I just thought. Well, if he's going to haul off and hit me, he'll hit me. But somebody's got to fight him. He'd be furious for a moment, but he was never unkind to me."

A television director who worked with Cash during those years had told me that "Johnny was completely irresponsible. He'd promise to do a rehearsal or a show and he'd never turn up. He was on his way out; nobody trusted him any more."

"Anyway," June said, "for a long, long time I never admitted that I cared for him, not to myself, not to anybody in the world. And then it really got to bugging me, you know? But . . . I don't know . . . I guess it all worked out for the best."

Her hesitation stemmed from the fact that at the time each of them was married to someone else.

"When I admitted to myself that I cared for him, it was a very difficult time for me. I'm not a fighter—you know? I never had raised my voice in my life or been violent in any way. But when you're on drugs like John was, you never know what they're going to be like. All kinds of weird things went through his mind. He was kind and gentle one minute and vicious and wild the next.

"I found myself coping with him in a way that was against my nature. I decided that if I had to fight, I would fight. Literally, if I had to pick up a baseball bat, I would do it. If I had to scream, I would do it. And it just wasn't me.

"There were times when we quarreled and I felt like I was fighting for his life. He was literally killing himself with the drugs, down to skin and bone, and he could have taken an overdose very easily and died.

"I told him that life was beautiful, wonderful, and great, that he had no excuse to treat himself this way. He had a God-given talent and he had no excuse for doing a bad performance—ever! You know, there's very few people like him in the world that have magnetism and are just . . . well . . . that are just the man he is. He's the greatest man

I've ever known in my life. And I just couldn't stand to see him destroy himself.

"In the end, I don't think I did anything for John. He did it himself. He just decided that he was a better man than the way he was behaving and he stopped taking the drugs."

There was a little more to it than that. June insists that John did not have any kind of psychotherapy, but he did talk to a close friend who was a psychiatrist.

"John and I had this good friend. Nat Winston, who was born near my home town. He was Commissioner of Mental Health for the state of Tennessee at that time, and I went to talk to Nat because I had to talk to someone about my relationship with John.

"He said, 'June, you are the most independent cuss I've ever seen in my life. You won't take a nickel off anybody and you always do just what you want to do. But if ever you decide that you really love this man and come hell or high water you're going to stick with him—and to heck with whatever that brings—and you let yourself become dependent on him, you'll come out of it all right.'

"John had been living alone in a little house on a lake in Tennessee, and once morning I took Nat and went out there. That was a few days after John had gotten out of jail in Georgia—he had taken so many pills that he was wandering around the streets not knowing what he was doing, and they put him in the jail to sleep it off.

"And Nat and I went out to the lake to see him and we all three talked. I told John that whatever happened, I was prepared to go along with him. And Nat said that if John wanted, he'd go out there every day and they could just talk. So for a couple of weeks Nat went out there and he and John would chat and John just got stronger and stronger. He stopped taking the pills, just stopped cold. That was a hard five or six years, but from the day he stopped, from that day to this, there's never been one angry word between us. I don't know what I'd do if he raised his voice to me now. I guess I'd just drift away and die."

This night's concert was the final one of the tour and I was afraid I might be bored seeing the same show for the third time. But as it turned out, it wasn't the same show at all.

Whatever that magic is that sometimes happens between performer and audience, it happened during this concert. I found myself carried away—clapping my hands and stamping my feet like everyone else. And when I looked around at the others in the entourage I saw that they felt it too; they were grinning and moving with the music as though they'd never heard it before. The show ended with the 12-verse "Children, Go Where I Send You," which built to a crescendo and left everyone exhausted. "Wow," the guy on the sound crew said, "that was really something! I'm glad you got to see a good one."

I stayed behind to talk to some people, and suddenly I realized that the bus that carries the troupe from the auditorium to the motel had left without me. Along with 100-odd fans who were hoping for a glimpse of the stars, I chased the bus down the street. When we caught it in stalled traffic, I knocked on the door, which opened for me and closed quickly on the fans. There is something frighteningly seductive about that—about the immediate sense of superiority that comes with being included where others are excluded—and I wondered if it is possible for any star to avoid feeling godlike, even Johnny Cash, who talks a great deal about God.

On stage Cash mixes piety with *machismo*, switching from gospel to love songs to lusty ballads. In Jacksonville he was asked to sing "Welfare Cadillac," a song about a welfare chiseler, and ignored the request. I had asked June about his politics and she said, "John's not left and he's not right. He once said to me, 'Don't ask me what I think about anything unless you want to know about the next five minutes.

My mind changes all the time. I believe in one thing one month and the next month I believe something else. I'm changing. I'm growing. I'm becoming.'

"I know," she added, "that John is troubled. I know that where he didn't used to take issue with anything, his heart hurts if he stays quiet now. His shoulders get heavy because he feels a responsibility for young people. They care about him, the young kids, and they're our future. How do you turn your back on them?

"John has never believed in war. I don't think anybody does. But you know, if you don't stand behind your country . . . I don't know . . . you've got to believe in the principles that this country stands on. But you ask John about these things."

"I think," Johnny Cash said the next morning, "that one thing about youth today is that they're not coming to understand the real truths of Christianity. They're looking for Jesus in drugs and He ain't there. Because drugs are the tool of the devil—that's the way I see them."

He and June were still in bathrobes, having breakfast. It seemed too early, after the excitement of the concert the night before, to be talking about drugs and religion, but the tour was over and he was eager to get home to Tennessee.

"Listen, you want to know about drugs and me? It's a miracle, and I mean a miracle, that I wasn't killed dozens of times. When I was taking pills somebody would give me another kind of pill and I'd take it without knowing what it was. And I'd mix it with liquor. Next thing I knew, I'd be waking up somewhere.

"Kids say that drugs turn them on to love, but I'll tell you, there's no such thing as love when you're on drugs. Drugs are the whole center of your life. You'll do anything to get them, betray anyone who's precious to you. Like I betrayed June. I'd lie to her, behave in cunning ways, if I had to, so I could get the pills."

I asked him if there had been something about his life, or something about life in this country, that had made him and so many people turn to drugs.

"I don't know. I'll tell you why I took them—because it felt good. There isn't anybody can get a kid off drugs by telling him it doesn't feel good. He *knows* how it makes him feel. For a while you're so stimulated your mind is like a high-speed camera clicking away at three hundred and sixty degrees and you see and know everything.

"There are all those beautiful visions, all right, and those realizations and feelings of love and awareness. But when you come down off it, you pass that line from ecstasy to horror. You go down the other side of that whole thing, and the going down ain't worth the coming up. Here's something. I wrote this poem when I was quitting that says the way I felt about it:

Are there ruined regions of the mind
Where reason didn't reach to draw the line.
Where the brain was pounded by some drug
And gave in till a hole was finally dug?
And who can know what part is the hole
And who can say what it does to the soul?

"I still worry that I might have damaged my brain with pills. I don't think so, but I'll tell you, even after three years off drugs, at least once a week I'll have a horrible nightmare. I've got pills in my pocket that I'm trying to hide from somebody, and I'm always falling down and cutting myself, and somebody's chasing me and I'm going to jail, and somebody's beating me. All kinds of horrible things. At least once a week. It was almost every night at first.

"I think the kids are wising up at an early age. If they start fooling around with drugs, I hope they do it while they're young and can see what it's doing to them and then they'll have the strength to get off it.

"I was older and it was harder for me. My body fought against it and saved me; I had a self-survival thing built into my mind in some way to help me fight it. But not everybody's so lucky.

"The thing I've tried to tell kids is that as long as the laws are as they are, it's a kind of ridiculous thing to smoke pot. Maybe I agree with what they say about the law being unjust. But until it's changed, and it'll be their turn to change it soon, they oughta stay away from it.

"They've got to have some kind of foundations and moral principles to their lives. And I think they can find it in the Bible."

"But," I said, "Christianity has been so misused, it's no wonder they reject its values."

"Yeah," Cash said, "but they don't have to relate to the bad things that have been done in the *name* of Christianity. They don't have to have any truck with wars that have been fought in the name of God, of all the ridiculous things. All this killing in the name of Christ—death to the infidels!—but kids don't have to relate to that crap. Because bad things were done in the name of religion doesn't mean religion is bad."

June, who had been packing in another room, came in on the tail of her husband's last sentence.

"I just believe in God so much," she said. "I wish everyone in the world had a religion of some kind. We think that if young people could find some kind of spiritual experience, it's better than drugs or anything.

"And they're searching for it. I know. The reason I think they wear old-timey clothes and a young girl would rather have a beaded bag from the 1900s than a new leather purse is that they're trying to go back to the things this country was founded on. If we don't have some kind of spiritual comeback, I think that we're going to be in really bad trouble. Our morals are deteriorating to the point where people will just disintegrate."

"That's the moral principles I was talking about," Cash said. "Here I am at the age of thirty-eight—I'm still as warm-blooded as ever I was. I enjoy my love life as much as any man could. My wife and I wouldn't be happy if we shared any of that with anybody else.

"I think all this free love is a passing plaything. June and I found what we want in this world, and it's beautiful, the love we have for each other. Doesn't that have something to say to young people? Like, look at us. This is the way it ought to be. I don't think there's anything in this world that could destroy my marriage to June. And there's all kinds of things that could come along and cause trouble. Another man, another woman, if we didn't watch out. And we have first to admit that we're both human so we have to guard and protect the happiness we have.

"Once in a while I notice another woman that really looks good—you know? And June understands that. We'll be driving along and see a girl in a short skirt and I'll turn completely around in my seat and say, 'Wow!' and she'll say, 'Get a good eyeful, honey. Oh ain't she pretty? Don't let her get by without seein' everything she's showin', honey.' But that's as far as it goes. I still look because I like to see a pretty woman. But I couldn't share June with anyone. It's a spiritual bond we have and it would be sin for anyone to come between us."

"Do you really think it's unnatural?" I asked. "The men in the Bible had as many wives as they could afford. What kids are saying is that the isolated two-parent family doesn't work anymore. And why shouldn't people be able to love more than one person?"

"Maybe it'll work for a while," John said. "As long as they're young and they've got all that fire and energy. But there's nothing lasting about it."

"It would be like cutting off my arm to share you, honey," June said.

"I guess that's part of this whole Women's Liberation business," John says. "I don't understand it at all. And June doesn't either."

"Well," June says, "I find my happiness from trying to make John comfortable and happy. And I try to take everything off him that would cause him worry. And he does me the same way. I try to be up first thing in the morning so I can bring him his coffee. And it thrills him to death if he can sneak down and get that coffee back up to me first. That is just a little thing, but we try to be this way. But then, if I gave and gave and he never gave to me, we would probably have trouble. He's kind and he pets me and he loves me and I know that—you see? That's all I need.

"I told my oldest daughter, 'Carlene, I hope that when you decide to marry, you find a man who's as nice to you as John is to me.' And she said, 'Forget it. There's only one of him!'"

In any event there aren't many like him. Mixing fundamentalist morality with sympathy, if not approval, for the life-style of the young, he seems in touch with people who are deeply divided from one another. A few weeks after I returned to New York I watched one of his television shows. His guests were James Taylor and Neil Young, both idols of the youth culture. Cash sang a new song he had written, which, he said, was inspired by his talks with college students. The lyrics said that he would continue to wear black (which he always does on stage) as long as there is hunger and misery in the world and as long as people are dying in wars.

I remembered something June had said: "John stands for what this country can do for poor people. If you've got the guts, you can make it. He's proved that. I've always felt God's hand was on John."

It's an odd combination of ideas, but maybe a hopeful one. A young rock-record critic recently reviewed a new Johnny Cash album and wrote that he never would have thought that a performer could "plug me and the people of Nashville into the same socket." And he concluded that if anyone could bring the American people together, as one leading political figure has promised, it would be Johnny Cash and not the politician.

II

"Cash's 'Gospel Road' Film Is Renaissance for Him"

by George Vecsey (1973)

JOHNNY Cash looks 10 years younger. He has lost the tension in his mouth, the burned-out look in his eyes that lasted after his self-destructive decade. He is 41 years old and he bounces like an athlete when he walks.

The general explanation for his good health and international fame as a country singer is that Mr. Cash has long since put the pills behind him and has an enduring love affair with June Carter, his wife since 1968. "They act like kids—always hugging and kissing each other," a friend said.

But that is not the explanation that Mr. Cash and Miss Carter give. They say the difference is his religious experience in recent years—"the coming back to Jesus," as he put it.

The new peace coincides with one of the major departures of Mr. Cash's career—creating the movie *The Gospel Road*, about the life of Jesus. It was filmed in Israel "with a lot of faith and a lot of June's money," he said smiling. That film, which had its metropolitan benefit premiere tonight at C.W. Post College, has reportedly cost the Cash family $500,000—with no immediate prospect of breaking even.

The movie is a documentary narrated by Mr. Cash (who also sings in it but does not play a role) and backed up with country music that is having a national renaissance these days. The film has been released cautiously by 20th Century-Fox, making its way northward and eastward after moderate success in the Fundamentalist South.

"The film is specialized," said Hal Sherman, co-ordinator of national promotions for Fox. "It's good quality but it has a very strong Fundamentalist opinion. In the South, people take the Bible more literally than in New York, Chicago or Los Angeles. Theater owners resist this kind of picture because traditionally people go to church on Sunday and they want entertainment from the movies. We'll schedule it where we get requests."

There was word that Mr. Cash was worried about the reception in the more liberal Northeast (the film will open in five theaters around New York next month). But he expressed no alarm in a brief visit to New York this week.

"We believe it's a film for everybody, even if they don't believe in Jesus, as long as they can stand Johnny Cash's singing," he said.

When he talks about feeling good, Mr. Cash smiles and gives the thumbs-up sign—some of the same positive mannerisms he has displayed in frequent television commercials for Amoco and other sponsors.

"You can't confuse John's religion with a commercial," said Robert Elfstrom, the young director who also acted the role of Jesus. "John did those things to make money so he could make this film. But John is trying to bring his Jesus to the whole world. When I would improvise something like picking up a rock and tossing it, John would say, 'My Jesus wouldn't do that.' It's very personal with John."

His feeling about Jesus is so personal that Mr. Cash does not easily describe how it developed. In the biography, *Winners Got Scars Too* by Christopher S. Wren, there is little feeling of Jesus as playing a personal role in the salvation of Johnny Cash from the hulking pill-popping rambler who came close to dying from overdoses.

Mr. Cash said he accepted Christ when he was 14 in a Baptist church in his native Arkansas. He admits, "I kind of got away from it in my

20s and 30s like so many young people did." But he says the acceptance has returned gradually in recent years.

The movie began with Miss Carter's dream in 1968 of John standing on a mountain in Israel holding a Bible in his hand, she said. They were in Europe and they flew to Israel for four days. Later they made an album there "but that wasn't what I had in mind," Miss Carter said. "About two years ago, John said, 'let's go back and do it your way.'"

Using Cash-Carter family and friends in major roles and collecting vagabonds and amateurs to play other roles, they went into the desert, sleeping three hours a night, taking their story line from *Thompson's Concordance*, a biblical reference book.

At first, Mr. Cash planned to film only the hands and feet of Christ but he soon realized that did not fit his personal feeling about Jesus as a real man who walked the country roads and dealt with people. So Mr. Elfstrom—tall and graceful with a very blond beard and long hair—carried a 200-pound oak cross on camera.

Back in New York, they added songs by Kris Kristofferson, John Denver, and Mr. Wren and others. Mr. Elfstrom said he believed the film would slowly be accepted as an artistic triumph. But the bookings have been cautious.

Tonight's performance was a benefit for the Metropolitan Youth for Christ, held in the Dome Auditorium here rather than in a New York theater because various officials felt it had a bigger audience of Christian and/or country music fans in the suburbs than in Manhattan.

A near capacity crowd paid $5 and $10 for an hour's show that was followed by the film.

"This picture is relevant in New York City also," said Mr. Cash. "At the end we show Christ dying on the cross in the desert. Then we show him dying in the same way with backdrops in New York, Las Vegas and Hollywood. Christ is real to me everywhere. I'm not looking to make money on this. This is my expression of faith."

"Interview with Johnny Cash"

by Peter McCabe and Jack Killion (1973)

The Gospel Road *was the focus of the interview with Johnny Cash that follows (which ran in* Country Music*). But as the interview turned away from the film, conversation revealed a mellow Cash. The fire in the belly that had prompted him to romp and stomp before the Folsom and San Quentin crowds in 1968 had dimmed. Cash now had a son, a stable relationship with a woman, and a new partnership with God. Inciting his audiences and stoking up on pills seemed not to match the pleasures of home and spirituality.*

When did you first get the idea to make the film Gospel Road*?*

It began about six years ago with a dream June had. We were in Israel for the first time and she said, "I dreamed I saw you on a mountain with a book in your hand talking about Jesus." At that time I didn't want to hear anything like that. It sounded too much like preaching.

We went on up into Galilee and we saw this mountain up at the north end of the Sea of Galilee. We didn't know what mountain it was, but we found out later it was Mount Arabel. And all around this area is the land that Jesus lived and walked—Magdala where Mary Magdalene lived, the place of the Sermon on the Mount, the mountain where He fed the multitude. June said that was the mountain she dreamed about. So we came back two years later and I brought a recorder, and the result of that trip was the *Johnny Cash And The Holy Land* album. We decided then that someday we'd come back and do a film.

You see, for somebody like me, who grew up singing Jesus songs all his life and who was raised up in a Baptist Church, going to Israel is like going home. You see the things you've been singing about all your life. You sing about the old oak tree at home all your life and you go home and there it is. You want to hug it.

Was that your only motivation?

Another thing happened about three years ago; I met Billy Graham for the first time. He called and said he wanted to come to Nashville to see me. I never had met him. He came down, we had a big meal and we sat around and talked a long time. I kept waiting for him to say what he came to see me about. Finally I asked him. He said he just wanted to meet me and talk to me about music, but another thing he wanted was to talk to me about gospel songs, Christian songs and songs about Jesus. This was just before the big Jesus song thing came along. He said the kids were not going to church, that they were losing interest in religion, and he said he thought that the music had a lot to do with it, because there was nothing in the church house that they heard that they liked. The latest thing that the kids can hear in church is "Bringing In The Sheaves" and "How Great Thou Art," and those are not the kind of things going on in religion that makes the kids say, "Hey, I like that. Let's go hear some more." There's nothing that they can relate to.

So he talked to me about myself and other song writers like Kris [Kristofferson], who think along that line, and he kinda challenged me to challenge others, to try to use what talent we have to write something inspiring, that would inspire people to sit up and take notice of religion and Jesus.

Well, first thing that happened, the night after he left, I wrote "What Is Truth." Just him coming to the house inspired me to write that, if you want to call it inspiration. But June and I also got to talking about the thing we'd talked about doing in Israel. We'd thought about making a kind of travelogue, walking the steps that Jesus walked and telling His story, and then we talked about taking some contemporary, country-style Jesus songs, having songwriters write them and telling His story with them. As it turned out, that was a rough concept of what the film was actually going to be. We didn't know it at the time. When we went to Israel we had two songs that we thought would probably be in the film. We had gone through all the church hymns, discarded them, not because they weren't any good, but because they didn't say anything to people today. We had "Jesus Was A Carpenter" and another Christopher Wren song called "Gospel Road."

We hired an Israeli film crew to supplement our crew that we took over there, and we decided since we'd gone to all the expense to take a bunch of people to Israel that we were gonna shoot the moon, and we were gonna make as good a film and spend whatever it took for the month that we had to spend over there. And that's what we did. We hired extras. We didn't try to make a little big movie. We didn't try to make a Cecil B. DeMille film. We used as few extras as we could, and at the times when there should have been a multitude of people, we didn't use anybody. We used sound effects, to try to make it seem like there was a multitude of people. Well, when we came back and started editing the film and putting it together, we saw the need of a song to help tell the story here and there. So a boy named Larry Gatlin came along, who wrote a song called "Help Me." Kris has recorded it now—Kris and Rita Coolidge. And it fit so well in the scene about Nicodemus that we used Kris' recording of it in that scene. We had Gatlin write two more songs, I wrote two or three for the film, and we got Joe South's "Children" for the sequence where Jesus is playing with the little children on the beach.

We spent a year picking songs and fittin' them in the film, and that's what we've got now, a musical drama with a bunch of good, new songs that I think people will enjoy hearing if they can stand my voice. One prerequisite for seeing this film is you've got to be able to stand Johnny Cash for 90 minutes. If you can't, then you don't need to go. But if you can stand me for 90 minutes, then you're gonna enjoy it because it's an excellent film as movies go. If it wasn't, 20th Century Fox wouldn't be spending a half a million dollars to promote it and make prints like they are.

Let me ask you about the financial side of it. Tucked away in a Newsweek *report was a suggestion that you consciously went out and raised a lot of money to make this film.*

No, I didn't go out and raise it. I had it. I guess it cost half to three quarters of a million dollars, somewhere in that area. I don't know what the cost is gonna be when they tally it up. But it was the first time anybody was ever stupid enough, if you want to call it that, to put up all their own money to make a movie. But that's what we did, and we did it for a very good reason. If we hadn't put up our own money, we couldn't have done it exactly the way we felt like we wanted to do it. We would have had to do it the way the financier wanted it done. And we could have taken somebody's money. We could've had our bank put up the entire amount, because we have a good reputation with our bank, and we had no doubt that we could've got the money. But we wouldn't have had the say and it wouldn't have been our personal film. And this is. This film has our personal feelings in it, and it's got our believability because we believe in what we're saying and what we're doing.

I think I understand the effect that you hope this film will have on other people—but what effects has the actual making of the movie had on you, your circle of friends and your family?

Well, it's had a great effect on a lot of people that have been associated with it, like the little crew that Robert Elfstrom [director] brought over. He referred to them as a bunch of blackguards, as a bunch of profane outlaws. The first day on the set, when they realized we were serious about the subject that we were making the film about, all the profanities stopped, and I think most of the drugs stopped—I'm not sure about that—and if there was any wenching going on, it was on the sly.

I had about a 30-minute meeting with this crew the evening that we got to Tiberius, Israel. We sat around on the floor, and I told them that whatever they'd done before, it didn't make any difference to me. Some of them had some pretty tough reputations; they'd been in the riots in Mississippi; some of these people that worked on this film had been in South American revolutions. I said, "We're beginning a film about a man that is my Lord, and you're working for me, and that's all I want you to remember, that we're making a film about my Lord. There's not gonna be any preaching; there's not gonna be any orders given; there's not gonna be any rules laid down." And I said after the first day of filming, "I think you're all gonna get into the spirit of the thing and believe in what we're doing." And the second day of filming, everybody was up at 3:30 A.M. cleaning equipment. We drove 20 miles and were on location when the sun came up ready to start shooting. It was that way every morning. This was the most devoted bunch of people that anybody could ever hope to have.

Will you make other movies after this one?

This is probably the first and the last film I'll ever want to produce because I don't want to be a film producer, if you want to call it producer, 'cause that's what I was on this. This is my life's proudest work that I wanted to produce, to lay down a story and put it on the screen, have people go and sit and enjoy it, and when they walk out of the theater, feel good about it. Not walk out of the theater saying, "Oh me, I'm a sinner. I've got to run and do something quick, to get right." It's the kind of thing that will make you think about your religion, but it's a beautiful film.

When Jack Hurst spoke to you last Fall for a story in Country Music, *he asked you when religion became important in your life. You said you didn't know, but you felt it had something to do with when John Carter came along and you and June "realized that you weren't children any more." Could you talk a little more about that now?*

Well, for seven years I tried about every dirty rotten thing there is. I took all the drugs there are to take, and I drank, and then when I married June, I decided all that was no good, that I'd run through every evil, dirty thing there is, and I didn't like it. I wanted to live, I saw a chance to find a little peace within myself. Everybody had written me off. Everybody said that Johnny Cash was through, 'cause I was walkin' around town, 150 pounds. I looked like walking death and they were turning and laughing at me. I saw it myself, many times, people saying, "Oh man, he's gone."

Well, it didn't take too much of that for me to say, I'll show you, that ain't all of me. I had June to hold onto, and my religion helped. My religion now is no different than it was when I was a kid, it's just that after a few years of adult life, I went down the wayward path.

Do you feel any sense of accomplishment from those years? I'm thinking particularly about the songs that you wrote.

Yes, there's a lot of things I wrote that I'm proud of through those years. And I feel that every time I went on stage, I tried to do a good job. There were some shows I missed, and some bad shows I probably did, but I'm not ashamed of it. Right now I'm not ashamed of a thing I did because when God forgave me, then I forgave myself, see. That's one thing that people like me have to learn to do, that after you've straightened up and stopped all that, and you know that God forgave you, then the big sin would be not to forgive yourself. So I'm not ashamed of all that rot that I did. I don't like to think about it. Some of it I've erased from my mind, so I don't think about it, and some of it I refuse to admit that I remember.

Do you think your audience has changed since you've moved more toward gospel music? I know many people found it easy to identify with what you were singing, and your songs appealed to anybody who had even the slightest troubled frame of mind.

You know, the accent is not all that much on gospel music. It's just that when I sing gospel music or record gospel music, I'm serious about it, whereas a lot of artists I know, every three or four years, or at one point in their career they say, "Well I think I'll record a gospel album now because it would be the thing to do and it would show the people that deep down I'm a religious person." That's the way I used to think about it, too. Now my last record was "Any Old Wind That Blows," and the one before that was "Oney." You know I'm still the same person that I always was. It's just that I'm serious about the gospel songs when I do sing them. I'm serious about this film, but there's a good chance that I might star in a film called *Old Fishhawk*, a story about an Indian. 20th Century is now trying to buy the rights for me to do that film, and it's got nothing to do with religion.[1]

I guess there are two things that have really influenced your life and career in the last few years. One, the fact that you stopped taking drugs, and two, the arrival of your son, John Carter.

Yes, John Carter's had a lot to do with it. You know, I used to go rabbit hunting and squirrel hunting, and killing all kinds of animals. But John Carter's almost three years old now. He's got all these animal books, and I tell him stories about animals, and I can't go killing any animals now. John Carter has had a lot to do with the change in me. I'm 40 years old, and all of a sudden this little, redheaded boy comes along. Everybody thought it was going to be a black-haired boy, but this little redheaded boy comes along who looks like June Carter and

[1] *Editor's note:* This film was never made.

follows me everywhere I go. I can't go anywhere in this house without him being right at my heels, and I enjoy all the quiet, nice, little things that three year old boys do. There's something strengthening about that. He's had a lot to do with it all right.

Did giving up drugs make you feel that this was the first time you'd stood up to something and really come through it?

There's been a lot of us that was on drugs and quit. There's been a lot of us who had the problem with alcohol and quit it. It takes a real man to be able to do it. It really does. But the toughest thing I ever did was to quit smoking. I can say that, and maybe I don't really mean that, because I made myself forget all those nightmares I had when I was trying to come off barbiturates. Before I married June and lived out here in this house on the lake, I used to get those pills by the hundreds or thousands, and I used to put a hundred of them in a sock and hide them between boards in the floor, or in the ceiling in the bathroom, or behind the light or something. Last week I found a box full of pills! They were not in a sock, but in a matchbox.

Merle Haggard incidentally knows where I used to hide my pills sometimes. I told Haggard where I hid 'em and I'm not going to tell you, but Haggard knows where I used to hide my pills when I wanted to carry 'em on me. But I found a box full of pills under the washbasin and I almost broke my arm to get to 'em. I knew that I had hidden some pills five years ago under that washbasin. I got down on the floor and I stuck my arm under there and the tips of my fingers touched a little box. It slid around a little bit, and I kept straining and skinned my arm to get to 'em, pulled them out and there was that box of yellow pills. Half yellow pills and half tranquilizers because I'd hide both kinds, so I could go up and come back down, too. I pulled this box of pills out and looked at 'em. Smelled 'em, that weird sticky smell they have, and I thought of a bunch of things I'd done while I was on 'em. I took them up to the bedroom and June and John Carter was laying on the bed. And I opened up that box of pills and said, "June, look what I found." I emptied them on the bed, and she said, "Oh, my God, no," 'cause she remembered a bunch of bad things, too. And I said, "Don't worry, let's go in here and flush 'em," and June and John Carter and I went into the bathroom and John Carter said, "What are you doing that for, Daddy?" And I said, "Because it's the thing to do, Son." I said, "That was bad stuff, Daddy flushed bad stuff." So we got rid of the pills. There may be some more pills at the house, but if I ever find 'em, I'll flush them too.

To change the subject a little, what do you think is happening in country music now? Probably you, more than anybody, in the last ten years have broadened the scope of country music, popularized it for a much wider audience.

That's happening, and will probably continue to happen, but when it's broadened, it can spread pretty thin. But I think better songs are being written than ever before. Tom T. Hall's "Watermelon Wine" is one of the greatest things ever written in country music. This is the kind of thing I love. It's philosophy, it's life, it's—and those are the kind of songs that are going to stay, no matter how wide the spectrum spreads. Songs like that are gonna make it. So I think that so long as people come along like Tom T. Hall writing great stuff like that, then country music is here to stay. Well, it's here to stay anyway, but I mean in a big way, 'cause there's some really good talents around. There's a young writer that we've got here named Dick Feller, who has just recorded for United Artists. He's going to be a big artist. I recorded a song of his, one called "Orphan Of the Road." I think as long as people like him keep coming along, country music's got a great future.

Do you see yourself moving more towards producing?

No, not at all. We've got the best studio at House of Cash, the finest one in Nashville. The feeling here is great. People love to record here, but I don't want to produce. I don't want to produce records. I want to do my own records, and that's it. I don't want to get involved in a bunch of business ends of the business. That's one reason why I'm still around and going, because I haven't stuck myself behind a desk. Although I've got a nice desk here, you won't find me behind it once a month. I don't like the business end of the business.

There was some talk recently that you were going to play more small halls. Is there anything to that?

Well, I'm not only playing small halls. I'm still playing the big halls, but I enjoy going to a town that I've never been in before, like a 100,000 population town. I just looked at the map and made up a list of towns that I gave to my manager last week, for him to check out. I like to play a smaller hall because the audience response is better in an auditorium of 3000 or 4000 people.

What effect, if any, has working with companies like American Oil and Lionel had on your career and your audience?

It hasn't had any effect on me. Those commercials I do for American Oil about every six months take three days of work and then I forget about it. Of course then my fans see me on TV. I don't really know what effect it has on them, except I get a few letters. I haven't had a half a dozen letters in two years offering any harsh criticism on those commercials. I really do use American Oil, up here at the station in Hendersonville, and I try to be realistic about things. I like to sing about trains and the old times and the good old days and all that business, but if my boy gets sick and I need a doctor, I don't want him to walk 15 miles. I want him to burn some gasoline to get out here.

I think there's always two or three ways to look at everything. The commercials I did for American Oil helped pay for things like the film, or part of it. So I use the money that I make to do a little good now and then. We're very active in a lot of charities, in mental health and boys' homes, so I don't have any apologies to make for anything that I do to earn income. I employ a lot of people here and feed a lot of children and I'm very proud of all the work that I do because there's a lot of thought and careful consideration that goes into all of it. It doesn't mean I don't make mistakes because I know I do. I've seen them. I do just about as many things wrong as I do right, but at least I'm doing what I feel is right at the time.

You pledged to support President Nixon and his policies in Indochina toward ending the Vietnam War. Do you feel you were right now that the war has ended?

The only thing I know about that is what I've read. One thing, *Country Music* magazine said something about me refusing to endorse the President. What was that headline? "Cash Is Cool To The Republicans?" Well I guess you could say that, but all I said was that I didn't feel that an entertainer had any business going to political conventions. I still feel that way. It had nothing to do with the Republicans or Democrats, or the President. I think the dignity of the office of President of the United States should be maintained and respected no matter who is our President. He is our President, and we the people have elected him whether you or I voted for him or not. As far as the war in Vietnam is concerned, that war just made me sick. I'm not supporting that war or any other war and whether or not Nixon did his best, I don't know, because I don't know that much about his job. I have to assume that he did because we believed in him enough to re-elect him.

Do you think there's been a big change in the American way of life since the sixties? Do you think we're going back to the fifties way of thinking?

No, I don't think so. Change is the whole process of life. Change is for the most part healthy, of course. We made a lot of mistakes in the sixties. We'd like to just erase that whole war from our history books. That would really be nice, except you can't forget the ones that died, and every time the war is brought up, you think of something that brings it home. Maybe Vietnam has taught us a hard lesson to not be involved in foreign wars. Maybe that's the lesson we've learned. I hope we have. Then all those things that happened in the sixties were solidifying and strengthening for this country. The riots, the campus riots—I was just reading a copy of the *New York Times* I have at the house from 1873, and in Washington, D.C., in 1873 there was a student riot, and there were burnings in effigy and bonfires out in front of the Capitol and students singing and dancing and drinking all night. Kids want to get out roaring, and get organized in their roaring and march while they're roaring. I don't think that's gonna stop. They're gonna let off steam however they want to. And sometimes they get serious about it and somebody gets hurt. I think we've learned a lot of lessons from the sixties.

What happened at your testimony on prison reform last fall?

I guess because I got a lot of attention from prison shows and albums, I get a lot of requests from people who want me to be involved in this and that program. One thing I did, I went with Senator Brock to Washington to testify before the Senate Sub-Committee On Prison Reform for some bills he was trying to get through. I told how I felt about prison reform and such, and about some things I had seen or knew about that go on in prisons. People say, 'well what about the victims, the people that suffer—you're always talking about the prisoners; what about the victims?' Well, the point I want to make is that's what I've always been concerned about—the victims. If we make better men out of the men in prison, then we've got less crime on the streets, and my family and yours is safer when they come out. If the prison system is reformed, if the men are reformed, if they are rehabilitated, then there's less crime and there's less victims.

Ever since I've been in the entertainment business, from the very first prison I played in 1957—Huntsville Texas State Prison—I found that a concert is a tension reliever. A prison is always full of tension, but sometimes it gets to the breaking point and there's trouble. I'm not saying that our concerts have prevented trouble, but who knows? They may have, because I've been called on by a warden here or there to do a concert when they've had trouble, and we've done it, and there's not been trouble. Here at Tennessee State Prison, I had a man come up to me and say, "I believe I can make it another five years. I know somebody out there cares, cares enough to come in here and sing for us." A concert does relieve a lot of tension because it makes them forget, it makes them happy, it makes them applaud, it makes them laugh, they tap their feet to the music. That's our purpose, to give them a little relief.

You seem to have acquired a great deal of tolerance and you seem to have mellowed a great deal. How do you see your life moving now?

I think I feel better on stage now than I ever did in my life. I worked a concert in Fargo, North Dakota, recently, and I never felt so good on stage as I did that night. I see myself on stage, if God lets me live, 20 or 30 more years. It's what I feed on, the performance and the audience reaction. It's what I love and that's all I want to do. I want to try to write and record better country songs. I've got my own studio here and just because it's the biggest and prettiest in town doesn't mean I'm going to fill it full of fiddles every time I record. I spend a lot of time in there with just my flat-top guitar. And another thing, talking about the future, I want to try to become a musician. I started taking piano lessons at the age of 40. I just had my first piano lesson about two months ago and I already know C, F and G7. That's one of the proudest accomplishments of my life is to learn those three chords on the piano, and I've got another lesson tomorrow afternoon, my third lesson. I'm trying to learn to finger pick on the guitar. Red Lane will laugh at this, but I'm trying to learn some finger picking. I learned my guitar lick from Norman Blake and Red Lane. I've been working on it. They don't know how good I'm gettin'. I'm gonna show 'em some day. Then I took my first piano lesson, I learned three chords and I practice them. And then Walt Cunningham, a young man that's been playing piano for us on some of our concerts, taught me how to vamp in 4/4 rhythm and everyday I practice on that. That's something I've never done in my life, sit down and play something. Strumming is all I ever did before.

Is John Carter interested in music?

Yes, he is very much interested in it. June and I did a show at a handicapped children's school last week. We took him with us because there's little kids there. I was right in the middle of a song when he bounded onto the stage and said, "I want to sing." I stopped the song and said, "What do you want to sing?" and he said, "I wanna sing 'The Cowboys And The Indians And The Sheep.'" So he started singing, and when he got through that I said, "Okay, Son, let's hear another," and he said, "Oh, The Wind Blows On The Cows." That's the name of another one that he made up. And the kids loved it.

But last week in Fargo, I brought him out on stage because he told me—now I know the people won't realize that John Carter is old enough to think like this, but he's 3 years old now—he said, "Daddy, I'm going to sing tonight." I said, "What are you gonna sing, Son?" And he said, "Peace In The Valley." So in the show when I got ready to do "Peace In The Valley," I called him out on stage and he sang the chorus with me. At the end of the song, he took a bow and went off, and they kept applauding, and he came back and took another bow.

When someone interviews you and you talk about your personal life, do you think that serves a purpose to cut through the stage image which I guess all performers have?

Well, when I'm on stage I feel like I'm really a complete person because that's what I feel like I do best and that's what I'm most alive and happy doing, performing. Any other part of me might be interesting to the people that like that image on the stage. Yes, I think it's realistic; it's justifiable, the interviews, the pictures of the life of the man that lives off stage. And I think in most cases it's an honest picture, like right here, because it's really the way I feel about things; when I sit down and talk to you and tell you about these things, it's the way I feel.

"*Penthouse* Interview: Johnny Cash"

by Larry Linderman (1975)

With celebrity comes public controversy, and in 1970 Cash confronted his first since his 1965 drug arrest in El Paso. Noting Cash's sympathies toward President Nixon and his policies, the administration had invited him to perform at the Evening at the White House *on April 17, 1970. Along with the invitation, according to a* New York Times *report, came President Nixon's request that the Man in Black sing "Welfare Cadillac," a hit about a shiftless father on relief written and recorded by Guy Drake. When news of the president's request hit the papers, social workers in Tennessee dropped their pens and clipboards. The* New York Times *reported that the state's commissioner of welfare shot off an angry letter to President Nixon, calling him insensitive: "The song's message that welfare recipients are cheats and the rest of us chumps is a grave disservice" ("Nixon Is Criticized for Song Request, 'Welfare Cadillac,'" March 28, 1970). As if observing a tennis match, reporters turned their eyes to Cash. Would he perform the song?*

Cash refused. But his support of President Nixon was unstinting, which highlighted one of the contradictions that many saw in Cash. How could this man who had expressed solidarity with oppressed peoples support a Republican administration, which many assumed to be insensitive to the disenfranchised? It would be a year or so before he publicly and clearly questioned an administration policy, the war in Vietnam. In 1971's "Man in Black," he wrote, "I wear the black in mourning for the lives that could have been /

Each week we lose a hundred fine young men." His next hit was "Singing in Vietnam Talking Blues," another protest.

In the following interview with Penthouse, *Cash—despite his cooled feelings toward Nixon—defended him in the controversy, claiming that Nixon himself never asked to hear the offending songs. And that was the just the tip of the political iceberg. Interviewer Larry Linderman queried Cash on topics such as Vietnam, prison reform, and the legalization of marijuana, and he drew from Cash his story of chatting at length with former Nixon aide H. R. Haldeman at the Watergate trials.*

In interviews, up to and including this one, talk about politics often eclipsed discussion of his music, but after this interview, he would rarely again be so vocal on political matters. Nor would he be given so much magazine space to voice his opinions.

IT has now been twenty years since Johnny Cash first surfaced as a singer, and in the course of establishing himself as the unquestioned king of country music he has recorded nearly 350 songs, sold more than 30 million records, and currently earns more than $3 million a year.

Almost equally pleasing to Cash is the increased acceptance he's won for country music. Prior to his emergence, such fabled Southern troubadours as the late Jimmie Rodgers and Hank Williams could win followings only along the corn pone circuit. Cash, as welcome at Carnegie Hall as he is at the Grand Ole Opry, brought country music to the cities. And also to the young—pop idols Bob Dylan and Kris Kristofferson are among the many youthful singer-composers strongly influenced by the Nashville-based balladeer. As we head into the second half of the seventies, Johnny Cash seems a sure bet to become the most dominant figure in the entire history of U.S. country music. For a man who was a failure as an appliance salesman at twenty-three, Cash has clearly come a long way since those early lean years.

Born in Kingsland, Arkansas, on February 26, 1932, John R. Cash, at the age of three, was brought by his parents to Dyess, Arkansas, where the Roosevelt administration had established a federally financed farm settlement to aid depression-poor families. Cash's hardworking father was given a twenty-acre farm, a small house, a barn, a mule, a cow, and a plow—and eventually paid back the government for everything it had advanced him. One of seven children, John (which is what his friends call him) grew up on a steady diet of fatback, turnip greens, and hard work—he was picking 350 pounds of cotton a day by the time he was fourteen. Following his high school graduation in 1950, Cash worked for two weeks on a Detroit automobile assembly line and then enlisted in the air force. After a four-year stint in Germany—where he learned to play the guitar—John returned to Memphis and a job selling appliances.

Cash was a lamentably bad salesman. "Maybe that was because I hated every minute of it," he recalls. To supplement his meager income, John formed a trio with local auto mechanics Luther Perkins and Marshall Grant, and they were soon playing church socials and county fairs. After doing a series of fifteen-minute Saturday afternoon radio shows in Memphis, Cash decided they ought to audition for Sun Records. In early 1955, their first recording, "Cry, Cry, Cry," sold 100,000 records across the South. "Folsom Prison Blues" came next, and when it rose to the top of the country music charts Cash quit his job—and has been singing country music ever since.

Johnny Cash is much larger up close than he appears to be onstage. A big, barrel-chested man whose face looks like it crashed into a wall, Cash looks raw, speaks plain—and is surprisingly gentle. At the same time, however, the passivity seems tightly controlled: Cash has an enormously strong personality that he underplays. His sidemen are more than suitably impressed by their boss and talk of him in terms approaching sainthood. And it often seems that's what he's aiming at.

In addition to being a remarkable singer and songwriter, Cash is also a consummate performer. Several times a year he plays week-long engagements at the Las Vegas Hilton (which has that gambling town's biggest showroom), and his usual complement of two SRO crowds a night don't leave disappointed. Cash is often onstage for one and one half hours, and virtually every song he performs has won him a gold record. June Carter, his wife of seven years, joins him for several songs about midway through the proceedings, and occasionally their four-year-old son, John Carter Cash, also gets into the act. (John and June have both been married before, which accounts for their six daughters.) Cash knows how to bend a lyric just so, and his gravelly, slightly off-key baritone seems able to dive into bottomless pits. Unlike a number of performers these days, Cash is better in person than on his records. And his records are superb.

After catching one of his midnight performances, the author met Cash the next morning in the Hilton's Imperial Suite, a spacious and dandy refuge reserved for whichever entertainer (Ann-Margret, Tony Bennett, Barbra Streisand, Bill Cosby, etc.) is currently headlining downstairs. Cash was stretched out on the carpet, dressed in one of the black shirt-and-slacks outfits he performs in (and apparently lives in as well). He quickly bounded up, got coffee, and then sat down to talk. Cash really can't abide Las Vegas—he doesn't gamble and the desert air never fails to play havoc with his throat—yet there are at least a couple of reasons he keeps playing the town. One is the six-figure weekly salary he draws from the Hilton. Another is the rousing reception he gets from high-rolling crowds who aren't country music buffs. Cash's singular ability to turn virtually any audience on to his brand of music provided a logical opening for the interview.

—*Larry Linderman*

Although the music scene seems to be composed of enemy camps, you've somehow become a superstar not only to country music fans, but also to folk, rock, and gospel followers. What accounts for that?

Well, to start with, I have no illusions about who Johnny Cash is: I'm a country boy and I'm a country singer. But I've always felt that a lot of country songs—especially the ballads—have something to say to everybody. It finally just gets down to how they're presented; are you gonna present a song to people in a way that'll get them feeling the same way you feel about it, or will you do it in such a way that people will end up thinking, "Nope, that's not for me." I think I was aware of this as early as 1956 when a song I wrote called "I Walk the Line" was one of the first so-called country songs to become a pop hit as well.

Musical innovations aside, what do you think your songs communicate to people?

Love. I sincerely love people. And I especially love children. Now that I have six daughters and a little boy and I'm forty-three years old, I've learned to appreciate children. So I have them in mind when I make my records, and I also have the church people in mind, because that's part of my life now, too. And I also have convicts in mind. I try to remember that the airwaves belong to everybody—*anybody* can turn on a radio—so I try not to put my music into a bag.

The same is true of myself, 'cause I've never wanted to be put in a bag either. You know, even in the fifties, people in the country music business in Nashville considered me some kind of unorthodox left fielder, mostly because I came down from Memphis, where Elvis and Carl Perkins and Jerry Lee Lewis and I had been putting out all that strange stuff on Sun Records. I thought a lot about being considered weird—and it was all right with me. I bought it. It's still all right with me, 'cause I still don't want to be put in a bag. And because of that, I'll continue playing to different kinds of audiences. Like prisoners—I just played an Oklahoma state prison and a Mississippi state prison. And before that, I played a Billy Graham crusade and a Sunday school class. I just think it's fascinating for a man to spread himself around, to walk through different doors, see different groups of people, and understand and feel what they react to. You learn a lot.

You've been extremely critical of the way prisons are run, and once said, "I don't see anything good coming out of prison. You put men in like animals and tear the souls and guts out of them—and let them out worse than when they came in." Exactly what did you mean by that?

I've got a good friend named Glenn Sherley, who wrote "Greystone Chapel" on my *Folsom Prison* album. He's been out of San Quentin for three and one half years now, and he'll tell you—and I've seen it—that the prison system, like it was and probably still is at San Quentin and Folsom and some of the other big hellholes, is just a school for crime. On top of that, prisons are terribly overcrowded. Tennessee State Prison, right in my hometown of Nashville, has about 5,000 inmates—and at night there's only thirty people to take care of the needs of all those guys. They don't even have a doctor assigned to the prison. Can you imagine that many people with no doctor on call? Listen, that's just an example of the lack of concern people have for prisoners. And we keep putting men into settings like that. It's as if we're all saying, "Okay, let's send this man who's offended society to the school for crime that we call our state joint." The result is that when the guy comes out he'll be able to pull off a bigger-and-better robbery, or kill somebody, and that's what's been happening.

Do you see any signs of change in the penal system?

Well, decent things are in the works in different places. Tennessee, for example, is trying to build about seven different regional facilities around the state—farms where first offenders and nonviolent criminals are sent. Some of these prisons-without-walls even have work-release programs—prisoners are allowed to go home on the weekends if they're sent to the facility that's in their area. A lot of prisoners in these places have been convicted of marijuana charges, and I personally don't think they should be in prison in the first place. But so long as the law stands against them, they should at least be put someplace where they can improve their lot and be trained towards going along with those laws.

Would you like to see all marijuana legislation abolished?

Well, I just think there's a lot of money spent on enforcing marijuana laws that could be spent for better causes. As to whether it's harmful or not: I smoked grass for a seven-year period during which I did everything. I was on amphetamines, barbiturates—and I smoked a *lot* of grass. But when I smoked it, I was usually on amphetamines, so I really can't say whether marijuana ever did me any good or any harm.

What first got you into drugs?

The same thing that gets anybody into drugs: they make you feel good. It was a thing I did gradually, and it felt so good when I first started taking pills in '58 that I just kept trying things that felt better. Drugs were an escape for me, a crutch—a substitute for what I now feel. I was looking for a spiritual high to put myself above my problems, and I guess I was running from a lot of things. I was running from family, I was running from God, and from everything I knew I should be doing but wasn't. I was rebelling, and really for no reason. So I wound up living from high to high, and the highs got higher—but the lows got lower. So low, sometimes, that I realized I was at the bottom, and that if I didn't stop I would die.

A lot of people who knew you then are still surprised that you didn't die.

Yeah, all my friends had me written off, and I think some of 'em are still mad at me 'cause I rewrote the script. But I almost accommodated them, that's for sure. My first marriage was in trouble when I lived in California, and I have to take the blame for that—because no woman can live with a man who's strung out on amphetamines. My first wife put up with me for years after I was hooked, but I'd go home and try to put all the blame for it on her, and then I'd get into my jeep or camper truck and head for the mountains. And I'd get so stoned every time I'd leave home to go into the desert or the mountains that I'd wreck whatever I was driving. I totalled a lot of vehicles, and I guess I must've broken twenty bones in my body—my toes, my jawbone, my nose, my fingers, my elbow, my foot, my kneecap. I don't know why I didn't kill myself then. I think it was because God was really good to me, which is why I'm where I am now spiritually.

During that seven-year period—from 1961 through 1967—what was your life like?

It was like I was living with a bunch of demons. I don't want to get deep into demons 'cause I don't know that much about demonology, but I used to get into the desert, and I'd start talking to them. I'd talk to the demons and they'd talk back to me—and I could hear them. I mean, they'd say, "Go on, John, take twenty more milligrams of Dexedrine, you'll be all right." And I'd say, "Yeah, but I've already had forty today." And they'd answer, "Take twenty more, it'll be good for you, it'll make you feel just fine." So I'd take 'em and then continue talking back and forth to the demons inside me.

That doesn't sound too healthy, John. How did you feel about it at the time?

I felt completely crazy—and I was. Really, I was *completely* crazy. One time I remember going into my camper truck and looking at myself in the mirror. I put my hand over my face and peeped through my fingers at myself and said, "Let's kill us." And then I said, "I *can't* be killed. I'm indestructible." Well, I looked myself right in the eye and said, "I dare you to try." So I got in that camper truck and started driving down a mountain. The truck turned upside down twice, but the only thing I broke was my jawbone, which still gives me a pain now and then. It was really a battle that raged within me for a long time—but somehow I survived.

What finally caused you to give up drugs?

God. The times when I was so down and out of it were also the times when I felt the presence of God, or whatever you want to call it in whatever religion you might follow. I felt that presence, that positive power saying to me, "I'm still here, Cash, to draw on whenever you're ready to straighten up and come back to life." Well, that's what finally happened, and I'm not playing church now. I was brought up in the church when I was a boy and I didn't play church then. The spiritual strength I have is real, it's solid, and I don't compromise it. It's something within me that nobody can argue about with me, because it's a very personal strength that I feel and that I draw on. That's what pulled me out of it. But there were people I used—like June Carter, who stuck by me all those years while I was on drugs and fought me, to the point of stealing my pills and destroying 'em whenever she could. And then feeding me and trying to get me back on my feet. Strangers were also used, like the sheriff in the last jail I was in.

Why had you been arrested?

I didn't really find out until the sheriff told me, 'cause I'd been so high at the time that I didn't know what I was doing. I'd been out banging on somebody's door, trying to get in to use the telephone after wrecking my jeep in the woods in north Georgia—I had no idea where. The next day I woke up in the Lafayette jail, and the sheriff there unlocked my cell and led me out to his desk. He put a tray on the desk and said, "Here's your money—and here's your dope. . . . Now get out of here and go kill yourself." I said, "What? What do you *mean*, 'go kill myself'?" And he told me, "You got the power to do it and you're trying to, so go ahead and finish the job. You don't have far to go." I said, "I don't want to kill myself." And he answered, "Of course you do. You almost did. When we brought you in here I called a doctor and he gave you a shot and put you to sleep. But he said you evidently want to kill yourself, so there's your dope—go ahead and do it." That was the turning point.

Are the religious songs you now sing in your shows a result of your giving up drugs?

No, I always sang those songs—but I never did sing them with the feeling and the free spirit I have since I quit the dope. You know, I used to sing "Were You There When They Crucified My Lord?" while I was stoned on amphetamines. I used to sing all those gospel songs, but I really never felt them. And maybe I was a little bit ashamed of myself at the time because of the hypocrisy of it all: there I was, singing the praises of the Lord and singing about the beauty and the peace you can find in Him—and I was stoned. And, miserable; I was climbing the walls. But regardless of how I felt inside, those songs have always been a part of me. They were the first songs I ever heard—and I know this sounds corny, but they're the songs my mother sang to me. Gospel songs are the ones I love the most, and I can never wait for the part of my show when I sing them.

Is that the high point of a night's work for you?

It's just *one* of the high points, because I really brighten up when my wife June comes out to sing with me. She's my spotlight, and there's a magic to her that just fires me up about the time I really start getting tired onstage. And I also enjoy singing things like "The Ballad of Ira Hayes," which is one of four Peter La Farge songs about American Indians that I've recorded. Peter was a great writer and through him I came to love the American Indian. We were very close just before he died about ten years ago, and I sat up a lot of long nights listening to his songs and stories about his people. I've always loved Indian legends, and by now I've got about a thousand books on the subject.

A number of press reports have stated you're part Cherokee. Are you?

No, I have no Indian ancestry. Some folks have said I do, but I can't find it anywhere—and I've got my family tree. Of course, when I used to get high, well, the higher I got, the more Indian blood I thought I had in me. And a lot of people wanted me to be part Indian, especially after I recorded the *Bitter Tears* album.

Have you performed those songs before Indian audiences?

I sang 'em at Wounded Knee eight years ago. I went there to help the Sioux raise money to build a school; back then Indians hadn't started to speak out for themselves, and neither had any national figures.

In view of your efforts on behalf of prisoners and Indians, a number of people were surprised when, after returning from a tour through Vietnam, you declared yourself "a dove with claws."

I thought that was *awful* clever of me at the time—and now I wonder where I ever got that stupid line. My thoughts about Vietnam really had to do with our boys over there. Like one night at Long Binh air base, a Pima Indian boy—crying, and with a beer in his hand—came up to the stage while I was singing "The Ballad of Ira Hayes," which is about the Pima Indian marine who helped raise our flag at Iwo Jima. At the end of the song, that young Indian asked me to take a drink of his beer, and with the tears running off his chin, he said, "I may die tomorrow, but I want you to know that I ain't never been so alive as I am tonight."

Things like that made me to want to support our guys, because I loved them so much. I knew they didn't want to be there, which is why I went over myself. I was asked to come to Vietnam and I was paid well, but right away we all got caught up in the whole thing. Pretty soon June, Carl Perkins, and I were doing seven and eight shows a day, sometimes for only ten people in a hospital ward. Anyway, please forgive me for saying I'm "a dove with claws."

Not long after your return from Vietnam you were invited to perform at the White House and created a stir when you refused to sing the two songs President Nixon had reportedly requested—"Okie from Muskogee," which puts down longhairs, and "Welfare Cadillac," which characterizes welfare recipients as cheats growing affluent on the public dole.

I think everybody got that whole thing wrong, because the president didn't ask me to do those songs—one of his secretaries did. I think they wanted me to believe that President Nixon was familiar with my music, but evidently they'd just picked up a copy of *Billboard*, found a couple of songs in the Top Ten—and then took it from there. I simply told them, "Look, 'Okie from Muskogee' is Merle Haggard's song, it's identified with him, and I won't do it because it wouldn't be proper. As for 'Welfare Cadillac,' well, I've heard the song once, I don't like it, and it doesn't say anything I want to say. If the request actually does come from the president, tell him that our program is already planned and that I certainly hope he'll be pleased with what we do."

Incidentally, I took my daddy with me to the White House that night, which is one of the main reasons I went. He was a soldier during World War I, and in 1916 he served with General Pershing's forces and helped chase Pancho Villa back across the Mexican border after Villa had burned down Columbus, New Mexico. My daddy's a patriot and gave me a sense of history and a strong love for my country. And I really enjoyed walking around the White House, seeing the paintings and other things—like the room where Andrew Jackson's mountaineers came and swung on the curtains and poured their moonshine on the carpets.

Anyway, that White House performance took place in 1970, and at the time President Nixon was very popular, but it probably wouldn't have mattered if I'd been asked during the start of the scandals—I would've gone, because it was a performance at the White House. I was glad to go.

Did Watergate upset you?

Yeah, it really made me sick—sick and ashamed. But Watergate is just another growing pain, another lesson for us, and I think eventually we'll be a greater country because of it. Right now, we're watching a housecleaning going on. You know, even though we're set up on a capitalistic system, Congress picked Rockefeller to pieces during the vice-presidential hearings; they really put him down because of all of his money. In a way, they were putting down the very system the government stands for, and I think that's some much-needed housecleaning right there. There are going to be quite a few changes made because of Watergate.

In time, we're going to see that the whole Watergate mess was one of the best things that ever happened in the U.S. I may be dead wrong, of course, but I think Watergate is gonna make us a better democracy: the people are going to rule. That's really what I say in "The Ragged Old Flag." We've had some hellish wars that have just about torn the country apart, and now we've had these scandals. Well, the flag is symbolic of the spirit of the people and of the way of life we've cut out for ourselves. Sure, our flag may have holes in it, and it may be ragged and tattered and torn—but it's still waving. It's going to overcome. The *people* will overcome—and our government will be set up the way the people want it to be set up. That's going on *now;* it may not look like it, but that's just because we're housecleaning.

And apparently—judging by your attendance this fall at the trial of Haldeman, Ehrlichman, et al.*—you don't wish to see any dust swept under the rug. What prompted you to show up in the courtroom?*

James Neal, the government's prosecuting attorney in the Watergate trial, is also my attorney, and he invited June and me to sit in on our way back from an afternoon with Billy Graham in Norfolk, Virginia. So we went, and we heard the tape of Nixon talking to Haldeman on June 23, 1972, which was a cover-up conversation.

I had a chance to talk to Haldeman. As a matter of fact, he was the first man I saw when I walked into the courtroom, and his mouth dropped open and mine did, too. He immediately turned to someone else and then looked back at me with an expression on his face like, "What in the hell is *he* doing here?" When the court took a recess I walked over to him and introduced myself and he said, "I tell you, James Neal is really giving me a lick today. Not only is he on the other side, but he's got my favorite entertainer on the other side with him." I told Haldeman, "Wait a minute, I'm not on any side. I'm here as a spectator. You're a piece of American history, whether you like it or not, and I'm just here to witness it."

He asked if we could have a cup of coffee together, so June and I went out with him and Ehrlichman, who never *did* say anything except hello. At the table, the first thing Haldeman asked was, "You've been on the hot seat, haven't you?" And I told him I sure had been—he was talking about the couple of times I'd been before a judge on pill busts. He said, "You know how it feels?" And I said, "Yeah, it don't feel good, does it?" Then he started to say, "Look, I just want you to know—" and I interrupted him and told him, "Wait a minute, you don't have to explain anything to *me*, I'm not here to decide what side I'm on, I'm only here to witness." He went on, though, and said, "I just want you to know that I did what I thought was right at the time. I was only trying to do my job."

I told him I wasn't questioning that, and then we talked about the music business.

After we left Washington, June and I talked about Haldeman a lot. I really liked him as a person, and he seemed exactly what a president of the U.S. needed for that job. I think he was doing what he was told to do, and also making a lot of recommendations on his own that he thought were right. And the whole thing still makes me sick.

Do you think you're becoming somewhat of a political radical?

No, I sure don't. I look at it the other way: I'm just tryin' to be a good Christian. You know, there's three different kinds of Christians. There's preaching Christians, church-playing Christians, and there's practicing Christians—and I'm trying very hard to be a practicing Christian. If you take the words of Jesus literally and apply them to your everyday life, you discover that the greatest fulfillment you'll ever find really does lie in giving. And that's why I do things like prison concerts. Compared to that, projects like the television series I did, for example, have very little meaning for me.

Did you enjoy weekly TV?

It was all right the first year, but I soon came to realize that I was just another piece of merchandise to the network, a cog in their wheel, and when the wheel started squeaking and wobbling they'd replace me with another cog. Besides that, I began to feel as if every part of my personal and family life was being merchandised and exploited; I felt as if they were stealing my soul. To get ratings, they immediately started putting guests on my show that I couldn't—if you'll pardon the expression—relate to. People about whom I felt nothing, and that just made me uncomfortable. Eventually I was walking around thinking, "I don't have to do this. What am I doing this for?"

If weekly television was such a bummer for you, why have you agreed to do a new series next fall?

Because it's a dramatic show that won't give me the same problems. I'm going to play a character named John Andrew Jackson Stone, a country boy who's been through Vanderbilt Law School and who's a detective in the Nashville police department. Actually, I'm playing Johnny Cash as a policeman. The character has always wanted to be a singer, and the Nashville music scene will be part of the show. The whole thing grew out of a guest shot I did on *Columbo* last year.[1]

What kind of acting ambitions do you have?

None. I've never had any ambition to become an actor, because I love music much, much more than I could ever love acting. But I think I'll enjoy playing myself in the series, and another good thing about it is that it'll keep me home for five months—we're gonna be filming in and around Nashville. That'll give me a lot of time to sit around and talk to songwriters, and that's important.

Why?

Because it winds up with me writing songs. Like, if I'm around Bob Dylan, well, he doesn't talk much. He's a very quiet, kind person who loves his wife and children very much. We're in different worlds—he's a few years younger than I am and from Minnesota, and to him, Johnny Cash was always somebody from the South who sang those country songs. I think he has a great respect for my work and I certainly have a great respect for *his*, but it's not like we can't wait to get together to sit down and write a song. Actually, we *did* write a song to-

---

[1] *Editor's note:* The television series Cash planned never came to fruition.

gether once when he visited me at home. We were fishing at my boat dock and when we sat down to eat lunch we wrote "Wanted Man"—and we could hardly wait to get through with that song so we could go back to fishing. What I get from him is the something I get from all great songwriters: inspiration. It's like, I'll hear something they've written and think, "Why couldn't I write that—that's the way *I* think, too." Maybe it's more like a challenge than an inspiration, because after I've sat around with guys like Dylan or Kris Kristofferson and they've gone, I'll think, "Yeah, that's a good song he wrote, but maybe I can do better." And at that point I'll start writing.

Do you have the same effect on other songwriters?

I think so. Especially when I have songwriters' parties at my house, which is every three or four months or so. We'll sit in the living room and pass the guitar around, and anybody there who sings and writes knows they're going to have to come up with something. That sure motivates *me* to write, because I know I'll be in the hot seat sometime during the night, so I've got to have a song good enough to compete with what these other people will present. It's really a thing we all look forward to, and sometimes those nights have been memorable.

One final question: The people who know you best seem to think you have a mystic destiny. Do you feel that way too?

I don't know what's in store for me, but I know there are things I'm going to do that I haven't touched on yet. I don't know what they are, but I feel it. It's almost like when I was seventeen years old and my mother heard me sing for the first time after my voice had dropped. She said, "God's hand is on you, you're going to be a well-known singer." I smiled at her and said, "Oh, Momma." But I knew it myself. Back then, the big deal was singing on the radio—and when I was seventeen years old, I *knew* that I'd be singing on the radio. And that people would know my name. So yes, I feel there are things I'm going to do, but I don't know what they are. I'm writing a book about my experiences and beliefs, but that's not it. And the TV series may work out, but *that's* not it either. I'm not yet sure what's meant for me, but I believe I've got a lot to do—and whatever it is, I hope it's worthwhile.

PART III
LEGEND

I listened to an old record of mine on the radio yesterday and I noticed a big change in my voice, in the way I say my words, the way I talk. I know I've lost a little of that, that Southern dialect I had. I lost a hell of a lot of it, actually. And I don't know where I lost it.

—JOHNNY CASH, *Newsweek*
FEBRUARY 2, 1970

Johnny Cash settled into the 1970s secure in his status as country music's foremost symbol, a status he retained until the early 1990s (when it crawled atop the hat of a rising star from Oklahoma named Garth Brooks). But even during the pre-Garth era it was increasingly Cash the legend, not Cash the innovator, who played ambassador. To the world, he remained the face of country music, while failing to remain the industry's cutting-edge and top-selling artist. Performers who had begun revving their engines in the 1960s—Loretta Lynn, Charley Pride, Willie Nelson, Merle Haggard—outsold Cash and, particularly in the cases of Nelson and Haggard, produced more interesting and influential music.

Fortunately for Cash, he still cast the longest shadow in country and could open any door in New York, Nashville, Hollywood, and beyond.

The late 1970s and the 1980s were undoubtedly prosperous for Cash. Hits like "There Ain't No Good Chain Gang" (1978), "(Ghost) Riders in the Sky" (1979), and "Cold Lonesome Morning" (1980) summoned the trademark Cash spirit along with respectable record sales, as did albums such as *Silver* (1979), *Johnny 99* (1983), and *Johnny Cash Is Coming to Town* (1987). And the television industry continued to beckon Cash: he appeared in *Columbo*, *Little House on the Prairie*, *The Muppet Show*, and other weekly shows; hosted a series of musical variety shows on CBS; and starred in television movies, including *The Pride of Jesse Hallam* (1981), *Murder in Coweta County* (1983), *The Baron and the Kid* (1984), and *The Last Days of Frank and Jesse James* (1986).

But as he kept choosing routes that carried him away from home and the Nashville studios, his music suffered. Spending more time in Hollywood and on lucrative international tours left little time to nurture his creativity and challenge the complacency that age and success bring. He wrote less, and in the studio he often teamed with producers who had little desire or ability to tap Cash's strengths: his stirring voice, his songwriting, his way of summoning utter bleakness in two minutes and forty-two seconds. Emblematic of the aimlessness that plagued him was the 1975 album *John R. Cash*. He allowed the Columbia Records brass to propose the songs and independently record a number of the instrumental tracks, over which he later laid down his vocals. Perhaps this decision can be understood in light of the times, when musicians and producers were exploring new methods of recording. But it stands in alarming contrast to Cash's earlier approach to recording, when he virtually ran the sessions, building the sound he wanted for songs he had written. Although *John R. Cash* produced two hit singles—"The Lady Came from Baltimore" and "My Old Kentucky Home (Turpentine and Dandelion Wine)"—it remains one of the few Cash albums that failed to make the charts.

As the '70s became the '80s, he who reinvigorated country music with rawness and hard-charging rhythm buried his voice and the trademark rhythm under a sheen of Nashville production. The boom-chicka-boom sounded computer generated, his voice often sank in the mix, and strings—real and simulated—polished what didn't need polishing. Cash the musician was in a spiral and in a little bit of denial. In a discussion of 1980s production in the May 1988 *Musician*, he told interviewer Bill Flanagan that "Nashville got to watering down and slickin' up the country music. . . . A lot of producers and record companies made the fatal mistake of continuing to try to record that kind of syrupy country music." Cash failed to say that syrup dripped from more than a few of his own recordings.

In his 1997 autobiography *Cash*, he blamed his doldrums on his record labels, a charge that certainly had some merit.

> Sometimes in the early '80s I really cared about recording, but sometimes I didn't. It was hard to get excited about an album project when I knew the people at my label had come to regard me as a long shot and, when the chips were down, weren't willing to put money and muscle into pushing my records.

Whatever the label did or failed to do, there is no denying that the singer's flagging sales had left him vulnerable. This was never more apparent than in the early 1980s when a young generation of performers amassed at Nashville's borders and charged into town. Many of the fresh troops belonged to a group known as the New Traditionalists. They included Randy Travis, George Strait, Ricky Skaggs, Rodney Crowell, and others who found a way to acknowledge in their music the classic sounds of Lefty Frizzell, Hank Williams, George Jones, Johnny Cash, and other pioneers and still appeal to young listeners. Journalist Ken Tucker called them "the most interesting and exciting thing to happen to the country music industry in years" (*Journal of Country Music* 11, no. 1, 1986). Sadly, Cash, a father to these men and women, was churning out exactly what were they rebelling against. The New Traditionalists galloped by him, nodding solemnly as they passed.

During this period, Cash's record sales only surged when he worked with other country singers. Most notable are the three albums he released as part of the Highwaymen, an all-star quartet that also included Waylon Jennings, Willie Nelson, and Kris Kristofferson. "Highwayman," the title track from the rugged group's first LP, rode the charts for twenty weeks in 1985, spending a week at number one in August. Cash collaborated with Waylon Jennings in 1986 to produce the album *Heroes*, which included a hit version of "Even Cowgirls Get the Blues," written by Rodney Crowell. Throughout the late 1970s and the 1980s, Cash also paired with George Jones, Karen Brooks, Hank Williams Jr., and other performers with measured success.

Trading on the nostalgia that he (and his audience) felt for his musical past, he also participated in projects with his old Sun buddies: *The Survivors* (1982) was a live album recorded in Germany with Jerry Lee Lewis and Carl Perkins, and *The Class of '55* (1986) corralled Cash, Lewis, Perkins, and Roy Orbison for a dreamy musical recollection of the Sun days. Such collaborations put Cash in the papers again and made a blip on the sales screen, but they failed to create momentum for his solo career.

Neither did a jump from Columbia Records to Mercury Records in 1987. His last hit for Mercury—a warning about the apocalypse released in 1990 not long after the Gulf War commenced—managed only a pallid sixty-nine showing on the country charts. As the Man in Black's work appeared increasingly moribund, Cash the man was in something of a spiral. In the 1980s, he weathered an attack by an ostrich he kept near his home, battled addiction to prescription medication once again, and underwent open heart surgery.

Such personal struggle converged with Cash's listless recording career to suggest his career was passing away.

"What Now, John Cash?"

by Patrick Carr (1974)

❁ ❁ ❁

"Cash Comes Back"

by Patrick Carr (1976)

❁ ❁ ❁

"Johnny Cash's Freedom"

by Patrick Carr (1979)

Patrick Carr is the writer most closely associated with the Johnny Cash story. He has written extensively about the man in the press, and when he began preparing a full-length Cash biography in the 1990s, the Cash people proposed that Carr instead collaborate with Cash himself on his second autobiography. Out came Cash: The Autobiography, *an engaging work that contained new details and perspectives on the musician's life and work. Carr's probing had obviously forced Cash to ruminate on matters that he had rarely touched in public discussion, topics such as his friendship with the late Johnny Horton and his opinions of producers with whom he had worked. Carr knew his subject well, and it showed.*

The Carr interviews with Cash included here appeared in Country Music *magazine during the 1970s; they were among the most revealing snapshots of Cash taken that decade. Because the national media spotlight on*

Cash had dimmed, it fell primarily to the country music press to scrutinize him in a substantive way. The many Cash biographies that appeared in the 1970s, including Cash's first autobiography Man in Black *and Christopher Wren's* Winners Got Scars Too *generally ended around 1970, so it is fortunate that Carr visited with Cash and prodded him to reveal his thoughts in the heart of the 1970s. We see the legend in transition, struggling to find solid recording ground and reacting to the changing winds in country music.*

I

"What Now, John Cash?"

by Patrick Carr (1974)

On Thursday, August 29th, *Country Music* Editor Patrick Carr sat down with Johnny Cash in a suite in New York's Plaza Hotel. It was not a good time to talk with Johnny Cash . . . both June Carter Cash and Carl Perkins had just been summoned home to be with their ailing fathers, leaving Johnny to carry his show virtually alone, and only three days after the interview, John Carter Cash (Johnny's son) was to be seriously hurt in a jeep accident . . . but the Man In Black talked with complete frankness and hope about the problems that have affected his music recently, and what he plans to do about them. The news is good.

I've been hearing talk to the effect that you're dissatisfied with some of your recent work, musically speaking. Is that true?

Well, I still feel like I'm growing, see. I feel like I'm just starting out in this business. I feel better than I ever did. I'm working harder at it. But I've made a lot of mistakes in the studio in the last two or three years, and now I'm doing two things. I'm going in two directions . . . which is kind of a strange thing to do at the same time. One is with Jack Clement. He and I are working together on some sessions. We've had one, and I don't know when we're having the next one, but we're not going to release anything out of those sessions until we have something we know is it.

Now, as far as going in the old direction . . . back to the Sun sound . . . my album, *Ragged Old Flag*, was exactly that. I just had the Tennessee Three, mainly on that album, and those were all songs that I wrote . . . the first album I've ever done of all my own songs. I'm not sure how bad the people want to hear the boom-chicka-boom. If they want to hear it, that is what we'll give them. So I'm trying a couple of things. Jack Clement and I work very well together sometimes. Sometimes we don't agree on anything, and I never know from one minute to the next whether we're going to be able to have a session together and work together for an hour. I don't know which direction his head's going, and he don't know where I'm going; and we're both a little egotistical and temperamental. We're going to have another session, and it may last for three days and nights . . . or it might last for three minutes. I don't know. But we're going to give it a try. We're going to give it everything we got. We both respect each other quite a bit. I certainly respect him. If I didn't, I wouldn't work with him.

But it's not that I'm frantically groping around for a hit. I'm not. Everything that I have released, I was proud of it at the time I released it. It was exactly what I thought I should release . . . but the public has a way of proving you wrong, you know. If they don't want it, they ain't going to buy it, and you don't try to cram it down their throats. You haven't seen a lot of big ads run by Columbia Records or anyone else on my latest product, and maybe they shouldn't have run big ads. Maybe they knew it wasn't what I should put out, and maybe I didn't know. But when I made a mistake, I always knew it. I didn't make the same mistake twice. I made a lot of different mistakes, which is a good thing to do, because I know not to make them any more, see.

So, when the songs come along, if Jack Clement and I are working right together, we're going to get something reminiscent of some of the things we had on Sun, I'm sure. We have a good sound on things like "Ballad Of A Teenage Queen," "Guess Things Happen That Way," "The Ways Of A Woman In Love," things like that. Jack produced "Ring Of Fire." We're going to work together. If we can't work together the next time we'll set another session, and that time, we probably can.

You mentioned two new directions in which you are working. What's the other one?

Well, back out at House of Cash . . . or rather, back at Ray Stevens' studio . . . I recorded a song called "The Lady Came From Baltimore," written by Tim Hardin. It's a great song, and it'll probably be my new single. Now, the Columbia Records people in New York requested that I do that song, and they're putting together twelve songs for me to record. The sound is going to be produced somewhere else. . . . I'll put down my voice, and what they're going to do with it I don't know yet. But they have a man producing the music that has produced some fine stuff. I think he knows what he's doing: If he doesn't, I won't fool with him anymore. His name is Gary Klein.

There'll be songs like "The Lady Came From Baltimore," "Reason To Believe," "Bird On The Wire"; an Albert Hammond song called "Smokey Factory Blues," a Dylan song, Mac Davis's "Stop And Smell The Roses," and I'm recording "The Night They Drove Old Dixie Down."[1] I'm recording an album of what we feel are some of the greatest songs written over the past five years that didn't really make it big by anybody else. Things that I have a feeling for.

---

[1] *Editor's note:* This album was released as *John R. Cash* in 1975. "Bird on the Wire," "Stop and Smell the Roses," and the Dylan song were not on the album.

They're also slightly out of the mainstream of country music, aren't they?

Right. But I think they could be called some of country music's best, really "Stop And Smell The Roses" and "The Night They Drove Old Dixie Down" are classics.

Do you have any contact with Dylan these days?

No, I haven't talked to Bob in quite a while. He's pretty busy. We got a studio full of things recorded together now, but we're not going to release them. I don't have any plans for them.

Why not?

Well, they're things we recorded on his last Nashville session. He asked me to come in and record a song with him, and I did. That was "Girl From The North Country." And then we just got on a kick. We did about fifteen songs together. He recorded "Big River" and "I Walk The Line" and "Folsom Prison Blues" and "Ring Of Fire" and all those, and I recorded a bunch of his songs. Then we started recording old standard like "Careless Love" and singing them together. They're very informal, kind of loose things. Some of them don't have a real beginning or a real ending, and I don't believe they're good enough to release.

What about Kris Kristofferson?

I talked to Kris three days ago. I had talked about recording an album of his songs and he was going to produce it, but then he went off to Mexico and did a picture, and I did another album. So we didn't have enough time to do it. But we're talking about doing it now, maybe after the first of the year. It'll be probably a double album of songs that he writes and I write, and a couple we're going to write together, and he'll probably produce it.

Will you be duetting together?

No, I don't know if we'll sing anything together or not. I don't think mine and Kris's voices will, ah, blend.

Are you happy with House of Cash?

I sure am. It's the best studio in Nashville. The biggest and the prettiest. But I don't run House of Cash. Reba Hancock does. I don't go into House of Cash but once every two weeks. No, I don't have that many business interests. I don't even know what's going on at House of Cash. I go in and see monthly reports and that's about it . . . or they bring them over to the house. I never sit behind a desk at House of Cash. Don't ever think I'm an office man. You'll never catch me there. I mean, I never sit behind a desk. Never. If I'm up in my office and somebody comes to see me, then I get round in front of the desk. I never let myself be a desk man. I don't have any idea how much House of Cash music made last year. None whatsoever. And I couldn't care less, because I'm doing what I want to do. I'm doing exactly what I want to do, concert-wise and record-wise. I'm doing what I believe in, and I'm proud of all the work I do. I'm going to put it out, and if the public doesn't want it, I'm going to say, "Well, they didn't want that song. I'm going to try and figure out what'll be the best thing for them on this next one."

Are you writing much these days?

Yup. The harder I work, the more I write. I just wrote a song called "Down At Dripping Springs" and I think Reba's pitching it to Waylon this week. And I just wrote one called "Committed To Parkview," about the people in my business that have to go to the nervous hospital for various reasons. I think Reba said she's going to pitch that one at Waylon, too. [laughs] I don't know what she's got against Waylon, but she's going to send that one over to Waylon, too.

But I write a lot of songs, and the only time I go into House of Cash it's to put a song down or record.

I've been using my own group to record with me . . . you know, the ones I use for concerts . . . but I'm going to use a lot of other people, and try different things, because it's apparent that what I've been doing is not what the people really want to hear. So I'm going to try to do something that they want to hear.

II

"Cash Comes Back"

by Patrick Carr (1976)

WHEN "One Piece At A Time" went to Number One on the country singles charts it was plain that Cash was back, and this time in high style.[2] Since the late Sixties, Cash's records have been rather strange—more the recorded evidence of a great artist floundering in confusion than the masterful products of Cash's own unique mold. The hardness, the humor, the songwriting genius, that rockabilly "magic thumb," were hard to find on those records, and most of them failed to reach the top.

Meanwhile, however, Cash was still a major force. His charisma continued to make him the most respected and perhaps the most interesting male country singer of our time, and it seemed that even if he never produced any more music from the top of his form, he'd still be The Man. But it also seemed that in place of John R. Cash the musician, we might have to settle for Johnny Cash the public

[2] *Editor's note:* "One Piece at a Time" spent two weeks at number one on *Billboard*'s country singles charts in May and June 1976.

figure—author, folklorist, preacher, patriot, figurehead and moral backbone.

Two years ago, when I interviewed him in New York, it seemed that Cash was aware of this theme, and didn't like it. We discussed his plans to return to the old Sun Records sound by recording with the Tennessee Three, producer/songwriter Jack Clement, and Waylon Jennings—his old colleagues from the crazy days which produced most of his strongest material and just about all of his big hits. My impression then was that some sort of life cycle had ended for Cash; that he was through readjusting himself to pill-less reality, finding his sanity and accomplishing the kind of goals represented by his religion, his family life, and the House of Cash, and that now he might be secure enough to begin playing again.

It was encouraging to watch Cash put his plan into action at the House of Cash with Waylon, Jack and company. Though no tracks from those sessions have been released, the music was legitimately great (if a disk ever surfaces, get it) and the event reestablished Cash's links with the musical world he helped create back in '56 (which is no small point; scratch today's Waylon Sound and you'll find the Cash/Clement style of the late Fifties).

The end result of Cash's decision was "One Piece At A Time" and the album named after that superb, funny, slapback single. The album definitely recalls the "old" Cash. The production is a rockabilly's joy, the singing there, in tune with the spirit, and the inclusion of hard-edged songs like "Committed To Parkview" and "Daughter Of A Railroad Man" does a lot to destroy the often saccharine, musically unimpressive memory of Cash's last cycle. The album stands, in 1976, as a decent example of the state of the art, and Cash is planning to follow it with more of the same, plus another delightful wrinkle—duet work with Waylon.

This time, I talked to Cash on August 10th in Valley Forge, Pa. He was, as usual, frank about his music, himself, and his politics.

—*Patrick Carr*

When I interviewed you two years ago, you said, "It's apparent that what I've been doing is not really what the people want to hear, so I'm going to try to do something that they want to hear . . ." It strikes me, after listening to the One Piece At A Time *album, that you've done just that.*

I meant what I said, see . . . right? I think that I did something they wanted to hear, and what they wanted to hear was what I've done best all along—and that's the three-chord ballad with the Tennessee Three. I'm glad that's what they want because I know how to do that.

Is that what you enjoy doing most?

Yes, it really is. It's what I enjoy most. I'm getting such a kick out of it, feeling the same things I was feeling twenty years ago in my music. It's a whole new discovery for me, y'know—like, "Hey, I remember how good this felt, and I remember when I did it like this, and *this* is the way it feels best." Y'know? I just recorded a song I wrote eighteen years ago and forgot about. A song called "It's All Over." It sounds like the things I was doing eighteen years ago, and that's the way I recorded it, with the Tennessee Three. It's a weeper, a love song. It's kind of like being reborn again. I started out with that old simple sound on Sun Records, and I enjoyed it, and the people enjoyed it. But then I went through kind of a period there. Y'know, the real problem was not that I wasn't enjoying what I was doing; it was just that I was looking for something new, seeing if there was a new way to do it. As it turns out, what I think I discovered was that the way I started with it, the old way I've always done it, is the way I really enjoy it.

During that whole period when you were messing around with arrangements and so on, were you in control? Was all that stuff your doing?

Well, I agreed to it. That came out of a meeting I had with some Columbia Records people. They came out to my concert in Las Vegas, and they talked about, "Let's try something. Let's try this arranger. Let's try recording with the Big Sound."

Was the arranger Gary Klein?

Yes. For that kind of stuff, Gary is the best there is. He really knows what he's doing. . . . They thought it was the way to go, and I didn't know for sure at the time. So I went along with it, and I let them select most of the songs—which was a mistake, because if I'm not personally involved in my music, it ain't going to be right. I'm not going to have a feeling for it when I go into the studio. So all that whole scene, as capable as Gary Klein is, was a wrong scene for me.

But I learned a lot, and somewhere along the line Gary and I will do something—something that requires the kind of taste and artistry he's got. But it's like, ah—please pardon me for getting into politics—it's like we learned from the Vietnam war not to send troops to Africa, y'know? [laughs] And by the same token, I learned from those production days with Gary Klein that *I* shouldn't do it that way any more.

These days you're choosing your own material, right?

Yeah. That's the big thing, too. These days I'm totally involved with it from the time I choose the songs until the thing is finished in the mix. That's another thing I didn't use to get involved in. After the session was over, I'd never be there for the mix. I threw a lot of good sounds away because I didn't give them my ideas, y'know?

Charlie Bragg works with me at the studio, and he's the one who harped on me about, "Go back to the old sound, go back to the old sound." My attitude was "Oh, I can *always* do *that*. I want to do something else." So he mixed it the way I wanted him to. I'd tell him how I wanted it, and that's the way he'd do it—under protest. He was a mighty happy man when I got into the studio with him when he'd called a session for mixing, and I said, "Let's put the slapback on there. Let's put the old Sun slapback on there and forget about quadraphonic sound and stereo and everything, and make it sound like 1957." And I enjoyed it! I didn't think I'd enjoy it, but I did, and I got to thinking

. . . "Cash, you got involved in selecting the song; you put it down the way you wanted it; you saw it through the session. It would be stupid now to stay out of the mixing—like getting a ship almost to the shore, then turning it over to somebody else in the middle of a storm." So now I go in with Charlie on the mixing, and I tell him how I want it. We have some disagreements, but it always comes out the way I want it. [laughs]

I'm really enjoying it. I guess that's the whole key to it. If I don't enjoy it, somehow the people out there know it. For some reason, they know it.

Well, they usually do, don't they? That's what most of those producers forget. But how did you come by "One Piece At A Time," John?

Don Davis found it, and called me. Wayne Kemp was going to record it himself, but Don asked him to let me have it. They agreed, and Don brought it out to me.

Did you know it was the one when you heard it?

Yeah, I knew it. I knew that was it.

That's your first Number One single in . . . oh, how long now?

I guess since "Man In Black." . . . No, since "Flesh And Blood," 1971. Five years.

It must feel kinda good.

It really does. It really does. It's a joy, y'know? I dunno, maybe it's 'cause I'm older now. I used to take those hit records for granted. Back when everything I was releasing was going to Number One or up in the tops, I kinda took it for granted. Like, I would never look at the trade magazines. People would say, "Congratulations on your Number One record," and I wouldn't even know it was Number One. But it's like everyone shared in the excitement of "One Piece At A Time" being Number One. Everybody in town would be calling the office or the studio, saying "It's number seven this week," and somebody would get a tip that it was going to be number four next week, and they'd call. So I started looking at the trade magazines. I still don't read 'em, but I look at the charts and see who's doing what and what's happening in the business . . . who's selling, who's not. It's kinda interesting—again.

See, I had a couple of side involvements that took a lot of time and energy—but those were awfully important to me, and they were what I wanted them to be. That was my movie and my book. And you've only got so much energy. Right now I'm putting my energy into my music.

What about Jack Clement? Anything doing there? Are you doing any work with him?

Well, Jack Clement is always around, and I feel like I am, too, and sooner or later Jack Clement and I will do something together again. We didn't do too bad on "Ring Of Fire" and "Ballad of A Teenage Queen" and "Guess Things Happen That Way," some of those—and we'll have some ideas that gel perfectly sometime, and we'll get back in the studio together eventually.

Is anything going to happen to those tracks you recorded with Clement and Waylon a couple of years ago—the first cut on "Committed To Parkview," "You're So Heavenly Minded You're No Earthly Good"—all those?

Ah . . . We had one that I really like, "Someday My Ship Will Sail." I think Waylon and I are going to get that one out and listen to it again and see if we need to do anything to it. Waylon and I just did another session, did you know that?

Yeah. Just this past Monday, right?

Yeah. We cut two tracks for a single together, "I Wish I Was Crazy Again" and "There Ain't No Good Chain Gang." I guess we're just going to call the record companies' bluff. They say we can't record an album together, but I think we're going to do it anyway, and then say "Here it is. Work something out." I guess we could both get in trouble, but I tell you what: I respect Waylon as an artist, and think he respects me. We've been friends for fifteen years and we always did enjoy working together, and just because we both happen to be professionals and make a lot of money for other people doing it, I really don't see where that should hold us back artistically. If we want to get back in the studio together, we're going to do it. I think these record companies ought to set up a subsidiary amongst them for people like us, 'cause we're going to cut an album together. No doubt. We might do some country classics like "Lost Highway," some of those old heavy things. And we'll do it.

You were talking about taking more control over your music. Did the One Piece At A Time *album really satisfy you on that level?*

No, it just kinda got me primed and cocked for more and better to come. Like, it slipped me back into a whole new world of music and directions . . . like, I just recorded an old Presley song, "You're Right, I'm Left, She's Gone," and I did it with trumpets like I had on "Ring Of Fire," and I've kind of got a sneaky feeling about that one. I *really* like the sound on it. I've always loved the song. . . . So we're going to do an album of the old Sun things, the old Memphis stuff, '53 to '56. That's my next album project, the second one after *One Piece At A Time.* Some of my songs, a couple of Presley's, maybe a Carl Perkins song, a Roy Orbison song. It's not just an attempt to recreate that sound. I think we can make it sound like today's market, like today's thing, y'know? 'Cause I really enjoy it, and I search my conscience, and if I sing something I really enjoy, then that's what I ought to do. It's not always commercial, but it's what I ought to do. It's like *One Piece At A Time.* It was really what I wanted to do. I couldn't have been happier, unless it had been a song of mine.

That song was—well, not exactly socially acceptable, you know what I mean? I mean, it was really nice to hear you sticking it to the car companies.

Well, it's maybe back a bit more towards a more realistic outlook on life, y'know? There's so many people that would like to rip off the factory. It's not a sentiment that's totally far out for me, because I worked at Fisher Body Company making 1951 Pontiacs in 1950. I worked as a punch press operator in Pontiac, Michigan, in the factory—so I kinda had an understanding about what I was singing.

Would you say that the sentiments of the song echoed your own feelings, then?

Probably did so. I was eighteen years old, broke, hitch-hiked to Pontiac, Michigan, got a job in the car factory and there was all this wealth of car parts rolling down the assembly line and these brand new '51 Pontiacs coming off the other end . . . I guess every one of us in that place had thoughts about driving home one of those things. Or someday owning this construction company. Y'know, everybody that's ever worked cleaning up trash for a construction company has had these thoughts at the back of his mind . . . "One of these days, I'm gonna *own* this construction company!" Well, I felt that way about Fisher Body Company. So when the song came along, it was like memory time for me.

There was a lot of pretty hot picking on the album—a touch of the old boogie-woogie there. Are we likely to be hearing more of that from you? It's not something you've done much of in the past.

Yeah, I think so. "City Jail," a song I just wrote for the next album, has that boogie-woogie in there. Jerry [Hensley] is on all my sessions now, so you'll be hearing more from him.

Have you been writing much lately?

Ah—I haven't written anything in about a month or so, but I write in cycles, y'know. Like, when I was getting ready to do this last album, I wrote like a house on fire. And when I get ready to work on the next album, *that'll* inspire me to write some more. Yeah, I have some ideas that I'll be working on.

You know, there's an awful lot of emotional range between a song like "Sold Out Of Flagpoles" and one like "Committed To Parkview."

Well, they're from two different slices of life, and life is made up of all kinds of highs and lows, ups and downs—emotions. "Sold Out Of Flagpoles" is the light, up side, and "Committed To Parkview" is the valley. "Committed To Parkview" was somewhere . . . I've been. I still write about things I remember. I still sing "Sunday Morning Coming Down" 'cause it's something you don't shake in seven years, that kind of life. You might have become a different person, you don't live that way anymore, but it's sure not easy to forget the bad times. For the time I was singing "Committed To Parkview" I was *there.*

Do you still have a bad time sometimes? Temptation? Despair?

No, I'm never in despair. I'm never depressed. I got a lot on my mind sometimes, and it might appear like I'm depressed, but I never am. Temptation, yeah. I haven't fallen to it, but it still gnaws at me. It's a daily fight. But I can't afford the luxury of taking a drink or taking a pill because I'd have to have another one if I did. I *know* that. 'Cause you see, even after I quit in '67, I goofed up a few times. Several times. Nobody read about it in the papers, but I did, like when I went to the Far East in '69 and when I was in California cutting the San Quentin album. There were three or four times when I had to keep relearning my lesson that I can't mess with it, or I'm dead. And I know that's where I'd be if I got back into that stuff. It's either a matter of life or death with me. I either don't do it and live, or I do it and die. That's the way it is.

Is it a hard fight?

No, it's not really, because I got it all together family-wise, love affair–wise and everything else. I'm very much in love with my wife. I don't have any desire to fool around, and I really don't like liquor anyway. I know I'd really get a kick out of the pills for a while, but I can't do that. No, I'm really happy. I really think I'm a well-adjusted man.

You carry a lot of responsibility . . .

Uh-*huh*. You bet.

You're a figurehead, a target . . . does that bother you?

Being a figurehead and a target and carrying a lot of responsibility? Yeah, I get, er, I really get tired of the responsibility I have to bear. But being what I am, and with the success that's come my way, that's all a part of it.

Sometimes I *really* get tired of it. Sometimes I really want to shake it all off and go sit under a tree all day and forget who I am and where I am. That doesn't happen very often, 'cause, you know, I *enjoy* being Johnny Cash, I really do. Today at that press conference, all that attention—anybody would have to be crazy not to like being admired and respected that much, to have all these people fly in from all over the country just to sit and talk to *me*. I enjoy being Johnny Cash most of the time. The only thing that really irritates me—and it really irritates me *badly*, to where I might use a little force—is these people . . . I've seen them at my office all day long, and I've seen them on the road between my office and my house, I've waited while they got out of my way so I can drive out of my driveway, I've stopped to take the pictures and sign autographs and talk to them (and I talk to them every time).

And yet, when I get ready for bed and I bed down with my family for the night, they come knocking at my door. *That . . . really . . . irritates . . . me*, and I'm not gonna be responsible for what I say and do. I'm sorry to say I've really been rude to a few people. I just explode, y'know, when they coming knocking at ten o'clock and say "I've driven a thousand miles, and you gotta talk to me."

But the responsibility of living up to people's expectations about what they want me to be—being a figurehead—I don't mind that. I got a lot of self-confidence. I can handle any situation I've been faced with in that line.

What kind of a feeling do you get about the industry these days, John? You know, about how the music's going, how the controls are operating . . . the Outlaws thing, for instance?

I think all of that's good, y'know. And it's nothing new. The more change there is, the healthier the whole picture is. We can't lay back on our accomplishments and achievements . . . you know, "when this runs out I'll just quit."

Now, so far as the directions in the business, the Outlaws, I think that's just another way of saying "new direction." Waylon, Willie, Tompall, all of them are saying the same things, but they're saying them differently, and as an artist I really appreciate that. Y'know, myself, back in '56, I had a hard time breaking into the country music community in Nashville. I came up to the Grand Ole Opry to talk to Jim Denny, who was the manager of the Opry. "I Walk The Line" was Number One. I had an appointment—finally, my manager had gotten me an appointment—but I sat in his outer office about two hours before he ever saw me. Finally he let me come in, and the very first question was, "What makes you think you belong on the *Grand Ole Opry*?" See, I was one of those Memphis rockabillies—had sideburns—from that Memphis school of Presley and Perkins and Lewis and Orbison and Cash. It was a wonder they even let us in the city limits, the way they looked down at us at the time. Elvis had had a bad experience there—a very disappointing, unsettling experience. But Jim Denny asked me that question. I believe I'd just read Dale Carnegie's *How To Win Friends And Influence People* or some such thing, so I sat back and collected my thoughts after such a brusque, abrupt invitation to conversation, and I said, "Well, I love country music—always sung it—and besides that, I have a Number One country record." He sat and looked at me for five minutes before he ever answered me, and then he said, "When do you think you can come up here?"

But that first night, I got the feeling backstage at the Opry that there were a few of them weren't too happy to have me there. A few of them were maybe afraid of the competition (something I've really learned to appreciate is competition), but there were some of them like June Carter who really made me feel welcome. She'd worked shows with Elvis, you know, knew the Memphis scene. Then there was Minnie Pearl, and Roy Acuff, Hank Snow . . . y'see, guys like Acuff and Hank Snow are smart enough to know that people's tastes change. How many decades had they been singing, even in 1956? Acuff's smart enough to know that new people are gonna come along and be accepted, but that doesn't necessarily mean the old ones have to go cut their throats. Hank Snow had befriended Elvis. There were a few small minds who wouldn't talk to us as we walked by, but I made it. It took a while, though.

But back to your question. Rebels are going to come along and if they're not accepted they're gonna rebel until somebody notices them. But the thing that has not been noticed about some of these rebels like Waylon is the *talent*. Who's going to deny Waylon's *talent*?

You have any gripes about the industry?

Well, the record companies in our business are all looking for the "crossover" record, and the Nashville hype is the big thing going around. These radio stations all over the country get a call from a promoter or publicist or public relations person in Nashville, saying "jump on this one, it's a crossover record." The whole deal is trying to cut a country song with a crossover sound, a crossover feel, so it'll get on the pop stations. My friend Hugh Cherry talks about us standing in danger of country music losing its identity or its net worth, maybe, by concentrating on crossover and *not* concentrating on good country, and I think there's a lot in what he has to say.

I'm proud of the fact that my big crossover songs—"I Walk The Line" or "Folsom Prison Blues" were *country*. In no way were they an attempt to cut a crossover song. They made it over into the other markets on their own merits.

The whole big thing now is to cut a record that'll blanket all the stations across the board, right off, and I think the music, the songs, the records are suffering. A lot of songs that could have been good country records aren't anything, because such an attempt was made to make them crossovers.

You know, take Waylon. I can't remember hearing a record Waylon cut that sounded anything like an obvious attempt to put out a crossover record. Every record I've heard of Waylon has just been Waylon.

John, who would you pick for the CMA Awards this year?

Male Vocalist, Waylon. Female Vocalist? Looks like Tanya Tucker. Country Music Hall of Fame—Merle Travis. Merle Travis or Kitty Wells. They both deserve it, even though I'm one of the finalists. I was really surprised when I saw I was on the list. I really felt twenty years older.

John, what do you think of Jimmy Carter?

I knew you were gonna get around to this. How many political questions you got there, Patrick? Looks like a bunch.

C'mon, John, you worry too much. That's my shopping list. There's only one question. Really, now—what do you think of him?

Well, I think Jimmy Carter is part of the whole air of positivity in politics that has come around recently in healing this country's experience from Watergate and Vietnam. Now, Jimmy Carter—some of those who say they're voting for him are doing it because they believe what he believes, and some of them are voting for him because he believes in *something*. Whether *they* do or not, they're voting for him because *he* believes in something. "I'm not sure *I* do, but I know *he* does, so I'll vote for him. . . . " That's the feeling I get from some people. I think he'll probably be the next president, and I think everything's gonna be all right. On the other side . . . well, you didn't ask me that, so I ain't gonna tell you.

Mr. Ford?

Looks like he's done a pretty good job.

JUNE CARTER: I like Jimmy Carter the best 'cause of family ties.

CASH: Jimmy Carter's June's fourth cousin, I believe it is. Yeah, they're cousins. *He* brought it up. He's the one who told her where the family ties lie. She was really surprised. He'd told her that before, kidding, y'know, but recently he told her the names—how they're related.

But I really think he will be the next president, and I guess that would be all right.

You feel OK about that, huh?

Yeah, I *think* I'm going to vote for him. I think I am. I'm not going to say for sure, but I *told* him I was gonna vote for him. That was about three months ago, and I haven't changed my mind yet.

Has he asked you to work for him?

Yes, he did. I haven't replied to that request except . . . Well, I don't think it would be fair for me to *campaign* for a presidential candidate and try to influence people that way. That's important stuff and big stuff, and I don't think I've got a right to exercise any such control over the people. Voting is kind of a sacred, precious thing in this country . . . You're the first person in the press I've ever told about voting for Carter. I'm not recommending that anyone else vote for him; I just think *I'm* going to.

I didn't *refuse* to work for Jimmy. Jimmy just mentioned that he'd like for me to make an appearance with him later on this year in a key place, but I'm not sure I'm gonna be able to do that.

Along with Jimmy Carter comes the whole notion that the South is going to be in the driver's seat if he gets elected. I wonder if you think that there's something about the South—some basic virtues, whatever—that might not go amiss in Washington? You know—the politics of love, the stress of family ties, all that?

Yeah, but you know, I think that's a false impression that those kind of things like solid family ties are characteristically Southern. Or that faith in God is characteristically Southern. I think that's a misconception, an untrue philosophy about the South. I think that if it holds true there, it holds true in Michigan.

I think that probably there may be a *spiritual* strength that's stronger in the South, in what people very loosely refer to as the Bible Belt. I think that anybody with that spiritual strength would be a better president, a better leader, that that kind of mood and atmosphere and reliance upon. . . . I think a man like that would do a better job. I'd feel safer with him in there, y'know . . . a man who relied upon that spiritual power to determine his decisions, that spiritual discretion, 'cause it gives him a sense of conscience, like a compass. And that really works—I know that for a fact, from personal experience. That conscience is awfully important, I think, when you're dealing with the lives of millions of people.

Again, I don't know if the South's got anything over any other part of the country along that line. They show more dirty movies in the

South than they do anywhere else . . . I just don't know. All this doesn't answer your question very well, but I don't know how to.

I think it does, y'know. You did raise the question of moral integrity—spiritual integrity—and that's not insignificant.

"Integrity" I guess, is the word I'm trying to say. I feel that Jimmy Carter has that integrity. Not that Ford doesn't—he has that compass, too—but we're choosing a new man, and Jimmy's my choice of the new ones that are on the horizon and trying for the job.

III

"Johnny Cash's Freedom"

by Patrick Carr (1979)

CASH was not like I thought he would be. Yes, he was big and charismatic and hot with the nervous energy that is his key to other people's attention, but he was also loose, funny, and very much alive. That, the first time I met him in earnest, was some four or five years ago. Maybe his mood had something to do with the fact that he was recording with his old room mate Waylon Jennings for the first time, and with his old producer/songwriter Jack "Cowboy" Clement for the first time since Sun days; certainly, it betokened something good in the wind for music fans.

This time around with Cash, it was obvious from the start that with his best album in more than a decade under his belt, he had committed himself back to fun and music with all his heart. When you think about it, you have to say that after all, he had more staying power, more strength, than any of those Sun boys.

We began, of course, by talking about music.

—Patrick Carr

The last time we talked, John, you spoke about making albums more like the old Johnny Cash. . . . You know, without a lot of fancy orchestration and stuff.

Yes, well, that's what we're trying to do. We're trying to make it sound a bit more like something that was done today, rather than back in 1955, but we had a lot of things going on the *Gone Girl* album. First of all we had fun making it, we enjoyed it. We had my people that I enjoy working with—the Carter Family, Jan Howard, my group—and Jack Clement came in and played rhythm guitar. He's always a ball on sessions—or usually, anyway. Yes, we enjoyed doing the album.

Larry Butler had been busy producing some big hit artist, and about the time that I wanted to do the album he was right in the middle of it. I had to wait a while, and I got a little frustrated, and he knew I got a little frustrated, and finally we got together on a date. We didn't have words or anything, but I wanted in the studio. You know—when I wanted in, I wanted *in.*

The album came after a trip that June and Jan Howard and Jack Clement and I took to New York City. We went up and saw a couple of plays, and we sat up at night and picked and sang, and we got into some old songs like "A Bar With No Beer" and "Careless Love" and "Always Alone" and "Born To Lose," all those old things. Then we got into bluegrass, up-tempo stuff. Then we got to doing Jagger and Richard's song "No Expectations," and Jack said "Let's do it bluegrass style." I said, "It don't quite fit bluegrass style, but let's do it up-tempo," so we got to doing "No Expectations." Jan Howard knew it—she'd sung it before on the *Grand Ole Opry*—so she gave us the words for it. So we sang "No Expectations" perhaps forty times during the whole evening, and when we quit singing it the people next door called the room and said, "Please play some more!" We thought we'd been keeping everybody up.

That's the kind of spirit we had in the studio when we recorded the album—you know, we were having fun.

The musicians know that, too, see. It's awfully important to the musicians to feel that the artist is not acting like a star and not acting like the boss; he's acting like somebody that you're having fun with. That's what my guys felt in that studio that day. They were talking and laughing and cutting up and kidding Jack Clement about this and that, trying to make him balance a glass on the top of his head and do different kinds of dances. So we just had a lot of fun. Everybody was loose and laughing, and that's what helped to make it work.

But way before that I did a lot of homework. I weeded out a whole lot of songs. There were a lot of songs I didn't record on that album that I *wanted* to record, because I've been looking for good songs. You know who I've been listening to a lot? Tom T. Hall. Tom T. Hall has got to be the greatest country songwriter alive. I went to the K-Mart to buy a Tom T. Hall album the other day, just to hear some more of his songs. So I've got some of his songs laid back that I want to do—things he did on albums and didn't release as singles. But he's got so much great stuff.

It's not only him, either. There's other people like Rodney Crowell. Rodney has some good songs, and I'm holding some of his. I wanted to do some more of his on the album, but I didn't have room for them. So I'm looking forward to my next album, and I'm going to do my homework before I go in. And if everybody's not enjoying themselves and having fun when we get in the studio, then we'll just go home.

Cancel the session?

Right. After all these years, I realize that it's not especially the quality of the studio, who's got the best equipment, who's got the best sound. Jack Clement Studio happens to have a *great* sound and *great* equipment, which is why I picked that studio at that time, but I may do another session at the old Quonset Hut, Columbia Studio B, where I recorded so many times. I think I may do my next album there, because it'd be like memory time for me. Back in the Sixties I was there so many times with the Statler Brothers and the Carter Family and my group, back in times when I was having my own particular kind of fun and everyone else was sitting around waiting for old Johnny Cash to get ready to record—but now I think we could go back in there and have a good time. We may go back there, or we may go back to Jack Clement's studio, but either way . . .

The key to it all is atmosphere, right?

Exactly. Well, first of all, there's the songs. So I'm going to do my homework. Do a lot of listening to Tom T. Hall and Rodney Crowell and some other people.

What other people?

Well, I really like John Prine and Steve Goodman. I got two of their songs I'm going to try, see if the feeling's right. I've got several songs myself. I've been writing like crazy. I've got enough for an album of my own things that I've written since we did the *Gone Girl* album.

Things sound good. Sounds like you're really cooking these days. . . .

Well, you know I've sold my recording studio 'cause I never was interested in it in the first place. I don't know why I ever wanted one out here. I guess I do, too: because I could get Charlie Bragg to run it, and I believed in him as an engineer. But now we've gotten rid of that studio, which became kind of a burden, and Charlie's got a good job somewhere else, and the girls downstairs are turning it into a museum—which leaves me free. I guess that's it. That's another word that is important in this, too, Patrick. I feel free, you know. If I want to go to California and record, I'll do it. I'm not saying I will, but I might.

It's getting some of that big Cash load off your back, all those responsibilities. . . .

That's right. They're usually the ones I want to bear anyway, but things like that studio you look back on and say, "Hey, that was a status symbol, an ego trip. What'd I do that for? That was stupid, don't do that no more." But I'm free, you see. I'm free to go where I want to and record with whoever I want to.

That seems to be the direction you've been heading in for the last three years or so.

Yes. Freedom is the word. Not only that kind of freedom we were talking about, but freeing yourself from ideas and preconceived notions about what is expected of you. I forgot all of that crap. Forget about that I don't think about what is expected of me anymore. I'm doing what I *feel* is right for me.

For instance, I have people who say to me, "I want you to sound like you did in 1955 on Sun." I can't sing that way any more, and people don't record that way any more. Well, there's one cut on the *Gone Girl* album, "I Will Rock & Roll With You," where I asked them to put that old Sun slapback on, and it's pretty much got that old Sun sound. So we'll give them a little bit of that if they ask for it, if people want to hear it. I mean, I can do that electronically. But honesty in performance and freedom of delivery, that's where it's at. I feel free in the studio now. I wish I could go back in and do the *Gone Girl* album over again, and if I did, do you know what I'd do? I'd do it *exactly* the way I did.

Has Jack Clement had much to do with this kind of spirit in you?

Well, I haven't seen him in about two months, but I'm going to call him and pick his brains and see what kind of songs he's got. Jack has got so many great songs that he's forgotten about, you know, and I have to sit down with him and swap songs. "Hey, here's one I wrote that I forgot about!" he'll say, and he'll sing this song that you know should have been a hit when he wrote it. So I'm going to sit down with Jack and see if he's got anything else I might record, and then I'm probably going to ask him to come play rhythm with me again, 'cause

I like to work with him. As a matter of fact, Jack Clement asked me to produce his next album.

Really? That's a switch, isn't it?

Yeah, that scared me so bad I haven't even answered him yet. I said, "What do you mean, produce you?" He said, "Oh come down and sit in and play rhythm with me and tell me when I'm doing something wrong." I said, "Man, you sure are giving me too much credit here. I'm not a producer. I don't want to be a producer." He said, "Well, just come on down, sit in with me and play rhythm with me." I said, "All right, I'll do that."

John, how did all this freedom business start? I mean, you really weren't like this a few years ago.

You know what? It's just going back to the basics of what it was like back before all the big years of success and all that stuff. It was freedom, and I'm just looking for that freedom again. I've seen that in people like Waylon. Waylon is more free inside, and free from the business world of the music business, than anybody I know. He demands his privacy, demands exclusiveness to be not involved in everything going around. I guess maybe that my late association with people like Waylon—like, I learned a lot from Waylon. I mean, I can handle people. I like people, and I can handle them by the dozen . . . you know, when they come to the shows, I can handle them backstage and all that—but Waylon handles them with so much patience because he knows that tomorrow, ain't nobody in the *world* gonna be able to find him because he's going to be hiding out resting somewhere. Tomorrow, everybody in the world will know where Johnny Cash is, 'cause I'll have a commitment somewhere. That's the way it's been, but I've become a little bit harder to get to. Maybe I'm going through the change of life or something, but I want more time for myself, and I want more freedom from worry and work and the hassle that goes on at the offices and the recording studios.

It's showing in the music, you know.

Well, I hope it'll show more the next time around. Like I said, if the feeling's not there, we won't record. We won't do it until the feeling *is* there.

What about working with Waylon? Are you still getting him into the studio with you?

Well, he and I have done two more songs, but the record companies are having a hassle over who's going to release it. We just did a duet that RCA Victor gave CBS permission to release, but I don't know about Waylon's status with his record company, so I don't know if that song's going to be released or not. So we got two things we're holding, and we don't have any plans to record anything more right now. We have talked about sometime doing an album if we can get enough songs that feel right, but we don't have enough songs yet. I don't talk to Waylon very often, really, 'cause he travels like I do.

What do you think about what Carl Perkins is doing these days, John?

I think it's great. He's really hot again in England. *Ol' Blue Suede Shoes Is Back*, that's a great album. Carl Perkins is better than he's ever been. He was always great, but now he's better than he's ever been, 'cause he's free too, you know? For a long time he was the opener for the *Johnny Cash Show*, and I never did feel right about it. I never did feel right about having an artist of his stature in that position. But that's what he wanted, and it worked for a long time. When he went off on his own is when he really came *into* his own, though. He's terrific. He's got it all together, in his head and his heart.

He's sort of like you seem to be right now—he's got his family and his music, and he's doing what he wants to do. He's free to play.

Yes, sir. He's the best there is, in his field.

You think things are loosening up in the country music business in general, John? Last time I asked you that, about two years ago, you said basically that maybe they were, but you weren't too sure.

I don't know. I don't read the trades. I look at the charts every week if *Cashbox* or *Billboard* or *Record World* happens to be on my desk, but I don't really know what direction country music is going in. *I'm* really concerned with which direction I'm going in.

Maybe you're pulling back from your role as figurehead of the country music business?

I didn't know that's what I was. I don't know what that means, really.

Yes. No good asking you that these days, is it?

They keep asking me every year to host the annual CMA Awards Show, and I kind of hope they don't ask me any more. I get a little embarrassed. Really, I keep thinking some of my peers are going to say, "Hey, what? We got to have him again?" But the network keeps asking for me. I enjoy doing it, but I know there's that other world of country music out there that is as important to the people as that CMA world. It's a weird thing for someone like me to say, but I know that there's two worlds of country music out there now. There's that CMA world and there's that other world.

What's the other world?

Well, there's Waylon and Willie and all the guys that you don't see on the CMA—great artists like Marty Robbins, Webb Pierce, Carl Smith, Ferlin Husky, Faron Young, Ernest Tubb, Hank Snow. All these are great, great country artists, and you don't see them on the CMA show. You don't see them as a guest or a presenter, even. The network is looking for names, for ratings, and they don't realize how important some of these names really are. But there's no greater country singer than Marty Robbins, and I've asked the last two years to get Marty Robbins on the show, and I get some kind of runaround. And I'm not really all that happy to be the host of the show for that reason. Tom T. Hall—have you ever seen Tom T. Hall on that show? That's what bugs me. That's what really gets to me, that the agent and I will talk it over, and he'll say, "Well, what do you recommend I do?" and he'll say, "Well, you're the only one that means anything to them ratings-wise." I say, "Well, I don't *believe* that." Then we'll talk about the people that are going to be on it. I'll say, "Are they going to have any of the people on it that they've neglected in the past?" He'll say, "I don't have anything to do with that." Then I'll finally get around to talking to the producer. "Oh, the talent's already set for the show."

That's about as far as I get. I guess it's about time that I did let them know that I'm really galled that they don't have great people like Tom T. Hall and Marty Robbins and Ferlin Husky on there. I mean, Ferlin Husky's an entertainer. He's one of the greatest the business ever had. And just 'cause he doesn't have a hot record right now doesn't mean he's not important. There's a lot of them out there that are important.

Then there's the other world of country music like Waylon and Willie or Charlie Daniels—oh, Charlie was on there this year—and the other guys who couldn't care less about the CMA or anything else that goes on, only with what they're doing and the way they want to do it, like I am right now. The way I feel about the *Gone Girl* album is I guess the way these guys feel about most everything in the business—"If it don't feel right, I ain't going to get in it." I get into a lot of things in the music business that don't feel right but I get involved in them because of who I am. Whatever that means.

How do you feel about Jimmy Carter these days, John?

I'm not going to talk to you about politics.

Can I press you on one point? When we last talked, you said that you hoped Jimmy Carter might just bring back a sense of honesty and Christian values to this country. Do you think that has happened, if only a little?

Well, it's happened to me personally, and it's happened to a lot of people around me. Jimmy Carter's been up and down in the polls, but I think he's been as good a president as a president can be. I can't imagine any man even being able to handle the job in the first place. Any man that can bear it and keep grinning like he does has to be quite a man. But I don't believe that he's directly responsible for any great Christian revival—no. There's been a lot written about his being born again, and it's become a joke in a lot of areas—even though it's not a joke, it's a spiritual truth—but no, no great spiritual revival has taken place in this country that I can see. As a matter of fact, I've seen more decadence in the last couple of years than I've ever seen before in my whole life, I believe.

But the churches are full. But you know what, Patrick? I read a book recently called *In His Steps*. It was written in 1896, and in this book the man talks about the Church and how it separates itself from the very ones who need it most—the poor, the needy—and this preacher challenges his congregation in this book to go out next week and do it as Jesus would do it. Whatever you do, whatever you say, you ask yourself, "Is this the way Jesus would do it?" and see what comes about. So there was a lot of people in the congregation took the challenge, and started going out among the poor people and giving them food packages. They started putting their Christianity into action. Stopped separating themselves in their beautiful white sepulcher of a church from the poor people, the hungry people in the slums and the ghettos. Like I say, the churches are full, but the slums and the ghettos are still full, and for the most part, the churches and the needy haven't quite gotten together yet. And until more people in the Church realize the real needs of the people, and go out rather than going in . . . I mean, to go into church is great, but to go out and put it all into action, that's where it's all at. And I haven't seen a lot of action.

One of the things I've always liked about you is that you are a committed Christian, and yet you still work and hang around with people who might be considered backsliders or might have supposedly non-Christian habits. Funky musicians, you know? And you seem to be able to inhabit both worlds.

Well, it's not like going both ways. I don't compromise. I don't compromise my religion. If I'm with someone who doesn't want to talk about it, I don't talk about it. I don't impose myself on anybody in *any* way, including religion. When you're imposing you're offending, I feel. Although I *am* evangelical and I'll give the message to anyone that wants to hear it, or anybody that is willing to listen. But if they let me know that they don't want to hear it, they ain't ever going to hear it from me. If I *think* they don't want to hear it, then I will not bring it up.

It's something that Waylon and I have never discussed, and we're the best of friends. We've got into some deep subjects, like—well, we got into religion a little bit; not much, but we got into some deep stuff. I never got into it with Kristofferson, really. Even when I was doing *Gospel Road* and he was around, we really didn't talk about it much 'cause, you know, some people are uncomfortable talking about it. But back to how Jesus did it, He was that way, and I'm just trying to be like him.

John, is there anything you'd like to say about Mother Maybelle?

Mother Maybelle Carter. I still get choked up. She was my fishing buddy. That was my relationship with her. I've just lost an old buddy. That's it, and I don't have too much to say. She was the greatest. She was the first and the greatest, and the music world will slowly but surely begin playing its tributes to her by people recording everything she ever wrote and recorded.

I was talking to Carl Perkins the day after she died, and he said much the same thing. He said that when he was on the road with you, he and Mother Maybelle used to sit up at night playing cards, and that's how he'd always think of her.

I did a lot of that. We'd play poker. We'd sit up all night playing poker with Mother Maybelle.

What about Elvis, John? Any last words on Elvis?

Well, what has not been said? Elvis was the greatest in his field, of course. I'd always admired him: Every show before I went in, I'd always watch every minute of his show from the side. But I didn't see Elvis for the last eighteen years of his life, so I didn't know him that well.

What did the commercialization after his death do to you?

Well, I didn't go out and buy a bunch of posters and junk they were selling but it's something I expected. I'll tell you what it's done, though—it's got him a whole new world of fans. Little kids. Every little kid loves Elvis Presley. Kids John Carter's age, eight years old. I take him to school, he's singing "All Shook Up" or "Jailhouse Rock" or something, every day. Every little kid knows Elvis.

Sounds sort of like 1953 all over again.

No, I'm talking about little bitty kids, you know?

Well, it makes a change from John Travolta, eh?

Right.

"Johnny Cash: Still Free"

by Noel Coppage (1983)

❁ ❁ ❁

"Hard Talk from the God-Fearin', Pro-Metal Man in Black"

by Mary Dickie (1987)

❁ ❁ ❁

"Heroic Survivor"

by David Sinclair (1989)

The following are three snapshots of Cash as he negotiated the 1980s. Noel Coppage's piece in Stereo Review *on* The Adventures of Johnny Cash, *an album that is virtually forgotten, demonstrates Cash's ability to release average to above-average material and still attract enthusiastic critical reaction.* Adventures *was undeniably a satisfying album, but it was hampered by the era's chronic overproduction and the absence of Cash's songwriting (he cowrote one cut, "Fair Weather Friends"). However, Cash's stature made it difficult to question him.*

In the second article, Canadian writer Mary Dickie visited with Cash for Graffiti *and found a middle-aged heavy metal fan. Cash's openness to heavy metal must have surprised Dickie, but Cash had always explored fields out-*

side his own: blues while selling used appliances in the streets of Memphis during the mid–1950s, folk after listening to an early Dylan album. The acceptance of heavy metal and other styles new to him might help explain his ease with Beastie Boys and Run-D.M.C. producer Rick Rubin in the 1990s.

The final article, David Sinclair's review of a London performance for The Times *(London), reveals that the sluggishness in Cash's studio may have been creeping into his concerts.*

I

"Johnny Cash: Still Free"

by Noel Coppage (1983)

THE *Adventures of Johnny Cash* on Columbia is the first whole Johnny Cash album produced by Jack Clement since the two were with Sun Records, launching the heyday of rockabilly, twenty years ago. Cash's bass-baritone voice has been exposed enough in the intervening years that it no longer seems startling, and Clement has become semi-civilized, but the collaboration suggests that old hands can still have fun making a record and that free spirits don't easily fade away. This one and 1980's *Rockabilly Blues* are Cash's best albums in recent years.

Cash was something else when we first heard him—that was the phrase we used: "The man is something else." Neither country nor rock-and-roll listening had prepared us for the spartan, primitive records he and Clement fashioned for Sam Phillips. Here he and Clement have achieved a kind of freshness that has little dependency upon nostalgia. There *is* a similar kind of simplicity, possibly born out of their going with what they've got: not an elective tick-tack guitar but an acoustic/mandolin wizard in young Marty Stuart; not the classic spare, bare-bones rockabilly song but some fine new ones by the likes of Billy Joe Shaver, John Prine, Roger Cook, Merle Haggard, Allen Reynolds, and Bob McDill. So the backing is mostly acoustic (with an appearance by a real string quartet), the instrumentation is just dense enough to cover the ground around the vocals, and Cash—as sometimes happens to low voices when they age—is a more accurate singer now than he was back when this all started.

Clement can still be rough. If you recall his production of Waylon Jennings's "Dreamin' My Dreams" a few years ago, you'll remember it hardly seemed mixed at all. Here he has Cash on top of the mike in a seemingly well-padded room on one cut and well away from it in what sounds like a hard-walled closet on the next cut. But if you listen closely to the one you're listening to at the moment, you'll more than likely find that the mix is exquisite and that it wouldn't quite have worked otherwise. Clement and Cash have changed the way they do things but not, fortunately, the spirit in which they do them.

II

"Hard Talk from the God-Fearin', Pro-Metal Man in Black"

by Mary Dickie (1987)

OF all the great country singers, Johnny Cash is probably the most enduring and definitely the most versatile. And, from his beginnings as a rockabilly singer in Sam Phillips' Sun stable in 1955 (he was groomed as Sam's next meal ticket after Elvis) through his protest albums, folk festival appearances and work on Bob Dylan's *Nashville Skyline* in the '60s, to his covers of John Prine and Bruce Springsteen songs and his '80s collaborations with Nick Lowe, Dave Edmunds and Elvis Costello, he's always had the closest ties to rock.

Cash has also always had that rebel outlaw image, what with his Man in Black look, his well-publicized bouts with the bottle and various pills (including a "lost year" spent in the company of Waylon Jennings) and the persistent, though false, rumors that he did time in jail. He was given a suspended sentence in 1965 for bringing amphetamines across the Mexican border, but it's probably his prison concerts, where he gets a roar of approval when he sings "But I shot a man in Reno / Just to watch him die," that have reinforced that particular myth.

Johnny's not an outlaw anymore, though. He's a 55-year-old religious family man who's been clean for five years, ever since a visit to the legendary Betty Ford Clinic (where he befriended Ozzy Osbourne, who needed a pep talk). He's busy touring with wife June Carter Cash, sisters-in-law Helen and Anita Carter and stepdaughters Carlene and Rosie Carter to support his latest album, *Johnny Cash Is Coming To Town*, his first for Polygram after CBS, his label of 28 years, dropped him abruptly last year (he's also promoting his latest book, *Man In White*, about Saint Paul). But Johnny's got an open mind and a healthy sense of humor (anyone whose song titles include "Dirty Old Egg Sucking Dog," "Flushed From The Bathroom Of Your Heart" and "Frozen Four Hundred Pound Fair to Middlin'" would), both of which are clearly evident when he speaks. And he's very much a rock fan, thanks in part to his son, John Carter Cash, who has his own heavy metal band and recently performed his first official concert. They've even written a couple of songs together, which John Carter will perform someday.

"I probably listen to more rock than country now, because of John Carter," Johnny says. "When he got into heavy metal, he got to playin' things like Iron Maiden, Metallica, Motorhead, Twisted Sister—all of 'em. I couldn't relate to a lot of it too much, but I could feel the excitement he was feeling in the music.

"You know it was right here in Toronto that I met my first heavy-metal artist," he continues. "That was Iron Maiden. I was doin' the *Tommy Hunter Show* and they were setting up across the street at Maple Leaf Gardens. I'd heard them, 'cause John Carter played them all the time, y'know. I had a break and I went over, and they were doin' a sound check. I walked into the auditorium just to feel the music. 'Cause you can *feel* it, not just hear it. I can feel it in my liver! I wasn't really paying attention to the musicians, and I had no idea they'd recognize me. But they stopped and started pointin' and talkin'. So I went backstage and had a cup of coffee with them and got to know them. I got some autographed pictures for John Carter. Well, he got so excited that I'd met them, and he wanted me to go to a concert with him.

"You know in Tennessee, Tipper Gore's got that campaign to censor rock lyrics. So to try to understand all the hoopla from her side and also to understand what my boy was into, I decided to go and see Metallica and Iron Maiden, and later Ozzy Osbourne, who I knew already. And what I observed were a lot of teenagers and young adults just lettin' loose and havin' a good time. 'Course there was grass smoking, but there's grass smoking at people's houses everywhere. I don't think I saw anybody drinkin'—they probably were, but I didn't see anybody—and all the kids were nice to me. I'd have them come by and shake my hand and say, 'Man, what are you doin' at an Ozzy concert?' And I said, 'I'm enjoyin' the show! Great light show!' Iron Maiden's also got a great show, with all the special effects and everything. And Metallica, you know, before that guy got killed, they were fabulous! Three musicians—just knocked me out. That's the way I started—just me and two others. I could see why John Carter was into it—it's exciting and it's fun, and it's good therapy for me.

"And I got to thinking about this business of censorship, and how presumptuous people are my age to think that they're finally going to do something toward raisin' their kids right by censoring three minutes of what they hear in a day's dialogue. They hear more obscenity from their friends at school than on all the rock records they could listen to. And they probably hear it from their parents, when they think the kids aren't listening. It's like when they censored Elvis on the *Ed Sullivan Show* in 1956. I thought it was so stupid. And that's how I feel about censorship of rock lyrics. I think it's absolutely ridiculous. If a parent hasn't been close enough to his kids to let them make their own decisions, then it's too late by the time they're ready to rock 'n' roll."

On the new album Johnny does a great version of Elvis Costello's classic hangover song, "The Big Light." Certain that there's another story behind this one, I ask him how he hooked up with Elvis.

"Well, I met him originally through Carlene (who's still married to, but separated from, Nick Lowe)," Johnny explains. "When he came to Nashville we had him and his band out at the house for dinner, and I got to know him even before I heard his music. Nice little guy. But you know Nick Lowe had a hand in producing his *King of America* album. And Nick sent an advance copy of 'The Big Light' to a DJ in Grand Rapids, Michigan, where he knew I was going to be. I listened to it and went back to Nashville and recorded it. It was the first song we recorded, and I still think it's the strongest one on the album. It feels like something I wish I'd written."

Johnny feels similarly about the two Springsteen songs he recorded—"Johnny 99" and "The Highway Patrolman"—and would like to work with him, as well as John Mellencamp. But other than those two, there are very few people he wants to work with and hasn't already. "When I had my TV show (1969–70) I worked with an awful lot of people," he says. "I had Joni Mitchell on, her first time on national television, Kenny Rogers, Linda Ronstadt. . . . " (Joni postscript: Johnny's first Canadian tour was in 1957, supporting his hit "Ballad Of A Teenage Queen." In each city there were Teenage Queen promo contests, and in Saskatoon the runner-up was, yes, Joni Mitchell.)

"I loved singing with Jerry (Lee Lewis), Roy (Orbison) and Carl (Perkins, in *Class of '55*). We could do an album of spirituals that would be a real knockout," he says. "I'd also love to do *Highwaymen II* (with Kris Kristofferson, Willie Nelson and Waylon Jennings). It's just a matter of getting the four of us together."

Johnny's most storied collaboration is probably the session he did with Bob Dylan around the time of the *Nashville Skyline* album, in 1969, which has never been officially released.

"I signed bootleg copies of it all over Europe, but I don't know how it got there," he says now. "We just went into the studio and started singing everything we could think of. Some of 'em have no beginning and no end—they don't sound very professional. But we had fun for about two hours—I think we did about 26 songs together. I've got the only copy I know of outside CBS, but I guess Bob has one too.

"We were just doin' it for fun, but it is frustrating, because so many people want to hear it. And whether or not it's good or bad, I'd like people to hear it. But I don't know where Bob stands on that, I don't see him much. And I don't know where the record company stands—I got no influence with them anymore."

Johnny's consistent songwriting and openness to rock, folk and blues have kept him on the charts for three decades plus now, and he's seen a lot of trends come and go, as well as a lot of people trying to copy his inimitable walking bass lines and loooow voice. How does he feel about country's latest upswing in popularity and its effect on his own audiences?

"Well, a year ago," he says, "the *New York Times* had an article on how country music had dropped so much in popularity. But in a year's time it's come an amazingly long way back up. And that's due mainly to artists like Dwight Yoakam, Randy Travis, George Strait, Steve Earle. Traditional country music goes full circle about every seven years, and right now it's ridin' on top. But a lot of things have happened to make young people rediscover me. Like the minor wave of rockabilly out there. When I get requests for songs from young people, it's always for the early '60s songs, or the Sun years. No later than 1970, 'A Boy Named Sue.' They know I was ridin' that crest of rockabilly from the beginning. Nowadays, you know, at my concerts there are a lot of young people out there."

III

"Heroic Survivor"

by David Sinclair (1989)

JOHNNY Cash's formerly dissolute lifestyle is catching up with him fast, but for a 57-year-old man who underwent open-heart surgery earlier this year and is currently suffering severe pain from an old leg injury, he did not look or sound quite the wreck that might have been expected.

Playing as the centerpiece of the month-long "Route 89" festival, he arrived, as usual, mob-handed with family and friends. Jostling for space at the microphones at the start and finish were his wife June Carter, his sisters-in-law Helen and Anita Carter, a son-in-law, Rodney Crowell (who opened the show), a former son-in-law, Nick Lowe, and the unrelated Elvis Costello, with whom he performed an appallingly slipshod duet on "Bottle of Inspiration."[1]

---

[1] *Editor's note:* The title of this song is "The Big Light."

In between the family shenanigans, however, Cash turned in a substantial performance in his own right. With sedate backing from his seven-piece band he strummed an acoustic guitar, and sang in the dark, hard drawl that has done so much to shape the course of modern country music.

His pitching was uncomfortably approximate during a quasi-gospel sequence of "Peace in the Valley" and "Jesus, My Soul's In Your Hands."[2] But for most of the time the depth and roundness of his baritone was outstanding as he hit twangy bottom Es with ease and performed with an authority that was rarely less than commanding.

The inevitable blackness of his clothing was relieved only by the gaudy glitter of an outsize belt buckle, and he continued to purvey the kind of mystique more frequently associated with movie characters than with a popular entertainer. So convincingly did he put across the many prison songs—"Folsom Prison Blues," "I Got Stripes," "San Quentin," "Green Green Grass of Home"—that one could easily forget that Cash has never actually been in prison himself.

His plangent description of how the Seneca American Indians were cheated out of their land rights suggested that Cash is still a long way from relinquishing his role as folk hero and champion of the underdog in favour of a comfortable routine of showbiz schmaltz.

Above all he seemed relieved simply to still be around, for which he thanked the Lord, effusively. "It just feels good to be alive and be with you."

---

[2] *Editor's note:* The title of this song is "Why Me Lord?"

"The Mystery of Life"

by Alanna Nash (1991)

Alanna Nash has proven to be one of the most enduring and sensitive of country music writers. A native Kentuckian and Columbia University School of Journalism graduate, she has written about Johnny Cash for almost twenty-five years. In her 1991 review of The Mystery of Life *album, Nash pinpointed a few of the nettles snagging Johnny Cash's recording career.*

JOHNNY Cash was a busy man last year—touring with his fellow Highwaymen, putting together a retrospective exhibit at the Country Music Hall of Fame, and recording *The Mystery of Life*. When it came to writing the album, however, Cash apparently was too busy, and so he rummaged through his attic and came up with an odd set of songs, several of which are so old they practically sport toupees.

There's "Wanted Man," for example, a mediocre and disappointing number Cash wrote with Bob Dylan in the late Sixties. Then there's a remake of Cash's hard-chugging Fifties rockabilly classic, "Hey Porter," and a duet with Tom T. Hall, "I'll Go Somewhere and Sing My Songs Again," that the two most likely cut years ago for another project. There's also "Beans for Breakfast," a funny but dated tune (it first appeared as the B side of a single some years ago) that casts the singer as a pathetic lout unable to care for himself once his woman has run out on him. Although it's sexist by contemporary standards ("wish you'd come back and wash the dishes"), it also contains an interesting reference to Cash's true-life firebug-and-drugs days of yore: "The house burned down from the fire that I built / In your closet by mistake after I took all them pills." But by far the strangest tune here is one in which Cash tries to join a cowboy metaphor with a religious theme, entoning, "My cowboy hero hat's off to the man who rode a donkey / He's the greatest cowboy of them all." Gag me with a prayer book.

The Cash aura is so strong, though, that even when he's bad (or in the case of much of this album, just weirdly off-center), he commands attention, both for his presentation and for the beauty and humor he finds in life's most mundane situations. His stature is such that he can put out an album like this one and make it work, after a fashion. Cash will eventually be reckoned the single most important country-music figure of the postwar era, and *The Mystery of Life*, for all of its shortcomings and its quirkiness, provides not a few of the reasons.

"Johnny Cash's Best Performance Was Off Stage"

by Dan McCullough (1989)

Amid the many stories of Cash's compassion for and connection with all people, no matter their race, status, or class, this column, by Dan McCullough of the Cape Cod Times, *stands out.*

As I pulled my truck into a parking place in West Barnstable this week, a song which I hadn't heard for years came on the radio. It was "Ring of Fire," a classic hit by the famous country and western singer, Johnny Cash. By the time I had backed into the parking place, the song was only half over, so I just sat there with the truck running and the radio playing, and listened to the rest of the song. I was already five minutes late for a meeting, but the song had me by the throat.

When the song ended, I shut off the truck, grabbed my books and stuff, and headed across the parking lot. I wasn't much watching where I was going that morning; the song had taken me back to my first (and last) Johnny Cash concert. It was at Boston Garden a few years ago.

Now, let's get one thing straight right from the start: I am not now, nor have I ever been, a big fan of country and western music.

Steve Goodman, the Chicago songwriter, once developed a formula for the perfect country and western song. I don't remember the rules exactly, but to write the perfect song one had to include: mama, trains, gettin' drunk, a motel, a pickup truck, a dog, jail, divorce, and a long-distance call.

I like that; I like it a lot. It probably tells you how seriously I take country music. One of my favorites is, "The Night I Talked to Jesus on My CB Radio" (a real song, honest!).

So anyway, back to Johnny Cash.

My friend, Bobby, is a Down's syndrome adult. You know, what we used to call "mentally retarded." His best friend, Gordon, is a congenitally brain-damaged adult. At the time this story takes place, both these guys are in their late teens.

Now I've known both these guys since they were babies. I'm Bobby's godfather, and Gordon's mother is a woman from my old neighborhood. I played ball with her brothers (Gordon's uncles) and we went to school together.

Bobby and Gordon grew up together and they were inseparable. What a picture they made together. Gordon was a black kid, over 6 feet tall, with long black fingers, long black arms and legs, and beautiful big brown eyes, which were only magnified by the glasses he wore because he was visually handicapped. Gordon was so skinny, he could hide behind a telephone pole, and often did, teasing Bobby. His 6-foot-plus frame could not have weighed 130 pounds. I could pick him up with one hand.

Bobby, on the other hand, had white Irish skin, blue eyes, also magnified by the glass frames of his handicap, and was built like a professional wrestler. He was 5 feet 6 inches tall, round-shouldered and strong as a little bull. He would often pick Gordon up in jest, much to Gordon's displeasure.

What a visual duet the two of them presented, walking down the street together or sitting on Bobby's front porch steps, talking things over. They went to separate schools but spent every free waking hour together. They were two of the most free spirits I've ever known. I didn't know anyone who knew them who didn't love them. They sure loved each other.

Oh yeah, Johnny Cash.

Well anyway, the one thing these two characters had in common was a passionate addiction for the music of Johnny Cash. They had Johnny Cash posters in their rooms, Johnny Cash albums and cassettes, Johnny Cash T-shirts, picture books, magazine articles, memorabilia, ad infinitum.

So one day, I read in the newspaper that Johnny Cash is going to be at Boston Garden. I think for a minute, maybe less, say to myself, "What the hell," and head up to Boston Garden. The guy behind the ticket window says, "How many tickets?" I tell him three. "Where do you want to sit?" he says. I tell him money is no object; I want the three best seats in the house.

Now I don't know where this next idea came from, but on the way home, I started to wonder what the possibilities might be of Bobby and Gordon getting Cash's autograph, or something. But I didn't know any Boston promoters or wheeler-dealers. I was just a guy who had two special friends who would give anything to have Cash's autograph, or maybe (Oh God! Could it possibly happen?) shake his hand.

Minutes later, I'm on the phone with Ernie Santasuosso, entertainment columnist at the *Boston Globe*. He had reviewed a rock concert earlier in the week, so I dialed the *Globe* and asked for him. The conversation began, "Hi, Ernie, you don't know me; we've never met, and I don't have any friends in the entertainment business, but I've got these two kids, special kids, friends of mine . . . "

Later Santasuosso says, "Give me your number; I'll see what I can do, and get back to you." (Sure, I think, he'll get back to me, all right.)

Twenty minutes later, the phone rings. It's Santasuosso. "Call this number at the Sonesta Hotel in Cambridge," he says. "Ask for Fred

Taylor; he's expecting your call. I just talked to him. He's at the hotel with Cash." (With Cash? With JOHNNY Cash? Hey, wait a minute, this is getting a little too close!)

Five minutes later, I'm talking to Taylor. He tells me to be at a certain place, Stage Door 3 or something like that, at 8 P.M. on the Saturday night of the Johnny Cash concert.

Four days later, I'm at Stage Door 3. I'm not alone. My two pals are with me. It's 7:55. There's a grey-haired cop looking very bored. We must have made a strange-looking trio. He doesn't ask us what we're doing there. I'm glad he doesn't, because I wouldn't know what to tell him. For all I know some guy is going to open the door, hand us two Johnny Cash ashtrays and some application forms to the Johnny Cash Fan Club, and say, "Enjoy the show."

I haven't told Bobby and Gordon anything except that we are going to see Johnny Cash live at Boston Garden. What could I tell them? I don't know what's going on here myself. The lights dim in the Garden, and, from our spot down below, in the run way, we can hear the show begin. Fifteen thousand fans are screaming and applauding. Bobby and Gordon are restless. They want to know why we're "down in the cellar." They've asked me 10 times already why I've given each of them a little pad and a pen. Neither of them can read or write.

My heart is heavy. I look at my watch; it's almost 10 past 8. Well, it seemed like a good idea, I think. It was worth a try. I take each of my pals by the arm, and begin to head up into the Garden proper. A voice behind me says, "Dan McCullough?"

I turn around. The guy in the doorway repeats the question. I nod my head. He beckons us. He leads us backstage to a spot near the main stage. "Wait here," he says. We wait. As we are waiting, I realize that it's the warm-up band that is on stage.

My back is to a dressing room area. My two pals are facing me. They are not having a good time. They are bored and confused. A minute later, I'm reviewing my first aid training, because it's clear that both Bobby and Gordon have gone into some sort of aphasiac seizure at the same time. Their eyeballs are frozen on an object behind me. I turn around. The object says, "Hi Dan, I'm Johnny Cash."

I'll never forget him. He treated those two kids as if they were the co-owners of the biggest music production studio in Nashville. I stood to the side; it was their show. The three of them talked as if they were just three guys back in their neighborhood. They told him about the special schools they went to; he told them bus and airplane stories. He spent a good half hour with them. I just could not believe this was happening.

Soon his people were calling him; it was show time, time for us to go. As they shook hands in parting, Bobby said, "I say a prayer for you every night, Johnny." Cash looked like someone had punched him in the stomach.

Then Gordon hit him with a left hook: "I don't pray for you every night, Johnny, but just on Sunday, when I go with my mom."

Cash couldn't speak. His eyes filled up. He looked at me, reached over, took me by the arm, and shook my hand. "Thanks," he said, "Thanks very much." I didn't feel much like talking myself.

We turned and walked away. Cash hollered after us, "What song would you boys like to hear?" Bobby and Gordon said at once, "Ring of Fire!"

Minutes later, we were in our seats with the other 15,000 fans as Cash strode on stage. I don't have to tell you what his first song was, do I?

So, country and western music? Naah, doesn't do much for me. But Johnny Cash? Well, let's just say I'm a big fan.

PART IV
BACK IN BLACK

But as it was fate swooped upon his head.

—SOPHOCLES

One morning in the mid-1990s, we woke up to find Johnny Cash leaning on our headboard, looming over our warm nest. A chill filled the room, like the cold you feel when you mistakenly leave the window open all night in late October. "Wake up," he urged in a hoarse whisper. "I've come back." Cash, his eyes urgent and his hair askew, unfurled his long black arm and pulled us from our bed in a dazed shock. He had something to show us.

The last we knew about Cash, he was traveling the roads and skyways, playing dates as if he were plugging a thriving hit. But there was no hit—and no radio airplay. We knew he was out there because the dented, majestic face periodically appeared in newspaper advertisements: Johnny Cash at Charlestown Racetrack in West Virginia, at Potter Center Music Hall in Jackson, Michigan, at the Easton State Theatre in Pennsylvania. The name popped up every February 26 in the Associated Press' list of birthdays, and short items about surgeries or visits to rehab appeared here and there. Fortunately, he skirted the obituaries.

But suddenly he was at the fore again, after sneaking out West to a thirty-one-year-old producer named Rick Rubin. There was this album called *American Recordings* on the market, an accompanying video, and talk of a revitalized, stripped-down J. R. Cash. It was the spring of 1994.

Rubin had produced young, blazing acts such as the Red Hot Chili Peppers, Run-D.M.C., and Danzig, and he saw in Cash the rebellious image (formed in a crucible of drug use, protests on behalf of the disenfranchised, and writers with romantic tendencies) that his young bands claimed for themselves. "I don't see him as a country act," Rubin told Christopher John Farley of *Time* in May 1994. "I would say he embodies rock 'n' roll. He's an outlaw figure, and that is the essence of what rock 'n' roll is."

Rubin taped Cash and his guitar, just Cash and his guitar, and when the final playbacks and sequencing had been done, the new partners pulled back the curtain and revealed music defined by dark themes and haunting vocals. His gravely hum was stark against the sparse instrumentation on *American Recordings;* it had not been allowed such prominence in productions of the previous fifteen years. The performances' desperation and aggression was the stuff of Cash's '50s and '60s, the stuff of Sun and San Quentin. Anthony DeCurtis, in the May 19, 1994, issue of *Rolling Stone,* branded the new album with five stars: "Not a feeling is flaunted, not a jot of sentimentality is permitted, but every quaver, every hesitation, every shift in volume, every catch in a line resonates like a private apocalypse." Cash finally had a producer who was thinking about him, thinking about the right ambience, songs, songwriters.

In reply, the mass media feverishly churned out coverage, intrigued by Cash's odd pairing with songwriters such as Glenn Danzig,

Leonard Cohen, and Loudon Wainwright III, and the reemphasis on his dark side. Consumers were jarred awake too. Ultimately, they propelled *American Recordings* to the twenty-three position on the *Billboard* country albums charts. A solo album by Cash had not climbed so high in sixteen years.

In 1998, shortly after Cash won a Grammy Award for his second American Recordings album *Unchained*, he and Rick Rubin ran an ad in *Billboard* featuring a younger Johnny jamming his middle finger into a camera lens. It was meant for Nashville. The Grammys generally recognize marketing potential over artistry, so it was curious that Cash and Rubin used the occasion of this establishment award to fire an "up yours" message at that very establishment, but his fans and the press took the bait and guessed that the old firebrand Johnny was at it again. Ignoring the preacher, patriot, and poet aspects of Cash's image, Rubin had successfully resurrected his buck-the-system side, finding in the process new acceptance for Cash among the young.

Unfortunately, as the Grammy was conferred, Johnny couldn't stand in the public spotlight that had swiveled around in his direction again. He was suffering from a Parkinson's-like disease that was attacking his nervous system. Doctors first diagnosed it as Shy-Drager syndrome, but they have since rejected that assumption. Cash had first felt the symptoms in October 1997, when he began walking backward involuntarily on a New York City street. Not long after, he canceled concerts and a publicity tour for his second autobiography so he could begin receiving treatment. He has since made only a handful of brief appearances. His public holds its breath and waits for his or the disease's next move.

In the early 2000s, the media spotlight has dimmed. Perhaps it will brighten again as it has so many times for Cash. However, for much of the last decade, the Johnny Cash story summoned the best music writers in America because once again Cash summoned great music. Cash's work in the 1990s achieved a quality equal to any he produced in forty-five years of entertaining. And if he is to quietly remain in retreat, nevermore to work again, the American material will be a proud cap to his career. He will have left the game on top, as Ted Williams homering in his final at bat. The American years have cemented his legacy. Country music may never again know so meaningful a career.

"Chordless in Gaza: The Second Coming of John R. Cash"

by Nick Tosches (1995)

Naturally the Journal of Country Music *(published by the Country Music Foundation in Nashville) took up the subject of the new Cash, choosing Nick Tosches for the task. Tosches, who had skewered Cash in the 1970s, seemed to have discovered a new, though grudging, respect for Cash in the 1990s. In doing so, he represented music journalism's renewed embrace of Cash: reporters deemed him to be once again cool and innovative. Tosches, the biographer of Dean Martin and Jerry Lee Lewis, elicited stories from Cash that had never been heard before, and, in pointing out the "tremor in his voice and manner," foreshadowed the physical difficulties that awaited him.*

HANDSOME Dick Manitoba, the lead singer of the Dictators, the punk-rock band that always hated punk, is an icon of sorts, if not quite to the world, then at least in his own neighborhood: a one-man school of cool, a patron saint, or, perhaps more accurately, heresiarch, of East Village rock & roll. He is telling me that the Dictators, who have not recorded for a major label in four years, are working on a new album.

"What do you call your shit these days," I ask him. I figure that "punk" and "new-wave," as marketing rubrics, have got to be as dead as the "champagne music" of Lawrence Welk.

"I have no fuckin' idea," he says. It's comforting to think that he, who's on the cutting edge, doesn't know either. But he does, and he doesn't like the sound of it: "Everything now is 'alternative.'"

"Alternative to what?"

"Who knows?"

He seems bored with it all. Except for this new album, *American Recordings*, by Johnny Cash, which, as we speak, has worked its way onto the pop charts, sandwiched incongruously between Sonic Youth and the soundtrack from *Crooklyn*. No matter that Handsome Dick was in diapers in the Bronx, that the East Village was still the Lower East Side, when Johnny Cash began his recording career. This album inspires in Manitoba a flood of enthusiasm that threatens to inundate coherency.

"Y'know, you listen to something," he says, his words gathering speed with every syllable, "you get a couple of, like, little—*boom-boom-boom*—from it, like this reminds me of this. My first impression was the way Springsteen was this big star who made this *Nebraska* record, which is, like, a haunting record of just his voice and guitars, and very sparse and very raw, and just, like, the embryos of songs. This is like that. In fact, the thing I love about Johnny Cash is the sound of his voice, the *physical* sound of his voice. It's like buyin' a book called, like, y'know, America or something. And if it had a voice, it would have his sound. That's what mesmerizes me about him. It's like a history book or something. This album is just that sound of his voice, with a little music sort of just, like, to have something to sing to." His effusion disperses, softens into glowing detumescence. "It's great."

Lord Byron said it: "Truth is always strange; stranger than fiction." The guy in the bar, forsaking *ottava rima*, said it better: life is funny. Two years ago, Johnny Cash, at sixty-one, was history, an aging, evanescent country-music archetype gathering dust in a forgotten basement corner of the cultural dime museum. He had not been able to break into even the country Top Twenty on his own in over a decade. But today, at sixty-three, there he is, up there with Sonic Youth. Walk into the huge Tower Records store in downtown Manhattan, and, amid the blare of the moment's rap, in the prominently displayed row of featured albums that make up Tower's Top Twenty-Five, there he is, on that black-and-white album cover, peering ominously forth, flanked by two dogs beneath a blustery sky in the Australian outback, robed in his full-length black duster, with his hands poised before him on his upright guitar case, as if to enfold in prayer or invoke the unspeakable or throttle the unseen intruder, the potential buyer, whom his grim gaze impales, looking like Luther and Lucifer, asceticism and evil, merged. Walk into Zapp Records, an ultra little shop across town on Bleecker Street, and there he is again, between the Cars and Nick Cave.

Little is heard these days of Jerry Lee Lewis and Carl Perkins, the other rockabilly legends who, like Elvis and Roy Orbison, both now beneath the dirt, came out of Sun Records in Memphis along with Cash in the fifties. George Jones, the only other living country singer of Cash's stature, has been relegated to the polyester purgatory of Opryland. Cash, on the other hand, has suddenly found himself commanding the ardor of the au-courant herd, holding forth, an unlikely Orpheus to pierced ears, on the stages of the sort of terminally hip clubs where one would sooner expect to find the Dictators than him: the Viper Room in Los Angeles, Emo's in Austin, Fez in New York. Bono, the ubiquitous leader of U2, sought him out and wrote a song for him to sing on the group's latest album. Even Ozzy Osbourne, the patriarch of heavy metal, has waxed reverent: "Not only do I admire Johnny Cash as a musician, but also as a man." Kate Moss appeared in his music video "Delia's Gone." The basic theme was lust murder. MTV deemed it beyond the pale, too hot to handle, and it had to be recut for broadcast.

His performance in December 1993 at the Viper Room, the Sunset Strip nightclub co-owned by Johnny Depp, was the most celebrated event there since River Phoenix croaked outside the joint two months prior, and received more notice than Mick Jagger's appearance there onstage two months later. "I can't believe I get to say this. Ladies and gentlemen, Johnny Cash," said Depp with an air of awe in presenting Cash to a full house that included Rosanna Arquette, Pierce Brosnan, Shannen Doherty, Juliette Lewis, Graham Nash, Sean Penn, Tom Petty, Randy Quaid, Henry Rollins, and members of the Red Hot Chili Peppers.

Also there that night was Rick Rubin. Barely thirty, Rubin was a kid from Queens, a Dictators fan, who rose, through his work with Public Enemy, Run-D.M.C., L.L. Cool J, the Beastie Boys, Slayer, Red Hot Chili Peppers, the Black Crowes, and Mick Jagger, to become one of the most successful and iconoclastic record-producers of the nineties. It was Rubin who brought Cash, when no one else seemed to want or know what to do with him, to his American Recordings. It was Rubin who resurrected him. The Viper Room was his idea.

"It turned into more than it was originally intended to be," he told me. "Originally, since John was coming to town and we were recording anyway, why not get up and sing a couple of songs at the Viper Room just for fun? And then, the day of the show, when he was deciding what he was going to do, his list of songs that he wanted to do kept getting longer, and I said, 'Well, as long as you're going to be singing that much, we might as well record it and see what it sounds like.' So, it was really more of an impromptu thing. It wasn't a planned thing at all." (Two of the songs recorded that night, the country chestnut "Tennessee Stud" and Loudon Wainwright III's "The Man Who Couldn't Cry," ended up among the thirteen of *American Recordings*.)

"It was really a magical event," Rubin says of that night on the Strip. "I think Johnny was really surprised at how interested young people were in him and what he does. It's odd to be in a place like the Viper Room, which is kind of a small but loud nightclub, and have it be so quiet. Having been to the club before under normal circumstances, it's nothing that you could imagine happening, that kind of silence and awe in an audience in that particular kind of a place."

What happened at the Viper Room happened again at Emo's during the 1994 South by Southwest alternative-music conference in Austin. According to Joe Nick Patoski, a senior editor of *Texas Monthly* and an inveterate follower of the Austin scene, SXSW is "for all of the none-of-the-aboves, the outsiders," and, last year, Cash "was the big sensation. His show, which was never really announced publicly, was the toughest ticket that they've ever had at South by Southwest. Emo's is kind of like a grunge-alternative-metal-tattoo-biker joint, and all these insiders, so-called alternative insiders, wanted in. It was, like, all of a sudden, Generation X fell head over heels for Johnny Cash."

When the album came out, *Rolling Stone* coupled it in a lead review with a new Sinatra release. Sinatra got four stars, Cash got five. Declaring Sinatra and Cash to be "brothers, blood on blood," the review represented an apotheosis of sorts, the imprimatur of ageless cool.

But why Cash? Why now? Surely it cannot be explained merely by the "legend and mythical stature," which Rick Rubin says brought him to Cash. For illumination, I turn from the Lower East Side, where Handsome Dick holds forth, to the Upper East Side, where Cash himself, dressed in black but neither Luther nor Lucifer, asceticism nor evil, meets me at Le Régence, in the Hôtel Plaza Athénée where he is staying while in town to tape the David Letterman show and a VH-1 special.

He orders an iced tea but barely touches it. Instead, as he talks, he fidgets with a box of matches. Though he quit smoking nearly a quarter of a century ago, he is quick to light the cigarette I draw. Within a few minutes, it is clear that Johnny Cash runs a lot deeper and through more unexpected places than most singers I have encountered. We end up talking about first-century history, a subject that enthralls Cash far more than the subject of himself. He tells me about his collection of silver denarii from the reigns of the twelve Caesars.

"But, for Tiberius, I have gold aureus, 'cause that's the period Jesus was . . ." His voice trails off. I mention Michael Grant's book *Roman History from Coins.*

"I got it," he says. "Got 'em all."

He refers to the "Twelve Caesars of the Republic," while in fact the Republic ended under Augustus, the second of the Casears. He pronounces "aureus" as "aur'us." And much of his history comes from antiquated works, such as *The Life and Epistles of St. Paul* by W. J. Conybeare and J. S. Howson. (When I mention another of Grant's books, *Jesus: An Historian's Review of the Gospel*, he seems unaware of it.) But his hunger for, and love of the history of the period is impressively sincere, strong, and, in his own self-schooled and rough-hewn way, erudite; and, in the end, I'm sure his grasp is no more unsure, perhaps less so, than my own. Immersed in the first century, we talk on. I've got the cigarettes, he's got the matches.

But, fuck, I'm here to make a buck, not have a decent conversation. Enough of this intelligent shit. The King of the Jews can wait. Back to the ever-elusive fucking angle: I ask him if he's surprised by the resurgence in his fame.

"Yeah," he says. "A lot of young people are tunin' in." He shifts the matchbox from one hand to the other. "It's strange too, they've found another category for me: alternative. I think that's kind of funny."

"Alternative to what?"

"I don't know."

We end up back in the first century. Cash on Roman times is like Handsome Dick on Cash. "I've read those kind of books as long as I can remember," he says. "I read *The Robe*, *The Silver Chalice*, all those books, in the fifties, the sixties. Josephus. Books about Masada. I was always interested in that period of history. Even as a kid I was interested in that period. As late as last night, in *Everyday Life in Ancient Rome*, I was lookin' at how they built a crane back then to lift a three-ton block of stone. I was lookin' at a drawing of a Roman crane. Just as efficient as the ones we got now. Fabulous.

"Unbelievable. I've always been interested in that. Solomon said it very well: There's nothin' new under the sun. And I just like to look at the origin of it all and see how smart we're not."

I remember interviewing George Jones, the only man who dominated the country charts more than Cash in the years since 1955, when both had their first hits. All Jones wanted to talk about, and only reticently, at that, were his cows. I prefer the Roman cranes by far.

"Then I got into the natural herbal cures that they had for everything. Roman vaccinations for smallpox and so forth. They would take someone with smallpox and take a little scab, and for the person who was bein' vaccinated, they would cut the skin a little bit, put the smallpox germs in there, and wrap it up, till that person had a big ugly sore but he didn't get smallpox. He was vaccinated. That's interesting to me."

Cash wrote a novel set in the first century, *Man in White*, about Saul of Tarsus, published by Harper & Row in 1986. The book was the product of much hard research and work, and he tells me it annoyed him to open *Spin* magazine the other day and read, in novelist Barry Hannah's article about him, that, while *Man in White* was "a highly literary effort" comparable to the work of Taylor Caldwell, "off the top I'd guess Cash didn't write it at all."

Cash shakes his head. "Nothing ever written about me has told it right."

What about *Man in Black*, his autobiography of twenty years ago?

"Even that," he says, explaining obliquely that it was written expressly for a publisher of religious books. He commends the journalist Christopher Wren's 1971 biography of him, *Winners Got Scars Too.* But nobody, he repeats, has gotten the story wholly right.

An opening if ever there was one. He says he'll be back home, in Tennessee, for a few days next week. If I come down, we can talk more then. As I would discover, he isn't just speaking idly. There was a lot that was not known about him, a lot he had never told, including a tale of murder that still haunted him.

The House of Cash, in Hendersonville, northeast of Nashville, is set back along the road now known as Johnny Cash Parkway. Years ago, when this big brick house with its six white pillars was all that stood here, it must have been a beautiful place. Today, looking out across the road, one sees Twitty City, the yahoo architectural legacy of Conway Twitty, and the International Village mall.

The ground floor of the House of Cash was, until recently, given over to the Johnny Cash Museum and Gift Shop. This museum was an eclectic array devoted as much to Cash's obsession for collecting as to the chronicling of his career. For the price of admission, one could behold not only Cash's 1948 eleventh-grade report card (all C's, an A for conduct), but also Chiang Kai-shek's writing desk, Al Capone's chair, Buffalo Bill's Winchester rifle, Buddy Holly's motorcycle ("on loan from Waylon Jennings"), and much else. A chained-off staircase leads to the homey suite of private offices that serves as the center of Cash's operations.

The night after I met him in New York, I watched him on the Letterman show. He was the Man in Black. Letterman introduced him as the world sees him: "an icon." He performed his song about tying up and killing Delia, then was gone. "I was frightened," said Letterman afterward in his trademark louche way. "Yeah," his acolyte, Paul Shaffer, chimed in. "He's scary." They were talking about someone, something, different from the man I had met earlier in the day. It was the age-old grand illusion at the heart of every racket, the shell game of flesh and fantasy; and it made me think of what Cash said about nobody getting it right.

Today, in Hendersonville, he is not the Man in Black, except for his leather loafers. He wears no socks, a dark blue shirt, tail out, and gray-and-blue cotton drawstring britches, more like pajama bottoms than trousers. He settles into the big chair behind his big desk and removes his shoes. I ask him about the business of nobody getting it right.

"Well, you know, it's hard for me to be objective about myself, but still I have an opinion about what happened and what it was like. To hear it described by somebody who wasn't there, who didn't see it and feel it, it's just not quite right, ever, with me.

"For instance, people say, well, he's been in jail seven times. It might be true, but every time was different and really most of 'em were accidents. I just accidentally wound up in jail.

"I'm a rambler and a loner, and after a concert at night, I would often go for a long walk or a drive, and I'd be picked up in the wrong part of town with no explanation about why I was there. Like one time, about three in the morning, I took a walk in Starkville, Mississippi, whistlin' and strollin' along and grabbin' a flower, smellin' the flower then throwin' it away. I got arrested and charged with pickin' flowers in this lady's yard, and I wasn't doin' that; I was walkin' along the sidewalk, happened to brush my hand against a flower, so I grabbed it and just kept on walkin' till the police got there. But the press: Johnny Cash was arrested in Starkville pickin' flowers, three A.M. Which I really was, but it's not the way I saw it at the time.

"I was never hurtin' anybody any of those times. Except myself. I don't know. I think that the way the world perceives me sometimes isn't quite right. They perceive an image rather than the real me.

"I read some of these things and I feel the reader's probably thinkin' I'm walkin' along in such a horrible state that pieces of me are droppin' off every few feet. And I'm in very good health at sixty-two. I don't take any kind of drugs. I don't drink. I don't eat right 'cause I don't wanna eat right. I wanna eat what I was raised on. But I don't overdo that. I been wearin' the same size pants now for fifteen years."

In New York, I had noticed a tremor in his voice and his manner. It was not the tremor of a nervous man. In fact, it seemed oddly a part of his strength: the low, insistent rattling and rumbling of a battened iron composure against the ever-pressing forces of a storm he had managed, through will, to subdue. In Tennessee, that tremor was still there, but it had subsided greatly.

"Yesterday I worked in the yard at my farm up in the country. I hoed my tomatoes, my okry. I dug around my roses, set out some fig bushes, worked around my grape vines. I do that kind of stuff. That's my therapy.

"Sometimes I can only grab two hours up there, but I do. It's one hour exactly to drive from here to there. I speed. I go eighty miles an hour, but I make it in an hour. It's such a peaceful place. A hundred and seven acres. An old log house. It's the most rural county in Tennessee—Hickman—and I live on the most rural part of it. Way back. I never take anybody there. Always alone. That's where I write. I draw, I pray, I meditate. I listen to the birds. Talk to them. I talk to the animals and the birds all day long when I'm up there. Aloud. I do. I stepped out this morning with my coffee cup on the porch and the mockin' bird's singin', so I start talkin' to that mockingbird, 'Thank you for the song.'"

Cash bought his farm twenty-three years ago, the year he recorded "Man in Black." That record represented a parting from the country-music establishment that was as real as his physical departure to Hickman County. Though it eventually became a hit, "Man in Black" was an antiwar song released at a time when country music stood firmly behind Nixon, nationalism, and the Protestant way of war, and radio was reluctant to accept it. (This was not Cash's first conflict with mainstream radio stations: the resistance to his 1964 single "The Ballad of Ira Hayes" was such that he took out a full-page ad in *Billboard* asking them, "Where are your *guts*?")

But the log house in the middle of nowhere was as much of a return as a departure. For that is where Cash is from: the middle of nowhere.

He was born, the fourth of seven children to Ray and Carrie Rivers Cash, on February 26, 1932, in Kingsland, Arkansas. His father, the son of a Baptist minister, was a World War I veteran who worked during those Depression years in the mills and on the railroad. When John was three, the family moved to a New Deal cotton-farming community in the northeast part of the state. It was there, in the desolate Delta flatlands, in a five-room house on a gravel road two and a half miles from Dyess, that John R. Cash grew up. The black-mud country of his youth was so forsaken a place that a common piece of rock, rare and exotic in that wasteland, captured his imagination and became a symbol of romance and possibility.

"You could see thirty miles from my front yard, it was that flat; and there was not a rock of any kind within those thirty miles. My brother and I went to the Boy Scout camp at Hardy. You gotta go through Hoxie to get to Hardy. Comin' back on the bus from camp, we all stopped to pee by the road. I went down to the riverbed, and there was a big slab of sandstone, probably two feet long, a foot and a half wide, two inches thick. I picked it up, took it to the bus, brought it home, set it right below the front doorstep on the ground."

That slab, which he called the Hoxie Rock, is still there, outside the shambles that was his boyhood home. As a teenager, John hated the cotton fields. He liked to sit on the porch steps with his feet on the Hoxie Rock, talking to his dog, listening to Smilin' Eddie Hill's "Noontime Roundup," which drifted across the Mississippi from WMPS in Memphis, singing the songs he learned from listening, singing the songs he made up. And thinking. Because, by then, something great and mysterious and dark had descended like a shadow on his world.

It came in 1944, when he was twelve, the year the Holy Ghost took hold of him during a revival at the First Baptist Church, the year he wrote his first, forgotten song. He and his older brother Jack were close. "Really brothers. Really close." One Saturday morning in May, fourteen-year-old Jack went to work at the school shop. John had wanted Jack to join him in fishing the big drainage ditch that ran through Dyess. But times were hard for the family. Ray Cash was plowing in the cotton fields from dawn to dark, and Jack, to help out, was earning three dollars a day cutting fenceposts at the shop.

When John came home from fishing, his father took him into the smokehouse. From a blood-drenched paper sack, he drew blood-drenched khaki britches and a blood-drenched shirt, and he laid them out on the smokehouse floor. They were Jack's clothes. The pants and shirt were slashed from the bottom of the rib cage down to the pelvis, and the belt was sliced in two.

"He was cutting fence posts," his father told him. "One got tangled up in the swinging saw and pulled him into it—jerked him in. He fell across the big table saw."

Doctoring could not save Jack, and John stood by with the rest of the family at Jack's hospital bed as he lapsed in and out of coma. "What a beautiful city," Jack said. "I wish you could hear the angels singing." Those were his dying words.

"The memory of Jack's death, his vision of heaven," Cash wrote in his autobiography, "have been more of an inspiration to me, I suppose, than anything else that has ever come to me through any man."

The story of Jack's death, as told in that autobiography, has been retold many times. Now Cash tells me it is not the whole truth. His brother's death, he says, was an accident only "in the family's mind." It was murder, he tells me, speaking slowly, deliberately, with the tone of one drawing words from an uncomfortable place.

"There was a neighbor that went down to the shop with him that day and disappeared after the accident. We couldn't prove anything, but I always thought of it as murder. My mother and daddy didn't. They never mentioned that boy. Nothin' was ever done about it." He tells me he is writing a novel, *The Hoxie Rock*, based on that twelfth year of his life.

"I almost have it finished. I overwrote it. I've got almost three hundred pages, on my Tandy computer. The ending is all I have to write, but I've got to go back and change and throw out a lot of stuff that doesn't fit, add a lot that should be in there. I'll do it."

From his earliest memory, he recalls his mother playing her Sears Roebuck guitar and singing gospel songs. All the Cash children had grown up under the sound of her music. Roy, the eldest of the children, had even formed a band, the Dixie Rhythm Ramblers, that played a few times on radio station KLC in Blytheville.[1] But then the war broke out; the Dixie Rhythm Ramblers went off to fight, and all except Roy were killed.

Around the time of Jack's death, Carrie Cash's guitar vanished—sold, John figured, to buy food, though he never asked. Three miles down the road was a friend, Jesse Barnhill, a boy who played guitar with a polio-withered right hand. John learned to make the chords that Jesse made.

---

[1] *Editor's note:* Cash is probably referring to KLCN in Blytheville.

Cash wanted nothing more than to escape the Delta barrens. After high school, he decided to join the service. He chose the air force and enlisted in the summer of 1950.

"I don't know, I guess I wanted to fly out of that Delta land. I just liked the image of flyin'. I knew I didn't want to be in the army. My father was in the army and I'd heard so many stories about how—course, he was World War I—how rough it was. Same with the marines. I didn't wanna be in the marines. I guess I wanted to fly out of that Delta land. I just liked the image of flyin'. I really wanted to fly, and I thought if I joined the air force, I might have a chance." But he never flew. Tests he took during basic training revealed an aptitude for high-speed radio intercept. After schooling in Russian Morse code, he was stationed in Landsberg, Germany, where he became a staff sergeant.

"I was in the United States Air Force Security Service. We copied Russian transmissions from their ground bases, radar stations, aircraft. We'd spin the dial till we picked one up. You could always tell the Russians from the Americans because the Russians were very meticulous and would always broadcast a little cleaner than the Americans.

"The first Tu-4 Russian jet bomber that took off from Moscow, I intercepted its transmission from my position in Germany. And he was sendin' thirty-five words per minute by hand, the fastest I'd ever heard a man send by hand, and I was copyin' him. We'd been listenin' for him. We knew that a jet bomber was gonna take off for the first time. I shouted to the chief, 'I got him!' They took my code into crypto, broke it down, and, within an hour, we knew everything that the U.S. government wanted to know about that Tu-4. I got a commendation from Washington on that.

"It was an exciting job," Cash says, but he never thought of making a career of it. "No. I wanted to get out and play music."

In Germany, he bought his first guitar, for twenty marks, "so cheap that it didn't even have a brand name, but in my eyes it was a D-45 Martin." He played with his thumb leading, a primitive style that precluded any finesse for melody; but his few rough chords carried his rough voice well. With three other servicemen in Landsberg, he formed an acoustic honky-tonk band—three guitars and a mandolin—called the Barbarians. They played beer halls until closing time or until they were too drunk to continue. A lot of the songs they played were written by Cash. The first song he wrote in Germany was a gospel song called "Belshazzar." Later, after a showing on base of the movie *Inside the Walls of Folsom Prison*, he wrote "Folsom Prison Blues," derived from a current Gordon Jenkins tune, "Crescent City Blues." He was discharged in July 1954. On his way home from Germany, he wrote a song called "Hey, Porter!"

Three years earlier, stationed in San Antonio, he had met a girl named Vivian Liberto, and the two had corresponded across the Atlantic. The month after he returned, on August 7, they were married in a Catholic ceremony by Vivian's uncle, a priest from New Orleans. They settled in Memphis, where John's kid brother, Tom, got him a job as a door-to-door appliance salesman for the Home Equipment Company. John also enrolled at the Keegan School of Broadcasting under the G.I. Bill. Meanwhile, his older brother, Roy, who worked in a garage, introduced him to a couple of mechanic friends who also made music: Luther Perkins, a Baptist preacher's son who played guitar, and Marshall Grant, who played bass.

He was a bad salesman, and broadcasting school failed to get him a job in radio. His true aspiration was still the same as it had been when he was a boy. "I just wanted to sing on the radio. So, matter of fact, after I met Luther and Marshall, place I worked for, where I was tryin' to be a salesman, although I couldn't sell, I got them to sponsor a fifteen-minute program on the radio where I'd sing my songs and talk about the products." The Home Equipment Company sponsored the show for four Saturdays, on KWEM, across the river in West Memphis, Arkansas.

Two days after Cash had returned from Germany, another unknown singer, Elvis Presley, had made his first commercial recordings for Sam Phillips's little Sun Records company in Memphis, and by summer's end, Elvis's "That's All Right" had become a local hit. Cash saw Elvis perform at a joint called the Eagle's Nest, and, in September, he was among the small crowd at Elvis's first big public appearance, singing on a flatbed truck at the opening of Katz Drug Store.

"I was living on advances from George Bates, the Memphis businessman who ran the Home Equipment Company. Finally, I got desperate. I called Sam Phillips twice, and he turned me down both times over the phone. First I told him I was a gospel singer, 'cause of that song 'Belshazzar' that I wrote. I thought that was my best. And he said, 'Well, I can't make any money sellin' gospel music. I'm not interested.' The next time I called him, I said, 'My name is John Cash. I'm a country singer.' He had forgotten that I'd called him before. And he asked me what I had, and I said I have a lot of songs I wrote, and I sing a lot of Hank Snow songs, Jimmie Rodgers, and cowboy songs. And he said, 'Well, call me back in two or three weeks and we'll talk about it. I'm pretty busy.' Which he was, with Elvis.

"So, rather than call him back, I took my guitar one mornin', real early, went down and sat on the steps of the studio until he got there. And he was in a good mood that mornin'. He put me in the front of a mike, and I sang about two hours. He kept sayin', 'What else you got? Let me hear more.' Then, after I sang all these other people's songs, he said, 'Sing somethin' you wrote. I want to hear your stuff.' So I sang him everything I'd written. I think he recorded it all that day, I'm not sure. Then he said, 'Do you know any musicians?' I said, 'Yeah.' I'd just met Marshall and Luther down at the garage, and I'd been with them at night at my house on my front porch, or their house. So he said, 'Come back with them, and we'll put somethin' down, see how it sounds.' I came back with them the next day, and the first thing I recorded was 'Wide Open Road,' a song I'd written in Germany. And then I recorded 'Folsom Prison Blues' and then 'Hey, Porter!' He liked all three of them, but he liked 'Hey, Porter!' best. And he said, 'We gotta have a love song. A weeper, a cryin' song.' So I went home and wrote 'Cry! Cry! Cry!' I came back with the two musicians and put that down soon after. That was February 1955. And the weeks started flyin' by, and I'd call, 'Am I gonna really have a record out?' And I thought I was gonna be on Flip Records, which was his subsidiary. I told Sam, 'Please don't put me on Flip.' I didn't like the name of the record label. And finally he told me, about the first of June, after waitin' since February 11, that he was gonna release my record, 'Hey, Porter!' and 'Cry! Cry, Cry!' And I said, 'What label's it gonna be on?' And he said, 'It's gonna be on Sun.' I never told anybody about that, my fear of bein' on Flip for some reason; I didn't like the name," he laughs. Sam released the record on June 24, a month to the day after the birth of John and Vivian's first child, Rosanne.

Cash had always gone by the name of John. It was Phillips who, with that first record release, made him Johnny.

"I knew absolutely nothin' about the record business. I mean, nothin'. I didn't know my record was out, and Sam walked up to me, handed me this big 78, and said, 'Why don't you take this down to WMPS and get Bob Neal to play it?' So I went down, got on Bob Neal's noon show, handed him the record. He played 'Hey, Porter!' and he liked it. He said, 'That's good, let's play the other side.' He reached to turn it over, dropped it and broke it. And I thought, Well, I did what I set out to do: I sang on the radio. That's it. I thought my career was over. I had no idea there was even another copy. I thought one was all there'd be.

"I went back to Sam, and he said, 'How'd it go?' And I said, 'Well, he played 'Hey, Porter!,' but he broke my record.' Then I started to get up and go home. Sam reached in a box and handed me two more, said, 'If you got time, take him another copy and he'll play it tomorrow.' And I looked, and here's a whole box of 'em." He laughs deep and hard. "That's how little I knew.

"Then on my way home, I heard it on KCIJ Shreveport, and I couldn't believe it. All the way from Shreveport. This was the miracle of the ages. T. Tommy Cutrer. And I thought, That's 350 miles—how can this be?

"Six weeks after my first record came out, Elvis asked me to be on the show with him at the Overton Park Shell, in Memphis. That was my first real major appearance, openin' the show for Elvis. August 5, 1955. And then I went on tour with him. The Colonel hired me to go on tour over the next few months, until he [Elvis] left Sun and went to RCA Victor." In November, "Cry! Cry! Cry!" appeared on the national country charts.

"You know what I felt like? That I'd have a better job. And I'd get to do what I loved. That I wouldn't have to waste my time knockin' on doors tryin' to sell people things that I didn't want 'em to buy.

"So I went out and booked myself at two or three little theatres in Arkansas, in my part of the country, in Mississippi County. One of them was Etowah, a little theatre, seated about sixty people, had a bedsheet for a screen.

"Then I went in to see Sam later on that week, and he said, 'Sonny James is playin' Halls, Tennessee, tonight, and you can sing a song on his show if you wanna come.' I got in my car right away and went to Halls, Tennessee, a few miles northeast of Memphis. That was Sonny James, one of my heroes, and he put me on to sing two songs.

"Then things really happened fast. The Louisiana Hayride called and wanted me on. I guested on there, and they asked me to stay. I became a regular. Elvis was on there. George Jones. Johnny Horton."

In 1956, his third record, "I Walk the Line," became a #1 country hit and crossed over to become a Top Twenty pop hit. He had written the song as a slow ballad and been against releasing the version that became a hit. "I wrote it backstage at a show with Carl Perkins in Gladewater, Texas. And when I recorded it, I recorded it real slow the first time. Sam played it back and he said, 'I don't like that arrangement. Let's speed it up.' And I wasn't gettin' any sound on my guitar speedin' it up, so I put paper in the strings to get that shufflin' sound and we picked up the tempo, and he kept sayin', 'Pick up the tempo, let's do it faster next time,' so we did, till it was—here, I'll show you exactly how I did it." He searches around for a scrap of paper, folds it, takes up a guitar, weaves the paper through the strings high up on the neck, begins to strum, a fast, rasping shuffle. It sounds great, just as it did back in '56, when it became one of the biggest hits of the year. "That's how I got the sound. But I didn't like the record when I heard it on the radio. I hated it. I called Sam from Ocala, Florida—I was on tour when it came out—and I said, 'That's the worst thing I have ever done. Please don't send out any more copies of "I Walk the Line" that way. I hate it.' And he said, 'Well, let's give it a chance and see.'" He laughs. "Course, the higher it climbed on the charts, the more I got to like it, and I started doin' it that way on stage. I got used to it."

For more than twenty years, the hits kept coming. He was more than a country singer. To much of the world, with his few, raw chords and his deep, raw voice, he was the avatar of country music itself.

By the summer of 1958, when he left Sun for Columbia and Tennessee for California, he had, like every other hillbilly singer, turned to pills to relieve the grind of the road. "Yeah. It was a universal. I mean, you'd call in the resident physician in a hotel and ask him for uppers, he'd write a prescription."

Over the course of the coming years, he became, in his own words, "a devastated, incoherent, unpredictable, self-destructive, raging terror." Between 1959 and 1967, he was arrested and jailed seven times.

A particularly notorious year was 1965: he was thrown off the Grand Ole Opry in Nashville for smashing the footlights with a mike stand (later that night, he crashed his car into a tree and suffered a broken nose and jaw); busted for starting a fire that destroyed more than five hundred acres of Los Padres National Forest in Southern California; and seized in El Paso for smuggling amphetamines and barbiturates in from Juarez. Though "Ring of Fire" in 1963 did much to resuscitate a flagging career, Cash's reputation as a country-music renegade soon became as problematic as his reputation as a sociopath. By the summer of 1964, he was hanging out with Bob Dylan and causing trouble with "The Ballad of Ira Hayes." Trouble, it seemed, both onstage and off, was what Johnny Cash was all about. By 1966, after the birth of four daughters, his marriage had come apart, and he returned alone to Tennessee.

Looking back on those years, he seems uneasy. "Well, y'know, like they say within the program, I have a disease of chemical dependency, and if I take addictive drugs, I'll become addicted again. So I don't do that. I don't crave any kind of mood-alterin' stuff now. But I did then.

"Usually speed. Then I got into tranquilizers. But mainly speed." He refuses to lay the blame on pressure, on stress, on anything except John R. Cash. "No! I took drugs because it made me feel good. I think that's why anybody takes 'em at first. It's like an alcoholic starts drinkin' out of the bottle, then the bottle starts drinkin' out of the alcoholic. The pills started takin' me. I survived with enough of me to stay alive, and God gave me back my sanity and the wisdom to know the difference in what I could choose and couldn't choose.

"The realization that I didn't need them anymore came to me many times. But being human and frail and of not much willpower, I'd go back to them."

I'd heard that in his amphetamine depths he had attempted to rob drug stores for pills.

"I never robbed," he says defensively. "I never used a gun."

"So, you never tried to break into drug stores," I say, figuring another rumor had been laid to rest. He doesn't say anything, then his stony face relaxes into a crooked grin.

"I did more than try," he says. "I just never used a gun."

The road came to an end in October 1967. Something lured him to Nickajack Cave, near the Tennessee River, outside Chattanooga. He had been there before. "It's the place where the Nickajack Indians used to live, where Andrew Jackson, General Jackson, had a battle there and killed a lot of Nickajack Indians. The legend was that their ghosts, the women and children, haunt that cave. And it was also a refuge for the Confederate soldiers in the battle of Missionary Ridge and Lookout Mountain. A company of Confederate soldiers hid out in that cave, stayed in that cave a long time. Their names and dates are carved in the stone inside. And I liked it there."

But this time he was there to die. "I was takin' forty to fifty Dexedrine pills a day. I weighed about a hundred and fifty pounds, and I'm six-one. It just felt like I was at the end of the line. I was down there by myself and I got to feelin' that I'd taken so many pills that I'd done it, that I was gonna blow up or something. I hadn't eaten in days, I hadn't slept in days, and my mind wasn't workin' too good anyway. I couldn't stand myself anymore. I wanted to get away from me. And if that meant dyin', then OK, I'm ready. I just had to get away from myself. I couldn't stand it anymore, and I didn't think there was any other way. I took a flashlight with me, and I said, I'm goin' to walk and crawl and climb into this cave until the light goes out, and then I'm gonna lie down. So I crawled in there with that flashlight till it burned out and I lay down to die. I was a mile in that cave. At least a mile. But I felt this great comforting presence sayin', no, you're not dyin', I got things for you to do. So I got up, found my way out. Cliffs, ledges, drop-offs. I don't know how I got out, 'cept God got me out."

But for two relapses, in early 1969 and the fall of 1983, he stayed out. In March of 1968, his first clean year in a decade, he took a new bride. Thirty-eight-year-old, twice-divorced, Valerie June Carter, the daughter of Mother Maybelle Carter of the legendary Carter Family, had been born into the country-music fold. In 1955, managed by Colonel Tom Parker and married to country singer Carl Smith, she toured with Elvis, who introduced her that year to Cash, and she became a part of Cash's show in 1961. Five months after the wedding, Cash lost his longtime friend and lead guitarist, Luther Perkins, who died following burns in a fire in his home. By then, Cash's new version of "Folsom Prison Blues," recorded live in Folsom Prison, had become his biggest hit since "Ring of Fire" in 1963. It was the first of a run of three #1 country hits, the third of which, Shel Silverstein's "A Boy Named Sue," recorded live in San Quentin, became the biggest hit of his career. It rose to #2 on the pop charts, and *Johnny Cash at San Quentin*, the album that featured it, became the best-selling album in America, hitting #1 and remaining on the Top LP charts for more than a year.

By the time "A Boy Named Sue" was released, Cash had his own television show. *The Johnny Cash Show* premiered, on ABC, in June 1969, with Bob Dylan as a guest star. Together Cash and Dylan sang "Girl from the North Country," the duet they recorded for Dylan's *Nashville Skyline* album.

A lot of people thought it a strange union, but not Cash. He had first heard Dylan in 1963, when John Hammond of Columbia gave him a copy of Dylan's second album. "I loved it so much that I wrote him a letter. I thought he was the best hillbilly singer I'd ever heard. I really did. I thought, he's gotta be from Mississippi, the best writer that ever came outa Mississippi." He grins, laughs, shakes his head. "And immediately I got a letter back from him. So we started swappin' letters. I'd write on airplanes, and I'd use air-sick bags as envelopes. A lot of letters we sent back and forth before we ever met, at the Newport Folk Festival, in '64. We met there, then we hung out some together in New York. He invited June and I to his home in Woodstock. He and I understood each other. So it just felt right for me to sing with him.

"He and I understood each other. I loved his music, I think he liked mine. And when he came to Nashville to do my show, he decided to come back and do the *Nashville Skyline* album. And we spent a lot of time together. He and his family stayed at my house. I was in the studio with him every day when he was recording. We did a lot of things together that was just two guys that loved that kind of music singin' together. We never thought about where each of us was comin' from. That never passed my mind. I didn't think it was strange at all that we were singin' together."

Cash was on top of the world in 1969, but by 1979, he was becoming a stranger in his own land. A new breed of country singers, young men who looked like male models and sang formulaic ditties with acting-school Southern accents, were taking over.

"The *Urban Cowboy* craze and all that. Nashville was recording songs for people in New York who were buyin' cowboy boots, people who thought it was chic to listen to country music. They were overproducin' everything that came out of here, embarrassing themselves and me too. So I kind of pulled back, just went on doin' my thing and forgot about tryin' to make really good records because nobody was really interested in 'em. I'd go in, turn in an album every couple of years, but never with a budget that could make it work. I kept hearin' demographics until I didn't want to hear it anymore."

Columbia dropped him. Mercury picked him up. But nothing happened. By the end of 1989, when he underwent double-bypass surgery and nearly died, he was becoming a memory.

"That was the lowest I ever been, after bypass surgery, when I got double pneumonia. I was layin', three doctors and June around my bed, and one of the doctors said, 'He's not gonna make it.' I tried to smile, I tried to laugh"—and he laughs when he recalls it—"but I had this tube down into my lungs and I couldn't move my mouth. All I could do was just roll my eyes, but I was tryin' to laugh, because I knew I wasn't gonna die. It was like that time in that cave, when I felt the presence of God sayin', you're not gonna die yet."

He was alive, but his career was dead. "I was at the bottom of my record sales. Everybody was sayin', 'well, he's no more.' I didn't like that. I just didn't like that at all. I said, 'I'm gonna do somethin'.'"

Cash had never heard of Rick Rubin. "He came backstage. I asked him, 'What would you want from me?' He said, 'I want the best Johnny Cash record that we can get out of you, whatever that is.' I got to thinkin', I never have done my best. So we agreed, after I went with him, that I'd bring in my list of seventy or so songs that I'd always wanted to record; I'd bring in my guitar, and I'd sit down in front of a microphone and just start singin' and see what sounded good." More and more, after these rough recordings, Rick would say, "That cut. Exactly like that. I want that on the album." Ultimately, Cash says, "we decided there would be nothin' on this album but my guitar and myself."

His version of the song "Delia's Gone," whose origins are lost in time, has a sociopathic edge that sets it apart from all other versions. (Cash himself first recorded the song in 1961. Bob Dylan recorded it on his own recent acoustic album, *World Gone Wrong*.) In its traditional form, he admits, "it was not quite as bloody and criminal-minded a song. I just decided that I'd make this man who kills Delia a little bit meaner than he already was. Tie her to the chair before he shoots her. Have a little more fun with her." Indeed, his "Delia" brings to mind the pointblank killer couplet of "I shot a man in Reno / just to watch him die," from "Folsom Prison Blues," back when it all began, forty years ago.

But it goes back further than that, really, back to that summer of murder and salvation. The obsession with death that runs through much of Cash's work possesses an oddly mystical pulse. Thus when he follows "Delia's Gone" with a song such as "Redemption," which he describes as "kind of a testimony" about "the redemptive blood of Christ," it seems, strangely but somehow naturally, the arsis and thesis of the same deep breath.

Neither Cash nor Rubin knows what's next. "I would say, we'll keep the quality of songs high and the personal rawness of it," Rubin says, "but I don't think we're going to make the same record again. The next record will probably be with a band, but I think it'll still be radically different than the records he's been making for the last twenty years."

Rubin recalls that rap singer L.L. Cool J came by the studio while Cash was recording. "I think he was very impressed," Rubin says. It makes sense. For all its posturing, all its sound and fury, rap's angriest assaults seem tame compared to Johnny's idea of having a little fun with Delia. And that, perhaps, is what it all comes down to: John Cash is real. In show business—or call it art, to con the suckers—in any racket, alternative or not, that is the rarest metal of all. Be it the Viper Room or the Montreaux Jazz Festival, which he played in July, or the Billy Graham Crusade in Atlanta, where he was at October's end, or the clay-eaters' Zion of Branson, where he played out much of the rest of the year; whatever stage he's on, Cash is Cash and that stage is just another Hoxie Rock.

In 1995, he isn't looking back, he isn't even looking sideways. "I'm on my way to doin' my best work right now," he says. "I've got another chance, and I'm grabbin' for the brass ring again."

Who knows? Like the man says: life is funny. One way or the other, I doubt if he'll be crawling off into any caves soon. He's got too much killing, and too much praying, to do.

Back in New York, I tell Handsome Dick that Johnny Cash, too, is alternative these days.

"Hey," he says, "you stay alive long enough, anything can happen."

"Johnny Cash, Austerely Direct from Deep Within"

by Jon Pareles (1994)

The New York Times *is perhaps the only major periodical in the nation that continued to closely follow Cash after the dimming of his torch in the 1970s. For twenty-five years, if Johnny Cash visited New York or appeared on a network television show, the Gray Lady usually put a reporter on the story. Five months into the Cash renaissance, the* New York Times *ran two stories surrounding the singer's September 14, 1994, appearance at Carnegie Hall: a preview that day and later a review. Both hewed to the story Rick Rubin was telling; both eschewed discussion of Cash's past, as recent* Times *articles hadn't, and both emphasized Cash the dark troubadour and his new connection with young audiences—audiences, as Neil Strauss noted in the preview, that "can relate to a mind that strays from what it knows is right." The concert review, included here, documents that Cash the performer had regained purpose, playing the classics but also unveiling for acceptance songs that helped him speak to a new audience.*

JOHNNY Cash knows that dignity makes the icon. Through a recording career that stretches back to 1955, his bass-baritone voice has gone from gravelly to grave; his demeanor has grown ever more somber and humble. But even in the 1950s, he was perfectly believable singing a line like "I taught the weeping willow how to cry." At

Carnegie Hall on Wednesday night, he sang with stoic calm about death, loneliness, love and Christian faith.

Mr. Cash has grown increasingly distant from the country-music business, which likes its singers young, optimistic and awshucks sexy. Mr. Cash's songs don't provide the cozy consolation of most country hits; they are more likely to tell stories of hardship and irrevocable loss. In "Oh Bury Me Not," the narrator recites a prayer that he will live up to the virtues of the wide-open country. The music then segues into the old song in which a dying young cowboy begs not to be buried on "the lone prairie," but he is buried there anyway.

In Mr. Cash's repertory, characters face unforgiving elements and indifferent fate; their faith and virtue will not necessarily be rewarded in this world. Even love songs, like "I Walk the Line" and "Ring of Fire," are about the dangers of temptation and the singer's stubborn resolve in fighting it off.

Mr. Cash is closer, now, to rock tastes for unflinching lyrics and stripped-down music. This year, he changed recording companies and released *American Recordings* (American), backing himself on an acoustic guitar. At Carnegie Hall, he performed alone and with the Tennessee Three, one of the leanest bands anywhere.

The Tennessee Three hark back to the rockabilly groups that backed Mr. Cash's first singles, with a few decades of subtlety added. While Dave Rorick slapped a bass fiddle, each of Bob Wootton's electric-guitar lines was pared down to essentials. W. S. Holland's drumming sounded like hoofbeats during "Ghost Riders in the Sky," a military tattoo in "The Ballad of Ira Hayes" and a steam locomotive in "Orange Blossom Special," in which Mr. Cash needed two harmonicas to play three chords.

Alone or with the band, Mr. Cash gave his songs an austere directness. He ignored the hoots and whoops that punctuated his songs at odd moments, maintaining a conversational directness and a courtly reserve. Mr. Cash never revealed the control behind his steely but unforced delivery; only an occasional dive into his deepest register showed that his tone is a matter of choice. By never overacting, Mr. Cash gives the impression that the song is speaking for itself; his determined simplicity honored songs like Leonard Cohen's "Bird on a Wire," Kris Kristofferson's "Sunday Morning Coming Down" and his own "Redemption," a stark meditation on the blood of Jesus.

The concert also included cameo appearances by Mr. Cash's daughter, Rosanne Cash, and his wife, June Carter. His daughter was self-effacing; his wife was extroverted, full of raspy inflections, hip swinging and arm flinging as they sang duets. Her antics set off his formality, making him seem like a loner even within his family. . . .

"Cash Conquers"

by Chris Dickinson (1994)

A seasoned journalist and critic, Chris Dickinson has never blanched in the face of prevailing opinion. In her tenure as editor of the Journal of Country Music, *she deconstructed and reconstructed the Garth Brooks myth and shed light upon homosexuals in country music. In her days writing for the respected* Chicago Reader, *Dickinson was a lone voice railing against Rick Rubin and Johnny Cash's romanticizing of Cash's sins.*

WHERE to start with Johnny Cash when there are so many precious Kodak moments to choose from? Like the time in 1965 when he was wrecked on pills and busted out the *Grand Ole Opry* footlights. Or his mid-60s bust in El Paso for amphetamine possession. Or the time he was attacked by an ostrich while walking through the field. Or his friendships with both genius-weirdo Bob Dylan and evangelist-weirdo Billy Graham. Or, or, or. Nearly 40 years after Cash first passed through the portals of Sun Records his songs and the personal stories behind them pour out in a mighty rush, the legacy of a great American artist, rebel, and flake.

But legendary status doesn't pay much these days in Nashville—just ask Merle Haggard. So at 62, Cash, in keeping with his consistently inconsistent choice of associates, hooked up with American Recordings label boss-weirdo Rick Rubin and recorded the conveniently titled *American Recordings* (1994). An avalanche of glowing press reviews followed its release. The born-again Cash was born yet again, only this time to an audience that wore crosses not as Christian symbols but as fashion accessories.

Notwithstanding all the media fuss, *American Recording* staggers under its own self-consciousness, starting with the cover photo of the album. Standing in a field against a cloudy sky like some dark Moses, Cash resembles the kind of pretentious icon Charlton Heston became after he made *The Ten Commandments* and started believing his own myth.

Given that weak pop and soft rock continue to dominate the country charts, it would be easy to embrace *American Recordings* as a fresh, back-to-basics move. But the overt calculation of this album's marketing keeps it from being anything approaching a modern classic. The music is for completists or neophytes only. Cash sings, accompanied only by himself on acoustic guitar. Rubin's production—which does nothing more than encourage the frequently flaky Cash by giving him free rein—has been compared, ridiculously, to the direction Cash got from Sam Phillips at Sun. At this late date, considering the enormous body of his work, it's probably unfair to expect Cash to have many new ideas in him. Covering songs by such disparate songwriters as Glenn Danzig, Kris Kristofferson, and Leonard Cohen serves as a masterful marketing tool by generating plenty of press, but "Why Me Lord" and "Bird on a Wire" were done far better by the original artists. These ultimately tired choices hardly constitute a reason for the alternative crowd to wet its collective pants.

But that is the crowd this album is so obviously courting. The "punk" anthem that's emerged is "Delia's Gone," a stark murder ballad told from the killer's point of view. Contemporary artists like Dwight Yoakam and George Thorogood have killed their women in song, but "Delia's Gone" is less about Delia and more about marketing to the hip crowd that believes "real" country must hew to the Appalachian dead-baby school of songwriting. This alternative faction sneers at any modern country artist who doesn't pretend he's auditioning for Ralph Peer at the historic 1927 Bristol sessions. Modernity is anathema, except when MTV rears its voracious head: the part of the ill-fated Delia is played by underwear model Kate Moss in the video version of the song.

So who is Cash in 1994? From listening to *American Recordings* it's hard to tell. But live there's no question—despite the hype surrounding his supposed reinvention as postmodern punk, Cash onstage is truly an overwhelming presence. At the Bismarck he proved that whatever self-indulgence and egotism he brought to Rick Rubin's living room stayed there.

Backed by his Tennessee Three, Cash stuck to spare and penetrating arrangements, many of which he first hashed out years ago in Memphis. It was easy to see why Cash's music has never been quite country or quite rockabilly but a unique amalgamation that got him inducted into both the country and rock and roll halls of fame. Unlike most country stars, he used no pedal steel, no fiddle. Upright bassist Dave Rorick worked his instrument in the rockabilly slap-back fashion, working the beat against drummer W.S. Holland's rhythms. Introducing guitarist Bob Wooton, Cash remarked, "He's been with me since Luther died," referring to his late, great sideman Luther Perkins. Perkins, who died in 1968, helped define the trademark Cash sound with his alternating-strings, idiot savant leads, epic statements of simplicity that were as distinctive as Cash's voice. Wooton rose to the terrible challenge of filling Perkins's impossible shoes. On the first number, "Folsom Prison Blues," he replicated with real emotion that immortal handful of guitar notes that's instantly recognizable as Keith Richards's opening lick on "Satisfaction."

The acoustic guitar Cash strapped on wasn't just for show. He strummed hard throughout, an integral addition to the snapping rhythms and primal beats of his band. His voice, always a heavy baritone that conveys deep meaning within a limited range, at times showed the toll of time and was hoarse and ragged. But he held up and got the songs out like he always has.

The first portion of the set played like a stunning American songbook, from "Get Rhythm" to "Ring of Fire." Halfway through he sat alone on a stool and accompanied himself on guitar, and even "Delia's Gone" rang with a true heaviness missing from his recorded version. Never mind that some in the audience laughed at several of the more gruesome lines; it seemed like a nervous response at being faced with Cash's unadulterated in-person rendition.

The utter cool turned weird when Cash brought out wife June Carter to join him and his band onstage. Dressed in a skirt suit and clunky pumps, Carter came on like a small-town businesswoman who'd stayed too long at happy hour. The hillbilly quotient went through the roof when Carter grabbed a mike and joined her husband in a caterwauling version of their famous duet "Jackson." Carter brought the evening down to an appropriate trash level, mixing in odd portions of schmaltz and deep-woods snake-handler fervor. Cash got through it all with aplomb and deserved a great deal of credit for not hiding this element of his life from the large alternative contingent that had turned out to see him.

Throughout the show audience members gathered at the edge of the stage, shaking his hand, passing him flowers, getting closer. There was truth in Cash's image; gone was the carefully fashioned golden calf that graces the cover of *American Recordings*, replaced by an even more awesome image that was personal and nakedly human. Kinda like Moses carrying those tablets down from the mountain and dealing with the folks at the bottom who'd taken to worshiping a false god.

"Johnny Cash: American Music Legend"

by Bill DeYoung (1996)

Johnny Cash's second album for American Records, Unchained, *generated almost as much press coverage as the first release. "With covers of songs by alternative bands like Beck and Soundgarden, and with Tom Petty and the Heartbreakers as its back-up band,* Unchained *will have a new generation walking the line with the Man in Black," proclaimed Al Weisel in* US Weekly *(February 1997).*

That same month, Stereophile *added, "The good news on* Unchained *is that the accent on Cash's voice heralded by* American Recordings *carries on here as Cash sings his butt off, striding through each song with a strength as American and cinematic as John Wayne riding the range in* The Searchers."

It was Cash come full circle. For Unchained, *he was back with a band: Petty's band, which played with the vitality and abandon of the Tennessee Two and compensated, as the Tennessee Two did, for his vocal shortcomings. The set list was a homecoming for Cash's favorite themes: salvation, rural life, desperation lurched to life in the singer's versions of Beck's "Rowboat," Petty's "Southern Accents," the Carters' "Kneeling Drunkard's Plea." He recalled the Sun days with renovated versions of "Mean-Eyed Cat" and "Country Boy," and indulged the sentimentality that often stymied his work with "Memories Are Made of This," the Dean Martin hit that he had relished singing in Germany with his air force comrades and on tour with his Sun buddies.*

Cash discussed Unchained *with writer Bill DeYoung while it was still under construction, claiming that despite the departure from the strictly acoustic approach of* American Recordings, *the set would recapture the first album's spirit. It did more than that.* Unchained *captured a Grammy and rivaled* American Recordings' *performance on the album charts, suggesting that the reengineered Arkansas Train still rolled.*

. . . What can you tell us about your new record with Rick Rubin?

This week I hope to finish it. I'm probably going to do four more songs this week; we've done about 20. We'll select 15 out of the 24, 25. There are some new songs, there are some old songs; some country songs, some rock songs, a little bit of everything. I'm working in the studio with Tom Petty and the Heartbreakers, and Marty Stuart, and one night a couple of members of Fleetwood Mac sat in on a song. We're just havin' a lot of fun.

So it's a more uptempo record than the last one?

Well, some of them are uptempo. And some are real soulful, you know? There's a couple of real heartfelt spirituals in this album. And there's a Soundgarden song in there, "Rusty Cage," a kind of countrified version of it that Tom and his band worked up. There's some old Hank Snow songs, a Don Gibson song, and the Hank Williams song "You Gonna Change Or I'm Gonna Leave."

Were the song selections entirely yours, or are you and Rubin close enough now to where you let him bring you songs?

We've always done that. We've always got a pile of songs for each other to listen to when we get together, choosing songs. A day like today, I've got four or five new songs I'm bringin' to the session, that we've all listened to and we thought we might take a shot at doing.

Maybe two Tom Petty songs, a Bob Dylan song, a Carl Perkins song and a Merle Haggard song.

Can I ask which two Petty songs?

"I Won't Back Down" and, let's see, what's the other one . . . [rustling paper]: "Goodnight, Baby"? No, "We're Alright Now."

And which Carl Perkins' song is it?

"Everybody's Tryin' To Be My Baby." And a Bob Dylan song from *Blood On The Tracks* called "You're Gonna Make Me Lonesome When You Go."

You still find new things in music all the time, don't you?

Oh, yeah, they're everywhere. You gotta look for 'em, though.

Is it a creative partnership with Petty?

It really is. That's all it is, really. I don't know, when I had the first session set up for this album, he called Rubin and said, "I want to come and play bass on Cash's sessions." Rick asked me, and I said "Tell him to bring 'em all." So he brought all the Heartbreakers with him. And they've been to every session since.

Marty Stuart was there for two weeks, but he had a tour booked and couldn't work any more. And I don't know who else might show up; you never know who's gonna drop in.

We hope to have the album out in July.

Was there a reason you chose to make this record different from American Recordings *or was it just evolution?*

I guess it's evolution. I've done that now, and I'm ready to go onto something else. There's some songs in this album that have that flavor;

they're so light acoustically that it's almost just me and a guitar. So I'll still have that feeling in this album, on some of the songs.

I had always wanted to do that; that's the way I naturally feel it. And everything I've ever done has been produced, you know, and other instruments put on it. *American Recordings* was closer to the way I started, with very sparse instrumentation. That's one thing that felt good about it. I always wanted to do an album with just me and my guitar, and I finally did it.

In the liner notes, you talk about how the guitar has to become an extension of you, where you feel it from the gut. Is that what you're talking about?

Right. The guitar and I have to become one, you know?

Was that album a risky proposition for you?

What did I have to lose? I had nothing to lose, and everything to gain. I believed in it, so did Rubin, so we went for it.

Were you pleased that it appealed to young audiences?

Very well pleased, yeah. It's gettin' better all the time. I just played a show at the House of Blues out here for a young audience, and it was really a lot of fun. Playing live shows is the best fun of it all.

Despite the things that happened with that record, you're still touring with the Family Show.

Well, I do the Family Show, and then sometimes I do tours that are promoted by alternative stations. That's just June and I and the Tennessee Three. And I focus on the rockabilly things, and do things from the last album. Of course, I do that on the Family Show, as well. We change the songs from time to time. I do some songs from *American Recordings*, and a couple from the new album. I sing with June. I love to perform with her, and I love to perform with my family. It's a show that sustained for about 30 years; it's what I do. So I have no intention of stopping doing it.

Is there a gospel segment in the current show?

Not especially a segment, but from time to time we do some gospel, yeah. I do it if I'm called to. I think I just like to share my faith, you know? I don't preach to people. I don't ever push it on anybody and I wouldn't sing a gospel song on any show if I didn't think the people would enjoy it. They seem to enjoy those as much or more than anything else. It's not that I'm proselytizing. I'm not out there tryin' to convince people, just to spread a little good news.

The themes on American Recordings *were rather stark. And one associates that sort of thing with you and your work. Why do you lean in that direction?*

I don't know! I really don't know. Of the 70 songs that we recorded, those are the ones that were chosen, the ones that were bleak, and stark, and some of 'em kind of bloody. But that's American folk music. "The Ballad of Jesse James" is about killin' people, and it was the biggest folk song in American history. Or "Folsom Prison Blues." "I shot a man in Reno just to watch him die." That's probably my most requested song. It's a fantasy trip that Americans like to take with some of their folk songs. And now their country and rock 'n' roll songs.

But they're story-songs that come right out of the Mississippi Mud, some of these songs like "Delia's Gone." They're interesting. They're pieces of Americana.

Yours is a distinctly American story, 40 years in the business. The things that you've gone through, and you're still here. Yet you have a huge following in Europe, don't you?

Yeah. We go there every year. The same songs sell over there that have sold over here. I poll the audience from time to time, every few years, and ask them what they want to hear. And my top requested songs are "Ring Of Fire," "Folsom Prison Blues," "Orange Blossom Special," "Sunday Morning Coming Down" and "I Walk The Line." No matter where I go, they're my top five requested songs. So they're kind of universal.

What's important to you? When you get up in the morning, what do you look forward to?

Doin' what I'm committed to do, and doing it as well as I can. Every day that goes by, I look back on what I've done. And if I did my best, I'm happy with it. If I'm not, there's a bad feeling in my gut. But if I know I've done the best I could do, and I feel good about what I've said to people, and what I've done, then I feel good about the day.

Is there something you haven't done yet that you'd like to do?

Career-wise, I'm not lookin' past today. And personally, I guess I'm not either, because I just want to feel good today. I want to have the energy that I need to do what I want to do. I mean, I'm 64, working with all these young guys, and sometimes I want to quit before they do. But while I'm there I want to give it all I got.

"Cash, Back"

by Ben Ratliff (2000)

❁ ❁ ❁

"Rays of Light from the Man in Black"

by David Brinn (2000)

❁ ❁ ❁

"Johnny Cash: *American III: Solitary Man*"

by Michael McCall (2001)

On the back cover of Unchained, *a stylized Statue of Liberty stands, its right arm, the arm of the torch, severed. Like the gravestone in Flannery O'Connor's "The Displaced Person," robbed of its cherub, symbolizing unrealized hope, the incomplete Miss Liberty suggests America's unfulfilled promise. Or the album's.* Unchained *promised to be the first in a string of similarly satisfying releases, but illness arrested such hopes. Any follow-ups seemed unlikely.*

However, in the summer of 2000, Cash and Rubin announced there would be a follow-up. After almost three years out of the public eye, Cash had begun to appear here and there, holding court at his wife's CD release party and appearing on a cable network tribute. He was anxious to launch new product in the market, and by the fall American III: Solitary Man *was welcomed with a short, intense hail of mostly gentle journalism.*

Virtually every reviewer praised this album, at least conditionally. A "but" followed every punch. The album was "less focused," but "still has a long lasting and special grace," ventured Carlo Wolff of the Boston Globe *(November 2, 2000). "His voice may be shaken," noted the* Irish Times, *"but his resolution remains undaunted" (October 21, 2000). Many critics refused to say that the sluggish, uneven quality of Cash's voice was just too poignant, too much like a prelude to demise.*

He had battled pneumonia, lapsed into a coma, and stayed out of the public eye, so the deterioration of Cash's voice shouldn't have been shocking. But it was. The bold baritone that on Unchained *reverberated like a train in a tunnel was now more withered than withering.*

Song selection also marred the album. Cash and Neil Diamond's "Solitary Man" were a poor match, for the song was a product of 1960s Tin Pan Alley, fantastic in the voice of Diamond, but trite in the voice of Cash. The same was true of "I Won't Back Down," its writer Tom Petty the definitive interpreter: Cash had nothing new to add, choosing the song one guesses because it put music to his admirable defiance. One of the exceptions on American III *was "The Mercy Seat." A composition that explores the mind of a death row inmate, Cash could relate to it, and he ripped into it, found every corpuscle of meaning, and delivered it knowingly.*

It was welcomed tepidly by the public. Of course, country radio left the album to languish, its content considered outside of accepted formats. It showed up on the Billboard *charts and made year-end critics' polls, but it failed to reproduce the excitement that its two predecessors had generated.*

The following are varied takes—one from Rolling Stone, *one from the* Jerusalem Post, *and the last from* Country Music*—on Cash's third American effort.*

I

"Cash, Back"

by Ben Ratliff (2000)

EVEN the best good ideas can get pushed too far, and, for Johnny Cash, *American III: Solitary Man* is one Rick Rubin–built cover album over the line. The point with the Cash-Rubin series, which started in 1994 with *American Recordings* and continued with 1996's *Unchained*, isn't really transformation, as Willie Nelson had done with his recent cover treatments of reggae and blues. The point is that Cash's baritone (still able, despite the onset of a neurological disorder) is elemental, the marrow of sadness; simply to bestow that dark voice on moody songs by a range of songwriters is statement enough.

Cash, solemn and ponderous, is the same in all the different rooms on this album, whether he's covering Neil Diamond or David Allen Coe or Will Oldham or the vaudevillian Bert Williams or himself. So the onus here lies on the production: I can't believe I'm making this complaint of a country record—they're usually so overproduced—but Rick Rubin's work is too timid; mostly, the shy combos of guitar, fiddle and accordian, or Benmont Tench's subliminal contributions on keyboards, make up the kind of severe meal that one is forced to think of as "tasteful."

It takes Nick Cave and Mick Harvey's overpoetic "The Mercy Seat," smack in the middle of the album, to represent what the album could have achieved: The song has a layered production, with organ, regular and tack piano, and accordian swelling and receding under Cash's onrushing, Leonard Cohen–like delivery. It's the moment of the greatest artistic risk; by the end of the record, we're back again to offhand drawing-room performances with the beautiful traditional song "Wayfaring Stranger."

There's nothing wrong with drawing-room performances; I can quickly think of a dozen country singers who ought to make a record like this. *Solitary Man* is good—better than good. But there are issues of repertory here; when you end up with Traveling Wilburys songs alongside pieces of silver like Cash's "Wayfaring Stranger," you start wondering how we got there.

II

"Rays of Light from the Man in Black"

by David Brinn (2000)

JOHNNY Cash's *American III: Solitary Man* is the third in a fruitful collaboration with "in" producer Rick Rubin, founder of Def Jam Records. Like its predecessors, *Solitary Man* is an unadorned, acoustic diamond in the rough, powered by stark arrangements, single-minded conviction, and a lot of heart, not to mention one of the most forceful and distinctive voices in pop music history.

On the rustic opening version of Tom Petty's "I Won't Back Down," when Cash warbles into his double bass boombox, "I'll stand my ground, and I won't back down" you just gotta believe him. With Heartbreaker Mike Campbell providing a driving acoustic accompaniment and Petty himself singing just a wisp of harmony, this is alternative folk/country coming from the source.

The disc is full of other inspired song selections, like Neil Diamond's title track, U2's "One" and a batch of Cash originals that are nearly as good. The man in black shows his awesome versatility when he tackles tunes by Will Oldham ("I See A Darkness") and Nick Cave ("The Mercy Seat"), which skirt on the edges of darkness. Cash brings such an authenticity to them, it's actually scary to hear.

Guests like Sheryl Crow, Merle Haggard, Heartbreaker Benmont Tench, whose palettes of keyboard color invigorate each tune, and Cash's wife June Carter Cash add a feeling of celebration to a disc that even at its most ominous, hints at salvation at the end of the tunnel.

III

"Johnny Cash: *American III: Solitary Man*"

by Michael McCall (2001)

No singer/songwriter ponders mankind's great questions—life and death, good and evil—with quite the same gravity as Johnny Cash. That the Man in Black has spent the last few years wrestling with his own mortality only seems to have deepened his resolve to confront those issues on record.

Solitary Man, as on the two previous albums on American Records that Cash made with producer Rick Rubin, finds him drawing from wide-ranging sources in his trademark deep, weathered tone—in this case, from U2's "One" to the pop standard "That Lucky Old Sun (Just Rolls Around Heaven All Day)" and from Tom Petty's "I Won't Back Down," to folk classics like "Wayfaring Stranger."

What binds these diverse songs is the spiritual core of each tune: In one way or another, the lyrics all deal with what life means, or pose questions about why we're here, where we're going and when we leave.

It's an ambitious undertaking, and one that Cash doesn't pull off quite as consistently as he did on his previous two American Records discs. But when *Solitary Man* really works, it's as powerful as anything he has done.

But problems run twofold. For one, Cash takes on a few well-known tunes that he doesn't quite make his own. Similarly, the tricky melody of "Lucky Old Sun" unduly highlights the frailties that now beset Cash and his voice.

On the other hand, Cash gets inside two unconventional choices with stunning effectiveness. Will Oldham's "I See A Darkness" finds an aging man locked in a dead-serious conversation about seeking inner peace, while acknowledging that the depraved temptations of his youth still pulse through his veins. Similarly, Nick Cave's "The Mercy Seat" is a wild-eyed cry from the death-row sentiment that Cash readily conveys, singing as if he were the one being strapped into the electric chair.

By now, of course, Cash's legacy is set. That he continues to pour himself so wholly and acutely into his music lends more evidence that he is an artist of rare conviction.

be a permanent member. I told Roy that I was wrapped up in touring and enjoying my shows, and that there was no way June and I could get back to Nashville 26 nights a year (at the time, the *Opry* required its members to play more shows each year than is currently mandated). I still have a great love for the *Opry*, though. I've always loved it, and I still do.

I also love Nashville. The happiest period of my recording career was when I was working here with Jack Clement in the '80s. He was, and is, a Nashville renegade himself. I guess I always gravitated to people of that ilk. I love Jack Clement, and I intend to do more work with Jack as time goes by.

Earlier, you said your next album will be your best ever. Are you competitive about your music?

I'm only in competition with myself. You can look back to my road shows, where I would have the Statler Brothers, Carl Perkins and others on stage with myself and the Carter Family.

Now we're off the road, and we're happier for it. When Maybelle and Helen and Anita (June's relatives and members of the Carter Family) died, June lost heart, and I was ready to quit the road. Those deaths had a lot to do with it. The sunshine went out of it, and the thrill of performing wasn't as great as it has been.

Thanks for your time this morning, Johnny.

Well, I wanted to talk to you, because this is where I live. Sony (American's manufacturer) were asking me about doing interviews with *USA Today*, the *Washington Post*, you name it. I said, first I'd like to talk to Nashville. So it's good to talk with you. I'm going out in the yard now to work on my grapevines.

BIBLIOGRAPHY

Books

Carpozi, George, Jr. *The Johnny Cash Story.* New York: Pyramid Books, 1970.

Cash, Cindy (introduction by Johnny Cash). *The Cash Family Scrapbook.* New York: Crown, 1997.

Cash, Johnny. *Man in Black.* Grand Rapids, Mich.: Zondervan Press, 1975.

______. *Man in White: A Novel.* San Francisco: Harper and Row, 1986.

Cash, Johnny, with Patrick Carr. *Cash: The Autobiography.* New York: HarperSanFrancisco, 1997.

Cash, June Carter. *From the Heart.* New York: Prentice-Hall, 1987.

Conn, Charles P. *The New Johnny Cash.* Old Tappan, N.J.: Spire Books, 1973.

Dawidoff, Nicholas. *In the Country of Country: People and Places in American Music.* New York: Vintage Books, 1998.

Dolan, Sean. *Johnny Cash.* New York: Chelsea House Publishers, 1995.

Edwen, David. *Great Men of American Popular Song.* Englewood Cliffs, N.J.: Prentice-Hall, 1972.

Escott, Colin, with Martin Hawkins. *Good Rockin' Tonight: Sun Records and the Birth of Rock 'n' Roll.* New York: St. Martin's Press, 1991.

Gaillard, Frye. *Watermelon Wine: The Spirit of Country Music.* New York: St. Martin's Press, 1978.

Gordon, Robert. *It Came from Memphis.* Boston: Faber and Faber, 1995.

Govoni, Albert. *A Boy Named Cash.* New York: Lancer Books, 1970.

Guralnick, Peter. *Feel Like Going Home: Portraits in Blues and Rock 'n' Roll.* New York: HarperCollins, 1989.

______. *Last Train to Memphis: The Rise of Elvis Presley.* Boston: Little, Brown, 1994.

______. *Lost Highway: Journeys and Arrivals of American Musicians.* New York: Vintage Books, 1982.

Hemphill, Paul. *The Nashville Sound: Bright Lights and Country Music.* New York: Simon and Schuster, 1970.

Herbst, Peter, ed. *The* Rolling Stone *Interviews: Talking with the Legends of Rock and Roll, 1967–1980.* New York: St. Martin's Press/Rolling Stone Press, 1981.

Hudson, James A. *Johnny Cash: Close Up.* New York: Scholastic Book Services, 1971.

Kennedy, Rick, and Randy McNutt. *Little Labels—Big Sound: Small Record Companies and the Rise of American Music.* Bloomington: Indiana University Press, 1999.

Logan, Horace, with Bill Sloan (introduction by Johnny Cash). *Louisiana Hayride Years: Making Musical History in Country's Golden Age.* New York: St. Martin's Griffin, 1999.

Malone, Bill C., and Judy McCulloch. *Stars of Country Music: Uncle Dave Macon to Johnny Rodriguez.* Urbana: University of Illinois Press, 1975.

Marsh, Dave, ed. *For the Record: Sun Records.* New York: Avon Books, 1998.

Moriarty, Frank. *Johnny Cash.* New York: Metro Books, 2000.

Nager, Larry. *Memphis Beat: The Lives and Times of America's Musical Crossroads.* New York: St. Martin's Press, 1998.

Norman, Philip. *The Road Goes on Forever: Portrait from a Journey Through Contemporary Music.* New York: Fireside Books, 1982.

Pleasants, Henry. *The Great American Popular Singers.* New York: Simon and Schuster, 1974.

Snow, Jimmy, with Jim Hefley and Marti Hefley (introduction by Johnny Cash). *I Cannot Go Back.* Plainfield, N.J.: Logos International, 1977.

Tosches, Nick. *Country: The Twisted Roots of Rock 'n' Roll.* New York: Da Capo Press, 1998.

Wren, Christopher. *Winners Got Scars Too: The Life and Legends of Johnny Cash.* New York: Dial Press, 1971.

Reference Books

Kingsbury, Paul. *The Encyclopedia of Country Music: The Ultimate Guide to the Music.* New York: Oxford University Press, 1998.

Larkin, Colin, ed. *The Guiness Encyclopedia of Popular Music.* Middlesex, England: Guiness, 1992.

Lewry, Peter. *I've Been Everywhere: A Johnny Cash Chronicle.* London: Helter Skelter, 2001.

Malone, Bill C. *Country Music USA*, 2d ed. Austin: University of Texas Press, 1985.

McCloud, Barry, et al. *Definitive Country: The Ultimate Encyclopedia of Country Music and Its Performers.* New York: Perigree, 1995.

Smith, John L. *Another Song to Sing.* Lanham, Md.: Scarecrow Press, 1999.

______. *The Johnny Cash Discography, 1984–1993.* Westport, Conn.: Greenwood Press, 1994.

______. *The Johnny Cash Record Catalog.* Westport, Conn.: Greenwood Press, 1994.

Smith, John L. (forewords by Johnny Cash and Johnny Western). *The Johnny Cash Discography.* Westport, Conn.: Greenwood Press, 1985.

Whitburn, Joel. *Top Country Albums, 1964–1997.* Menomonee Falls, Wisc.: Record Research, 1998.

______. *Top Country Singles, 1944–1993.* Menomonee Falls, Wisc.: Record Research, 1994.

______. *Top Pop Singles, 1955–1993.* Menomonee Falls, Wisc.: Record Research, 1994.

Periodicals

The following is by no means an exhaustive list of newspaper, magazine, and journal articles about and related to Johnny Cash. In total, it represents but a thin spine in the library of Cash literature. I came across most of the articles while reviewing articles for inclusion in the Reader, *and I list them as a resource for those who seek more information about Cash.*

Allen, Bob. "Good Outweighs the Bad on Quartet's Second LP." *Baltimore Evening Sun*, March 8, 1990.

Anderson, Brett. "Unbroken." *Salon.com*, May 18, 1999.

Arnold, Gina. "Family Fun at the County Fair." *Berkeley Express*, June 21, 1989.

Bemis, Jay. "Cash Worth the Wait." *Ottawa (Kans.) Herald*, April 11, 1988.

Berkowitz, Kenny. "No Regrets." *Acoustic Guitar*, June 2001.

Boehm, Mike. "Cash Flies Flag at Celebrity." *Los Angeles Times*, January 29, 1991, Orange County edition.

Bomstad, Sharon. "Johnny Cash Brings His Show 'Back to the People.'" *Wilmar (Minn.) Tribune*, August 19, 1989.

Bowdon, Bill. "Cash Ties Drug Bout to Ostrich." *Little Rock (Ark.) Democrat*, June 23, 1989.

Bowman, David. "Paint It Black: A Prayer for His Holy Hipness." Johnny Cash." *Salon.com*, December 5, 1997.

Braun, Saul. "Good Ole Boy." *Playboy*, November 1970.

Brinn, David. "Rays of Light from the Man in Black." *Jerusalem Post*, October 31, 2000.

Brown, G. "Memorable Telluride Show Keeps Cash's Legend Alive." *Denver Post*, June 21, 1997.

Carr, Patrick. "Cash Comes Back." *Country Music*, December 1976.

______. "Johnny Cash's Freedom." *Country Music*, April 1979.

______. "The Magic Thumb." *Country Music*, July/August 1980.

______. "What Now John Cash?" *Country Music*, December 1974.

"Cash Guitarist Dies of Burns." *Nashville Tennessean*, August 6, 1968.

"Cash Supports POW/MIA Cause." *VFW Magazine*, April 1989.

"Cash to Gear Show to Country Music." *Billboard*, November 1, 1969.

Cash, Johnny. "Ballad of a Teenage Queen." *Cash Box*, June 14, 1980.

______. "Don't Forget Number Two." *Country Music*, July/August 1980.

______. "Gospel Road: A Dream." *Music Journal* 31, no. 7 (1973).

______. *The Rambler*. Columbia Records KC 34833. 1997

______. "Why Country Music Has Swept U.S." *U.S. News and World Report*, February 27, 1978.

Cash, Rosanne. "1-800-TRY-CASH." *Spin*, December 1996.

______. "Songs My Daddy Sang Me." *Joe Magazine*, no. 3 (1999).

"Cashing In." *Time*, June 6, 1969.

Chambers, Andrea. "Johnny Cash Changes His Tune—from a Boy Named Sue to a Saint Named Paul." *People*, November 3, 1986.

Considine, J. D. "Without the Likes of Johnny Cash, Country Music Would Be Pretty Dull." *Baltimore Sun*, January 20, 1979.

Cooper, Peter. "Hello, This Is Johnny Cash." *Nashville Tennessean*. October 22, 2000.

Coppage, Neil. "Johnny Cash: Still Free." *Stereo Review*, March 1983.

Cotter, James F. "Cash Performs Bluesy, Rhythmic Show." *Middletown (N.Y.) Times Herald Record*, November 1, 1988.

Cromelin, Richard. "Johnny Cash: Unchained." *Los Angeles Times*, November 3, 1996.

Dangaard, Colin. "The New Johnny Cash." *Atlanta Journal and Constitution Magazine*, December 4, 1977.

Danker, Frederick E. "Country Music." *Yale Review* 63 (spring 1974).

______"Country Music and the Mass Media: The Johnny Cash Television Show." *Popular Music and Society* 2 (winter 1973).

______. "Johnny Cash: A Certain Tragic Sense of Life." *Sing Out!*, September/October 1969.

______. "The Repertory and Style of a Country Singer: Johnny Cash." *Journal of American Folklore* 85 (October-December 1972).

Davis, Hank. "Johnny Cash: The Sun Sound." *Goldmine*, December 20, 1985.

Dearmore, Thomas. "First Angry Man of Country Singers." *New York Times Magazine*, September 21, 1969.

DeCurtis, Anthony. "Johnny Cash Won't Back Down." *Rolling Stone*, October 26, 2000.

______. "Recordings Their Way." *Rolling Stone*, May 19, 1994.

Deen, Dixie. "'Everything Ain't Been Said.'" *Music City News*, January 1966.

DeYoung, Bill. "Talk Talk: American Music Legend, Johnny Cash." *Goldmine*, July 19, 1996.

Dickerson, Jim. "The Sun Session: Together Again in Memphis." *Rock and Roll* 29, 1986.

Dickie, Mary. "Hard Talk from the God-fearin', Pro-Metal Man in Black." *Graffiti*, October 1987.

Douglass, Tim. "5,000 Welcome Johnny Cash to Regal." *Meramac Valley (Minn.) Transcript-Pacific*, August 22, 1989.

Drowne, Tatiana Balkoff. "Johnny Cash: The Man, His World, His Music." *Films in Review* 21, no. 3 (1970).

Dunn, Jancee. "Johnny Cash." *Rolling Stone*, June 30, 1994.

Durchholz, Daniel. "The Last American Hero." *Request*, June 1994

"Empathy in the Dungeon." *Time*, August 30, 1968.

Farley, Christopher John. "Dream Album." *Time*, May 9, 1994.

Flanagan, Bill. "Johnny Cash, American." *Musician*, May 1988.

Foyston, John. "Roarin' Down the Highway." *Portland Oregonian*, September 26, 1990.

Fricke, David. "American Stars 'n' Bars: Living History Steals the Show at SXSW." *Rolling Stone*, May 5, 1994.

______. "The Ten Million Dollar Quartet." *Rolling Stone*, October 24, 1985.

"Friends of Cash Share Good Times, Bad Times, Life, Love and Music." *Country Music*, July/August 1980.

Friskics-Warren, Bill. "June Carter Cash's Full Account." *Washington Post*, June 20, 1999.

Frook, John. "Johnny Cash: The Rough-Cut King of Country Music." *Life*, November 21, 1969.

Gallagher, Dorothy. "Johnny Cash: 'I'm Growing, I'm Changing, I'm Becoming.'" *Redbook*, August 1971.

Gent, George. "Welk Show Among 11 Programs Dropped from ABC Fall Slate." *New York Times*, March 20, 1971.

Ghiani, Tim. "Real Life: Praying for Cash, Covering Illness—and Reflecting." *Nashville Banner*, November 19, 1997.

Giles, Jeff, with Maggie Malone. "The Kids Are All Right." *Newsweek*, May 2, 1994.

Gillis, Frieda Barter. "Johnny Cash: Slightly Terrific." *Rustic Rhythm*, May 1957.

Gleason, Ralph J. "It Looks as if Elvis Has a Rival—from Arkansas." *San Francisco Chronicle*, December 16, 1956.

Goldstein, Richard. "Johnny Cash, 'Something Rude Showing.'" *Vogue*, August 15, 1969.

Gordinier, Jeff. "Cash and Carry." *Santa Barbara (Calif.) News-Press*, July 30, 1993.

"Gospel Parley to Open." *New York Times*. June 12, 1972.

Gould, Jack. "TV: Johnny Cash's Life." *New York Times*, March 17, 1969.

Green, Ben A. "Johnny Cash Achieves 'Life's Ambition,' Wins Opry Hearts." *Nashville Banner*, July 16, 1956.

Green, Doug. "Bob Wooton: Pickin' for Cash." *Country Music*, July 1980.

Greenspun, Roger. "Screen: Johnny Cash Onstage and Off." *New York Times*, January 24, 1970.

Grevatt, Ren. "Johnny Cash." *Music Business*, March 13, 1965.

Gross, Ben. "Johnny Cash-es in Again on Country Music Show." *New York Daily News*, April 18, 1969.

"Guitarist Seriously Burned in Home Fire." *(Nashville) Tennessean*, August 4, 1968.

Guralnick, Peter. "John R. Cash: I Will Rock 'n' Roll with You (If I Have To)." *Country Music*, July/August 1980.

Hajari, Nisid. "Next Big Resurrected Legend." *Entertainment Weekly*, February 18–25, 1994.

Hannah, Barry. "Big Country." *Spin*, July 1994.

Harrington, Richard. "Walking the Line." *Washington Post*, December 8, 1996.

Haun, Harry. "Palance, Cash Blaze." *Nashville Tennessean Sunday Showcase*, November 9, 1969.

Hilburn, Robert. "'Important Music Comes from the Gut.'" *Los Angeles Times*, April 25, 1994.

______. "Johnny Cash Looks Back with a Smile." *Los Angeles Times*, February 2, 1992.

______. "Nothing Can Take the Place of the Human Heart: A Conversation with Johnny Cash." *Rolling Stone*, March 1, 1973.

______. "Q&A with Johnny Cash." *Los Angeles Times Calendar*, April 25, 1994.

Hoekstra, Dave. "The Man in Black Lives His Life Close to the Earth." *Chicago Sun-Times*, September 11, 1988.

Hoffman, Jan. "Some Girls Do: Rosanne Cash Walks Her Own Line." *Village Voice*, July 5, 1988.

Hoger, Dave. "Healthy Cash Delights Fans." *Jackson (Mich.) Citizen Patriot*, March 12, 1989.

Holden, Stephen. "Johnny Cash, the Fatalist as Patriarch." *New York Times*, December 19, 1992.

Hunter, James. "Dancing Inside the Ring of Fire." *New Country*, August 1994.

Jacobson, Mark. "New Adventures of the Man in Black." *Esquire*, August 1994.

Jahn, Mike. "20,000 at Garden Hear Johnny Cash." *New York Times*, December 7, 1969.

"Johnny Cash Checks Back into Alcohol, Drug Treatment Center." *Lakeland (Fla.) Ledger*, November 26, 1989.

"Johnny Cash Comes to Town." *Record and Show Mirror*, September 26, 1959.

"Johnny Cash Enters Betty Ford Drug Center." *Washington Post*, December 21, 1983.

"Johnny Cash on Life, Music and His Devotion to Family." *Cash Box*, June 14, 1980.

"Johnny Cash Sells Film on Jesus." *New York Times*, February 3, 1973.

"Johnny Cash: American III: Solitary Man." *Irish Times*, October 21, 2000.

"Johnny Cash: Unchained." *Stereophile*, February 1997.

Johnson, Robert. "Gleason Signs Cash for 10 Guest Spots." *Memphis Press-Scimitar*, January 7, 1957.

Jones, Peter. "Johnny Cash Comes to Town." *Record and Show Mirror*, September 26, 1959.

Joyce, Mike. "The Well-Trod Roads of the Highwaymen." *Washington Post*, March 11, 1990.

Judd, Ron. "'The Man in Black' Filled Spotlight on Pavilion Stage." *Bremerton (Wash.) Sun*, January 16, 1988.

Kaye, Elizabeth. "The Memphis Blues Again." *Rolling Stone*, November 21, 1985.

Kienzle, Rich. "Johnny Cash's Greatest Hits." *Country Music*, July/August 1980.

La Farge, Peter. "Johnny Cash." *Sing Out!*, May 1965.

Larson, Tom. "Town Gives Cash a Regal Welcome." *St. Cloud (Minn.) Times*, August 19, 1989.

Lewis, Randy. "A Walk on the Dark Side." *Los Angeles Times*, April 25, 1994.

Light, Alan. "Outlaws Still Loom Large." *Rolling Stone*, April 5, 1990.

Linderman, Larry. "Penthouse Interview: Johnny Cash." *Penthouse*, August 1975.

Logan, Nick. "His Music Makes Cash a Myth." *New Musical Express*, October 18, 1969.

Longsdorf, Amy. "Problems Plague Cash Show." *Allentown (Penn.) Call*, August 7, 1988.

"Luther Perkins, Cash Guitarist, Rites Set." *Nashville Banner*, August 6, 1968.

Lydon, Michael. "'Ain't Nothin' Too Weird for Me.'" *New York Times*, March 16, 1969.

Maclaren, Mike. "Johnny Cash in Kernersville." *Kernersville (N.C.) News*, October 27, 1988.

Mansfield, Brian. "Johnny Cash Sees the Light." *USA Today*, April 15, 1999.

Margheret, Frank, and Allan Parrish. "Cash, Perkins Differ on Origin of 'Blue Suede Shoes.'" *Willoughby (Ohio) News-Herald*, September 29, 1988.

Martin, Patti. "Dream Becomes a Reality." *Asbury Park (N.J.) Press*, February 25, 1988.

Maschal, Richard. "A Man 'For the People.'" *Washington Post*, February 16, 1973.

Maynard, Joyce. "Cash Sings Gospel of Old Values." *New York Times*, November 19, 1976.

McCabe, Peter, and Jack Killion. "Johnny Cash." *Country Music*, May 1973.

McCall, Michael. "Johnny Cash, American III: Solitary Man." *Country Music*, February/March 2001.

McCall, Michael, and Rex Graham. "Johnny Cash to Have Heart Surgery." *Nashville Banner*, December 15, 1988.

McCullough, Dan. "Johnny Cash's Best Performance Was Off Stage." *Cape Cod Times*, April 9, 1989.

McDonald, Richard. "Cash Tells of Plans for Record, 'Badman' Role." *Tom's River (N.J.) Observer,* March 2, 1988.

McLellan, Joseph. "A Singer Named Johnny Cash." *Washington Post,* November 19, 1975.

Miller, Floyd. "Back from Drugs: The Triumph of Johnny Cash." *Reader's Digest,* September 1970.

Morden, Darryl. "Concert Review: Johnny Cash." *Hollywood Reporter,* February 27, 1996.

Morris, W. R. "Legend Credits Guitarist Established Sound." *Music City News,* May 1979.

Nakahara, Liz. "Cashing in on the Craze for Country." *Washington Post,* June 21, 1982.

"Narcotics Rap Costs." *Variety,* March 16, 1966.

Nash, Alanna. "Johnny Cash, American Miracle?" *Stereo Review,* August 1994.

______. "Johnny Cash: The Mystery of Life." *Stereo Review,* April 1991.

______. "Johnny Cash: Weathering the Storm." *Stereo Review.* March 1986.

______. "The Remarkable Johnny Cash." *Stereo Review,* March 1984.

"Nixon Is Criticized for Song Request, 'Welfare Cadillac.'" *New York Times,* March 28, 1970.

Nussbaum, Albert. "When Johnny Cash Visited Leavenworth." *Charleston, W.V., Sunday Gazette Mail,* October 7, 1973.

O'Connor, John J. "TV: Baryshnikov, Johnny Cash and 'Feather' Are on Tonight." *New York Times,* December 6, 1976.

______. "TV: 'The Pride of Jesse Hallam' Stars Johnny Cash." *New York Times,* March 3, 1981.

Okon, May. "Cash on the Line." *New York Sunday News,* March 29, 1959.

Orr, Jay. "Man in Black—with Petty and June—Conquers Tinseltown." *Nashville Banner,* February 26, 1996.

Ortega, T. "My-Name-Is-Sue-How-Do-You-Do, Johnny Cash as Lesbian Icon." *South Atlantic Quarterly* 94, no. 1 (winter 1995).

Ouellette, Dan. "Johnny Cash Does it Again." *San Francisco Chronicle,* November 3, 1996.

Pareles, Jon. "Johnny Cash, Austerely Direct from Deep Within." *New York Times*, September 16, 1994.

Patterson, Jim. "Ring of Fire." *Country Music*, June/July 2001.

Peterson, Richard A. "The Dialectic of Hard-Core and Soft-Shell Country Music." *South Atlantic Quarterly* 94, no. 1 (winter 1995).

Pick, Steve. "Cash's Newest Shows a Craftsman's Touch. *St. Louis Post-Dispatch*, February 16, 1990.

Pond, Neil. "Johnny Cash: His Music, His Faith, His Demons." *Music City News*, May 1987.

______. "Middle Age Can't Slow the Man in Black." *Music City News*, May 1997.

Pond, Steve. "Johnny Cash." *Rolling Stone*, December 10–24, 1992.

"Pop Goes the Cash." *Rock and Roll Songs*, February 1957.

Purvis, Ray. "Cash: The Real Thing." *West Australian*, March 10, 1994.

Rader, Dotson. "'I Can Sing of Death, but I'm Obsessed with Life.'" *Parade Magazine*, June 11, 1995.

Ratliff, Ben. "Cash, Back." *Rolling Stone*, October 26, 2000.

"Recording Star Released." *El Paso Times*, October 6, 1965.

"Review Spotlight on . . . " (Review of "I Walk the Line"). *Billboard*, January 7, 1956.

Robertson, Nan. "Cash and Country Music Take White House Stage." *New York Times*, April 18, 1970.

Roland, Tom. "Cash Gets Pneumonia in Hospital." *Nashville Tennessean*. November 15, 1997.

______. "Parkinson's Stops Cash Book Tour. *Nashville Tennessean*, October 28, 1997.

______. "There's More Life, and Another Book, from the Man in Black." *Nashville Tennessean*, October 21, 1997.

Rush, Diane Samms. "Writer: Illness Won't Stop Cash." *Boston Globe*, October 31, 1997.

Saal, Hubert. "Johnny on the Spot." *Newsweek*, February 2, 1970.

Sachs, Bill. "Folk Talent and Tunes." *Billboard*, May 20, 1957.

______. "Folk Talent and Tunes." *Billboard*, April 29, 1957.

______. "Folk Talent and Tunes." *Billboard*, April 6, 1957.

______. "Folk Talent and Tunes." *Billboard*, February 23, 1957.

______. "Folk Talent and Tunes." *Billboard*, February 16, 1957.
______. "Folk Talent and Tunes." *Billboard*, February 18, 1956.
______. "Folk Talent and Tunes." *Billboard*, October 8, 1955.
______. "Folk Talent and Tunes." *Billboard*, September 17, 1955.
Sakol, Jeannie. "The Grit and Grace of Johnny Cash." *McCall's*, July 1970.
Salamon, Ed. "Johnny Cash Tells the Stories Behind His Greatest Hits." *Country Music*, July/August 1980.
Salata, Valerie. "Cash Can Carry Center Audience." *Costa Mesa, California, Orange Coast Daily Pilot*, January 24, 1988.
Sasfy, Joe. "The Sterling Simplicity of Skaggs." *Washington Post*, September 26, 1982.
Sawyer, Kathy. "Johnny Cash Walks New Line." *Nashville Tennessean Showcase*, April 20, 1969.
Schleier, Curt. "Johnny Cash Plays to Crowd." *Investor's Business Daily*, November 16, 2001.
Schoemer, Karen. "Johnny Cash, an Enduring American Icon." *New York Times*, May 3, 1992.
Segal, David. "Reaping the Johnny Cash Crop." *Washington Post*, May 21, 2000.
Seiler, Andy. "Johnny Cash 'Feeling Better.'" *USA Today*, December 15, 1997.
"Seven in Cash Family Hurt." *New York Times*, September 3, 1974.
Shaw, Bill. "Easing Back with Johnny Cash." *People*, July 11, 1994.
Shelton, Robert. "Johnny Cash Sings to a Full House." *New York Times*, October 24, 1968.
Shockely, Donald G., and Richard L. Freeman. "Johnny Cash on Prison Reform." *Christian Century*, September 30, 1970.
Shuster, Fred. "Outlaw No More, Cash Still Walks the Line." *Cleveland Plain Dealer*, April 7, 1995.
Silber, Irwin. "'Hootenanny Hoot!'" *Sing Out!*, December 1963/January 1964.
Sinclair, David. "Heroic Survivor." *London Times*, May 15, 1989.
"Singer Cash Bailed Out." *San Jose News*, October 6, 1965.
"Singer Guilty on Drug Charge." *New York Times*, December 29, 1965.

"Smart Money Says Johnny Cash Is the One to Watch This Year." *National Observer*, June 2, 1969.

Snider, Mike. "Johnny Cash Sings Cyberspace Blues." *USA Today*, September 17, 1997.

"Son to the Johnny Cashes." *New York Times*, March 4, 1970.

Steinfels, Peter. "Gulf War Proving Bountiful for Some Prophets of Doom." *New York Times*, February 2, 1991.

Sterritt, David. "Country Voice Heard Round the World." *Christian Science Monitor*, August 26, 1976.

Strauss, Neil. "New Rebel for the 90's: Meet Johnny Cash, 62." *New York Times*, September 14, 1994.

Sutton, Terri. "This Godfather of Gloom Finds Light in the Darkness." *New York Times*, May 22, 1994.

"The House That Cash Built." *TV Guide*, March 27, 1971.

"This Week's Best Buys" (Review of "Cry, Cry, Cry"). *Billboard*, October 22, 1955.

Thomas, Karen. "Cash Fingers Critics." *USA Today*, March 13, 1998.

Thomas, Michael. "Johnny Cash: Old-Time Original Made for the Fair." *Modesto (Calif.) Bee*, August 3, 1989.

Thompson, Howard. "Country Music Flows for NBC Series." *New York Times*, July 27, 1973.

Tosches, Nick. "Chordless in Gaza: The Second Coming of John R. Cash." *Journal of Country Music* 17, no. 3 (1995).

Trakin, Roy. "An Exclusive *Hits* Dialogue with Johnny Cash." *Hits*, May 2, 1994.

Trescott, Jacqueline. "'The Pride of Jesse Hallam': Johnny Cash and the Illiterate's Write of Passage." *Washington Post*, March 3, 1981.

Troop, Don. "Cash Tells of Personal Battles." *Fayetteville Northwest Arkansas Times*, June 22, 1989.

Tucker, Ken. "Johnny Cash: Boom Chicka Boom." *Spin*, April 1990.

______. "Why Ricky, Reba, and George Are Hard at It." *Journal of Country Music* 11, no. 1 (1986).

Tucker, Stephen R. "Pentecostalism and Popular Culture in the South: A Study of Four Musicians." *Journal of Popular Culture* 16, no. 3 (1982).

"Unchained." *Stereophile*, February 1997.

Vecsey, George. "Cash's 'Gospel Road' Film Is Renaissance for Him." *New York Times*, December 13, 1973.

______. "Country Music Fans Have Fans, Too." *New York Times*, June 14, 1974.

Von Sternberg, Bob. "Tiny Town Hits Jackpot as Cash Draws a Crowd." *Minneapolis Star-Tribune*, August 19, 1989.

Vovcsko, Jerry. "Cash Shows His Talent and Grit at Indian Ranch." *Worcester (Mass.) Gazette*, August 29, 1988.

"Walk That Line, Cash." *Music City News*, April 1965.

Weisel, Al. "The Man in Black Sees the Light on 'Unchained.'" *US*, February 1997.

Williams, Bill. "Man in Black Returns to the Fold." *Kingsport (Tenn.) Times-News*, January 10, 1986.

Wilson, John S. "Newport Folk Festival Becomes Music Bazaar." *New York Times*, July 19, 1969.

Wolff, Carlo. "New on Disc, Johnny Cash, American III: Solitary Man." *Boston Globe*, November 2, 2000.

Wood, Gerry. "Johnny Cash, American III: Solitary Man." *Country Weekly*, February 8, 2001.

Wood, Tom. "Cash, Fans Mark 40 Years." *Nashville Tennessean*, April 23, 1995.

Woods, William C. "Native Son, Nice People." *Washington Post*, December 10, 1973.

Woodward, Ken. "A Country Jesus." *Newsweek*, January 29, 1973.

Woulfe, Molly. "Cash Fumbles Through Rialto Performance." *Herald-News (Joliet, Ill.)*, June 23, 1990.

Wren, Christopher. "The Restless Ballad of Johnny Cash." *Look*, April 29, 1969.

"Write Is Wrong." *Time*, February 23, 1959.

Zimmerman, David. "New Breed of Fans Is Caught in His Current." *USA Today*, November 2, 1988.

CREDITS

Excerpt from *Winners Got Scars Too: The Life of Johnny Cash* by Christopher S. Wren. New York: Dial Press. Copyright © 1971 Christopher S. Wren. Reprinted by permission of Sterling Lord Literistic, Inc.

"Fork in the Road" and "Seven One Night Stands" from *Man in Black* by Johnny Cash. Grand Rapids, Mich.: Zondervan Press. Copyright © House of Cash 1975. Used by permission.

"Johnny Cash: The Sun Sound" by Hank Davis. From *Goldmine*, December 20, 1985. Copyright © 1985 Hank Davis. Reprinted by permission of author.

"Johnny Cash Achieves 'Life's Ambition' Wins Opry Hearts" by Ben A. Green. From the *Nashville Banner*, July 16, 1956. Copyright © 1956 Irby Simpkins. Reprinted by permission.

"It Looks as if Elvis Has a Rival—from Arkansas" by Ralph J. Gleason. From *San Francisco Chronicle*, December 16, 1956. Copyright © 1956 San Francisco Chronicle. Reprinted by permission.

"Gleason Signs Cash for 10 Guest Spots" by Robert Johnson. From *Memphis Press-Scimitar*, January 7, 1957. Copyright © 1957 the *Commercial Appeal*, Memphis, Tennessee. Used with permission. No additional reproduction or distribution of this article in any form is permitted without the written approval of *Commercial Appeal*.

"Write Is Wrong." From *Time*, February 23, 1959. Copyright © 1959 Time Inc. Reprinted by permission.

"Johnny Cash" by Peter La Farge. From *Sing Out!* magazine. May 1965. Copyright © 1965 Sing Out! (The Sing Out Corp.) Used by permission. All rights reserved.

"When Johnny Cash Visited Leavenworth" by Albert Nussbaum. From the *Sunday Gazette Mail* (Charleston, W.V.), October 7, 1973.

Excerpt from *The Nashville Sound: Bright Lights and Country Music* by Paul Hemphill. New York: Simon and Schuster. Copyright © 1971 Paul Hemphill. Reprinted by permission of the author.

"Something Rude Showing" by Richard Goldstein. From *Vogue*. Copyright © 1969 by Conde Nast Publications. All rights reserved.

"First Angry Man of Country Singers" by Tom Dearmore. From *New York Times Magazine*, September 21, 1969. Copyright © 1969 by the New York Times Company. Reprinted by permission.

"Johnny Cash: 'I'm Growing, I'm Changing, I'm Becoming'" by Dorothy Gallagher. From *Redbook*, August 1971. Copyright © 1971 Dorothy Gallagher. Reprinted by permission of the author.

"Cash's 'Gospel Road' Film Is Renaissance for Him" by George Vecsey. From the *New York Times*, December 13, 1973. Copyright © 1973 by the New York Times Company. Reprinted by permission.

"Interview with Johnny Cash" by Peter McCabe and Jack Killion. From *Country Music*, May 1973. Copyright © 1973 Russell Barnard. Reprinted by permission.

"*Penthouse* Interview: Johnny Cash" by Larry Linderman. From *Penthouse*, August 1975. Copyright © 1975 General Media Communications, Inc. Reprinted by permission of *Penthouse*. All Rights Reserved.

"What Now, John Cash?" by Patrick Carr. From *Country Music*, December 1974. Copyright © 1974 Patrick Carr. Reprinted by permission of the author.

"Cash Comes Back" by Patrick Carr. From *Country Music*, December 1976. Copyright © 1976 Patrick Carr. Reprinted by permission of the author.

"Johnny Cash's Freedom" by Patrick Carr. From *Country Music*, April 1979. Copyright © 1979 Patrick Carr. Reprinted by permission of the author.

"Johnny Cash: Still Free," by Noel Coppage. From *Stereo Review*, March 1983. Copyright © 1983 Hachette Filipacchi magazines. Reprinted by permission.

"Hard Talk from the God-Fearin', Pro-Metal Man in Black" by Mary Dickie. From *Graffiti*, October 1987. Copyright © 1987 Mary Dickie. Reprinted by permission of the author.

"Heroic Survivor" by David Sinclair. From *The Times*, London, May 15, 1989. Copyright © David Sinclair/Times Newspapers Limited, London 1989. Reprinted by permission.

"The Mystery of Life" by Alanna Nash. From *Stereo Review*, April 1991. Copyright © Alanna Nash 1991. Used by permission of the author.

"Johnny Cash's Best Performance Was Off Stage" by Dan McCullough. From the *Cape Cod Times*, April 9, 1989. Copyright © Dan McCullough 1989. Used by permission of the author.

"Chordless in Gaza" by Nick Tosches. From *The Journal of Country Music* 17, no. 3, 1995. Copyright © Nick Tosches 1995. Reprinted by permission of the author and the author's agents, Scovil Chichak Galen Literary Agency, Inc.

"Johnny Cash, Austerely Direct from Deep Within" by Jon Pareles. From the *New York Times*, September 16, 1994. Copyright © 1994 by the New York Times Company. Reprinted by permission.

"Cash Conquers" by Chris Dickinson. From *Chicago Reader*, September 16, 1994. Copyright © Chris Dickinson 1994. Used by permission of the author.

"Johnny Cash: American Music Legend" by Bill DeYoung. From *Goldmine*, July 19, 1996. Copyright © Bill DeYoung 1996. Used by permission of the author.

"Cash, Back" by Ben Ratliff. From *Rolling Stone*, October 26, 2000. Copyright © 2000 Ben Ratliff. Used by permission of the author.

"Rays of Light from the Man in Black" by David Brinn. From the *Jerusalem Post*, October 31, 2000. Copyright © *Jerusalem Post*. Used by permission.

"Johnny Cash: American III: Solitary Man" by Michael McCall. From *Country Music*, February/March 2001. Copyright © 2001 Country Music Media Group. Used by permission of the author.

"Hello, This Is Johnny Cash" by Peter Cooper. From the *Nashville Tennessean*, October 22, 2000. Copyright © 2000 the *Tennessean*. Used by permission.

INDEX

ABC-TV. *See also* TV
  Johnny's show on, xvi, xxiv, 83, 87, 98–101, 242
Accent, of Johnny, 94
Acting ambitions, 158. *See also* Movies; TV
Acuff, Roy, 182, 270–271
Ads. *See* TV
Albums, of Johnny, 42, 92. *See also* Singles/songs of Johnny
  The Adventures of Johnny Cash, 199, 200
  American III: Solitary Man, xxiii, 262, 263, 264, 267,
  American Recordings, xxi, xxii, 218–220, 222, 224, 248, 251, 252, 253, 254, 257, 258, 259, 263
  Ballads of the American Indian, 56
  Bitter Tears, 56, 58, 104, 153
  Blood, Sweat and Tears, 56
  The Class of '55, 164
  Gone Girl, 187, 189, 190, 194
  Heroes, 164
  The Holy Land, 110, 127
  John R. Cash, 162, 168
  Johnny 99, 162
  Johnny Cash at San Quentin, 242
  Johnny Cash Is Coming to Town, 162, 202
  Live at Folsom Prison, 74–75, 242
  Live at San Quentin, 75, 179
  The Mystery of Life, xx, 209–210
  One Piece at a Time, 171, 172, 176, 177, 178
  Ragged Old Flag, 167
  The Rambler, xiv
  Rockabilly Blues, 200
  Silver, 162
  Unchained, 219, 255, 256, 261, 262, 263
Alcohol, 56, 61, 105, 119, 179–180, 230, 240, 270
Allen, Steve, 48
American lifestyle
  change in, 137–138
American Oil, xvii, 136–137
American Records, xxi, xxii, 224, 248, 251, 252. *See also* Albums, of Johnny
  marketing of Johnny by, xxii
American West, The (magazine), 91
Amoco ads, 125
Ann-Margret, 146
Apollo moon landing, 73

Appliance salesman, 45, 52, 144, 145, 200, 235, 238
Arnold, Eddy, xvii
Arthur, Illinois, country fair at, 94–100
Articles
  on Johnny, 41–50
  mistakes in, xxv
Artistic freedom, 39
Audiences, xxii, 90, 98, 114, 126, 127, 139, 146, 247, 254
  ads and effect on, 136–137
  diversity of, 88, 92, 95, 111–112, 147
  gospel hymns and, 133
  Grand Ole Opry, 90
  Indian, 153
  magic between Johnny and, 118
  nostalgia and, 164
  polling of, 259–260
  young, 258
Auditoriums, 110, 136
Autobiographies, of Johnny Cash
  Cash: The Autobiography, 163, 165, 219
  Man in Black, xxiv, 26, 88, 143, 164, 166, 228, 255
Autographs, 81–82, 98, 203, 213
Automobiles, 150–151, 178
Autry, Gene, 97

Ball, Earle Poole, xiii
Ballads, xix, 52, 73, 108, 118, 147, 239. *See also* Songs
  mournful, lonesome, 45
Baptist, 22, 31, 52, 128
Barbarians, the, 235
Baritone voice. *See* Voice
Barnhill, Jesse, 233
Baron and the Kid, The, 162
Bates, George, 236
Bean, Woodrow, 67–68
Beastie Boys, xxi
Beatles, The, 89
Beck, 255
"Belshazzar," 235
Bennett, Tony, 146
Berle, Milton, 48
Betty Ford Clinic, 202
Beverly Hillbillies, The, 91
Bible, 27, 121, 122. *See also* Christians; God; Jesus
  belt, 185–186
Big D Jamboree, 3
"Big Light, The," xix
Billboard, 3, 45, 73, 154, 171, 193, 219, 231, 262
Biographies, xxiii, 166
"Bird on the Wire," 168
Blake, Norman, 140
Blocker, Dan, 99
Blood on the Tracks, 257
"Blue Suede Shoes," 3, 49, 79
Bono, 223
Books
  religious, 228
Boston Pops, 91
Boyhood
  music and connection to, 35
Bragg, Charlie, 174–175, 189
Broadcasting, 48
Brooks, Garth, xx, 161, 251
Brooks, Karen, 164
Brother, death of. *See* Cash, Jack
Bugs Bunny, 27, 28

Business
Johnny on, 136, 170
Butler, Larry, 187

Cadillac(s), 47, 51
Campbell, Glen, xvii, 87, 92
Campbell, Mike, 264
Career, 50, 260, 267
chronicling of, 228
effect on, 136–137
listless, 164
low-point of, 68
in music, 234
resurgence in, 226
"Careless Love," 169
Carmichael, Hoagie, 49
Carnegie Hall, 144, 247, 248
Carruthers, Bill, 99
Carter, Anita, 60, 202, 206, 271
Carter, Carlene, 202, 204
Carter, Ezra, 109
Carter, Helen, 60, 202, 206, 271
Carter, Jimmy, 183–185, 195–196
Carter, June. *See* Cash, (Valerie) June Carter
Carter, Maybelle Mother, xviii, xviii*n*2, 60, 96, 109, 196–197, 242, 271
Carter, Rosie, 202
Carter family, 2, 58, 75, 80, 96, 112, 187, 189, 242, 271
music history of, 109
songs of, 96
Carter lick, xviii*n*2
Cash, Carrie (mother), 5, 231
battery radio of, 16
on hearing Johnny sing, 159
household problems of, 11
on selling of wildcat pelt, 12
songs of, 2, 52, 152, 233
Cash, Jack (brother), xxiv, 5
alleged murder of, 26, 228, 233
on angels singing, 33
bandaged fingers of, 31
coma of, 31, 32
death of, 25, 232–233
funeral of, 34
gangrene of, 32
hallucinating of, 32
in hospital, 29–30
imitation of Bugs Bunny, 27–28
kind words of, 34
on morphine, 31
premonition of, 26–27, 159–169
reading letters, 31
on vision of heaven, 33
Cash, John Carter (son), 114–115, 146, 203, 268
accident of, 166
heavy metal band of, 202
heavy metal concerts with, 203
influence on Johnny, 133–134
interest in music, 140
religion and, 132
Cash, Johnny
in 1950s, 147, 149, 172, 177, 201, 218, 223, 234, 238
in 1960s, xv, xxii, 59, 113, 137–138, 150, 171, 179, 188–189, 218
in 1970s, 90, xv, xvii, xviii, xix, xxii, 144, 155, 161–164, 165–166, 221–246
in 1980s, xix, 162–164, 199–207
in 1990s, xix, xx, xxiii, 200, 218–220, 221–246

appearance and stature of, 52, 80, 89, 100, 132, 145, 207
birth of, 5, 231
charisma/persona of, 80–81, 111, 145, 171, 267–268
dark side of, xxi, 58
daughters of, 46, 51, 105, 113, 146, 240
debut of, xiv
early years of, 1–3, 106–107, 145, 232
extended family of, 105–106
false re-emergence of, xix
first memory of, 8
on first wife, 150, 240
on forgiveness of self, 132
as greatest country singer of our times, xvii, 161
House of, 105–106
on June, 113, 122, 124, 180
move from Memphis to Los Angeles, 41
nickname of, 18, 93
on performing, 141
as standard bearer, xv
style of, 100, 107
on tours, 49–50
waning of, xviii, 163
Cash, (Valerie) June Carter, xvi, xxii, 71, 74, 75, 79–80, 84, 86, 99, 113, 146, 151, 154, 156, 157, 166, 182, 184–185, 202, 206, 242, 249, 254, 258, 265, 268
CD release party, 262
as comic emcee, 96, 112
dream of John, 126, 127
graciousness of, 114–115
Grammy for "Ring of Fire," 107
interview with, 114–123
on Johnny's drug recovery, 109, 115–117
on Johnny's sickness, 269
marriage to, 60, 105
phone call to, 70–71
on visiting prisons, 79, 102
Cash, Louise (sister), 5
Cash, Ray (father), xiv, 5, 98, 232
on 1937 flood, 16–20
on acceptance by ERA, 8
construction job of, 11
at courthouse in Rison, Arkansas, 7–8
on Jack's death, 28–29
on life in Dyess Colony, 14–15
on move to new house, 8–9
on ownership and value of farm, 20
signing of final home contract, 9
at White House, 154–155
on wildcat and chickens, 12
Cash, Reba (sister), 5
Cash, Rosanne (daughter), 1, 105, 237, 249
My Old Man (book), 267
Cash, Roy (brother), 5, 233, 235
Dixie Rhythm Ramblers and, 233
on foiled bank robbery, 21
on Ray Cash, 11
Cash: The Autobiography (second autobiography), 163, 165
Cash, Tom (brother), 235
Cash, Vivian. *See* Liperto, Vivian
Cashbox, 193
Causes, xxi, 56, 74–76, 84–86, 88, 93, 98, 99, 107–108. *See also* Indians, American; Prisons
Cave, Nick, 263, 264, 266

CBS, xvi–xvii, xviii, 91, 192, 202, 205
Censorship of lyrics, 203–204. *See also* Lyrics; Songs
Chart(s), 176, 205, 222, 223. *See also* Country music
  country, xviii, xix, 48, 49, 55
  failure to make, 162, 164
  Highwaymen and, 164
  pop record, 48
  popular, 58
Cherokee background, xxv, 88, 92, 100, 153. *See also* Indians, American
Cherry, Hugh, 183
"Children," 129
Choral embellishment, 38–39
Christ. *See* God
Christian(s), 252. *See also* God; Jesus; Religion
  Johnny as committed, 196
  three different kinds of, 157
Christianity, 119, 121, 126, 195
Church, 22
  socials, 52
  special prayer for Jack in, 30
Clark, Dick, 41
Class of '55, 205
Clay, Andrew Dice, xxi
Clement, Jack (Cowboy), 38, 55, 172, 186, 187–188, 200–201, 271
  working with, 167, 168, 176, 190–191
CMA (Country Music Awards), 183, 193–194
Coe, David Allen, 263
Cohen, Leonard, 218, 249, 252, 263
Collecting, obsession for, 228
Colonization Project Number One, 7, 12–13
Colony Herald, 15
Columbia Records, xv, xx, 55, 58, 67, 92, 167, 168, 242
  first songs with, 56
  new methods of recording at, 162, 173
  prison album recordings for, 101–103
  switch to, 39, 53, 239
  switch to Mercury Records, 164, 244
Columbia Studio B, 188
Columbo, 158, 162
Commendation from Washington, 234
Commercials. *See* TV
Common man, 88, 94–95
Competition, 271
  appreciation of, 182
  between labels, 39
Concert(s), 206, 268. *See also* Prisoners; Tours; specific concerts
  Arthur, Illinois, 94–100
  benefit, 104
  John Carter Cash, 202
  prison, 74–75, 139, 202
  at San Quentin, 38
  schedules, xx
  sluggishness in, 200
Contracts, 50
Convicts. *See* Prisoners
Cook, Roger, 201
Coolidge, Rita, 129
Cooper, Gary, 50
Coral Records, 45

Cosby, Bill, 146
Costello, Elvis, xix, 201, 206
  meeting with, 204
Cotton, xiv, xvii, 6, 25, 92, 106, 112, 145, 232
  first planting of, 10
Country (Tosches), xviii
Country music
  artists, 45
  Carter Family and, 109
  changing winds of, 166
  crazy for, 90–92
  crossover record and, 182–183
  Depression era and, 112
  direction of, 193
  full circle of, 205–206
  future of, 135
  homosexuals in, 251
  king of, 144, 239
  at Leavenworth, 78
  new breed of, 243
  only African-American star in, 85
  pain and tragedy in, 35
  roots of, xix, xxii
  sales, 48
  seriousness in, 35
  shows, 87–88
  Sun Records unique development in, 36
  syrupy, 163
  tours and, 110–114
  two worlds of, 193–194
  Western, 90–92, 92
Country Music (magazine), 127, 137, 165, 262. *See also* Charts
  interview with Johnny, 166–171
Country Music Hall of Fame, 183, 209
"Cowboy Who Started A Fight, The," xix
"Crescent City Blues," 235
Crooklyn, 222
Crow, Sheryl, 265
Crowell, Rodney (son-in-law), 163, 164, 188, 189, 206
Cunningham, Walt, 140
C. W. Post College, 124

Dalhart, Vernon, 35
Daniels, Charlie, 194
Danker, Frederick, xvii
Danzig, Glenn, 218, 252
Daughter. *See* Cash, Rosanne
Daughters, of Johnny, 46, 51, 105, 113, 146, 240
David Letterman show, 225, 228
Davis, Don, 175
Davis, Scott, 108
Death, 150–151, 241, 244, 248
Def Jam Records, 264
"Delia's Gone," xxii, 223, 229, 244–245, 252–253, 254, 259
Demographics, xx
Demons/devil, 70, 150, 223. *See also* Drugs
Denny, Jim, 181, 182
Denver, John, 126
Depp, Johnny, 224
Depression-era, xiv, 5, 16, 23, 90, 100, 111, 112
  shortcomings with, 107
Detroit stadium, 92
DeYoung, Bill, 256
Diamond, Neil, 262, 263, 264
Dictators, 221–222, 224
Dirksen, Everett, 97

Disco, xvii
Dixon, Braxton, 71
DJ Kool, xxi
Doodlum, 9, 16
Dorsey Brothers, 47
Douglas, Kirk, xvi
Drake, Guy, 143
Draper, Rusty, 45
"Dreamin' My Dreams," 201
Drug(s), 133, 143, 179, 203, 218, 230, 268, 270
  Betty Ford Clinic, 202
  cancellations from, 95–96
  Carter Family's help from, 109
  crawl back from, 74, 92, 104–105, 164
  embarrassment from, 67, 68
  God and, 110, 119, 121, 123, 125, 127, 151
  hiding of, 134–135
  kids on, 120–121
  in Mexico, 62–63, 202, 240, 251
  Nickajack Cave and, 241–242
  nightmares on, 120
  on plane, 64–66
  on reasons for taking, 120, 149, 240
  robbing for, 241
  Sheriff Jones and, 68–70, 151–152
  temptation and, 179–180
  as tools of devil, 119, 150
  tractor incident on, 70–72
  use of, xxi, xxiv, 59–62, 104, 149, 239
Drums
  addition of, 38
  snare, 37
Dyess, Arkansas (hometown), 1, 22, 48, 145, 231
Dyess Colony, 5–23, 145
Dyess, W. R., 7, 12
Dylan, Bob, 58, 83, 88, 89, 98, 99, 112, 144, 168, 200, 201, 209, 240, 242–243, 244, 251, 257
  album liner for, 85
  collaboration session with, 205
  influences of, 57
  Johnny on, 85
  on Johnny's show, 242
  Nashville Skyline album and, 85, 89–90, 243
  recording Johnny's songs, 169
  recording with, 169
  writing songs with, 158–159

Eagle's Nest, 236
Earle, Steve, 206
Ed Sullivan Show, 48, 204
Edmunds, Dave, 201
Elfstrom, Robert
  as Christ, 125, 126, 130–131
Embarrassment, 68
Emo's, 225
Equipment, 188
Europe, Johnny in, 259–260
Evening at the White House, 143

Family history, 52, 97, 98
  on clearing of twenty acres, 9–10
  flood in Dyess Colony, 16–20
  living costs of, 9
Family Show, 258
Fan(s), 59, 69, 74, 197, 211–215, 267
  clubs, 47, 53
Farmers, 5, 94, 102
Father. *See* Cash, Ray
Federal Emergency Relief Administration (FERA), 5

homesteaders and, 7
in Mississippi County, Arkansas, 6
Feller, Dick, 135
Ferguson, Gene, 58
Films. *See Gospel Road*; Movies, of Johnny Cash
Finances, 47, 50, 100–101, 146
unspectacular, 51
Fishing, 26–27, 47, 49, 101, 106, 159, 196–197
Fleetwood Mac, 256
Flood of 1937, 16–20, 25, 97, 112
Folk movement, 56–58, 57, 74, 88
creating own, 93
gap between hillbilly and, 58
Folsom Prison, 74–76, 77, 88, 92, 148. *See also* Concerts; Prisons; Prisoners
four shows at, 101–103
inmates, 101
Ford, Gerald, 184, 185, 186
Freedom, 190, 191–192
Frizzell, Lefty, 56, 163
Frugality, 16

Gaslight coffeehouse, 57
Gatlin, Larry, 129
Generation X, 225
Germany
songs written in, 235, 236, 237
staff sergeant in, 48, 106–107, 145, 234–235
Gibson, Don, 256
"Girl from the North Country," 90, 169, 242
Gleason Enterprises, 47
Glen Campbell Goodtime Hour, The, xvii, 84, 87, 92
God, xviii, xxv, 70, 72, 109, 112, 121, 139, 268, 270. *See also* Baptist; *Gospel Road*; Jesus; Religion
death and, 241, 244
drugs and, 68–69, 71–72, 109–110, 150–151
first hope and faith in, 25
forgiveness of, 132
in interviews, 110
like feeling, 118
religious experience of, 124
Goodman, Steve, 189, 211
Gore, Al, 268
Gore, Tipper, 203
Gospel, 2, 109, 112, 236, 259
Gospel hymns, 55, 56, 69, 89, 91, 118, 152
audience and, 133
Billy Graham and, 128
Gospel Road, The (Johnny's film). *See also* Movies
bookings for, 126, 196
effect on crew of, 130–131
finances used for, 124, 126, 130
first idea for, 127–128
Johnny as producer for, 131–132
released by 20th Century-Fox, 124
shooting of, 129
songs used for, 126
strong fundamentalist opinion of, 125
very personal to Johnny, 125
Government, 155. *See also* Politics
foreign policy, 85–86, 99
Graham, Billy, 112, 156, 245, 251
on gospel songs, 128
singing for, xxi, 148

Grammys/awards, of Johnny's, xxiii, 107, 219, 256
Grand Ole Opry, xxiv, 41, 49, 144, 187, 270–271
audience, 90
first appearance on, 42, 43–46
floodlight smashing at, xxi, 251
hard time breaking into, 181–182
The Johnny Cash Show taped at, 83, 98–99
joining cast of, 42
mold breaker of, 93
resentment toward, 42
return to, 42
thrown off, 240
Tokyo, 91
Grant, Marshall, 2, 35, 45, 49, 68, 107, 145, 235, 236–237
building a bomb, 49
competent string bass of, 36
on Johnny's drug problems, 60
Guitar, 2, 78, 97, 140, 145, 233, 244, 252, 253, 258, 268
first, 107, 235
Martin, 92, 235
Mother's, 52
paper in neck of, 37, 239
and primitive playing style, 235
rhythm, 36
Gulf War, 164. *See also* War, Johnny on
Guns, 49, 51, 101, 241
antique, 63

Haggard, Merle, xvii, 77, 154, 161, 201, 251, 257, 265, 270
on Luther Perkins' picking, 38
Haldeman, H. R., 144, 156–157
Hall, Tom T., 135, 188, 189, 194, 209
Hammond, Albert, 168
Hammond, John, 242
Hancock, Reba, 170
Hardin, Tim, 168
Harvey, Mick, 263
Health, of Johnny, xxiii, 221, 240, 262, 263, 267, 268, 269
leg injury, 206
open heart surgery, 164, 206
Parkinson's-like disease, 219
Heart surgery, open, 164, 206
Heavy metal, 199–200, 223
band of John Carter, 202
Hee Haw, xvii, 87, 91
"Help Me," 129
Hensley, Jerry, 178
Hickman, Tennessee, 230
"Highway Patrolman, The," xix
Highwaymen, 164, 209
Highwaymen II, 205
Hilton hotel, Las Vegas, 60–61
Hippies, 95, 99, 113. *See also* Youth
Holland, W. S., 38, 248, 253
Hollywood Bowl, 92
Hollywood Palace, 83
Home Equipment Company, 235, 236
Hopkins, Harry, 13
Horton, Johnny, 165, 238
House of Blues, 105–106, 258
House of Cash, 135, 168, 172, 189–190, 228
happy with, 170–171
Howard, Jan, 187
Hoxie Rock, 232, 233, 245
Humbleness, xxv, 44, 68
Hunting, 133

Huntsville Texas State Prison, 139
Husky, Ferlin, 193, 194

Illnesses
drives for, 104
"In the Ghetto," 108
Indians, American, xxi, 58, 84, 98, 100, 104, 107–108, 113, 207. *See also* Causes; Prisons
Nickajack Indians, 241
Old Fishhawk, 133
Pima Indian at Iwo Jima, 56, 153–154
Inside the Walls of Folsom Prison (movie), 235
Inspiration, 128, 159
Integrity
moral and spiritual, 185–186, 247–248
Iron Maiden, 202, 203
Israel. *See Gospel Road*

Jack Clement Studio, 188, 189
Jackie Gleason Show, 41, 47, 50
Jagger, Mick, 187, 224
Jail, 103, 202, 229, 239–240. *See also* Prisons
in El Paso, 66–67
Johnny in, 59–61, 207
in Lafayette, 68, 151–152
James, Sonny, xvii, 238
Jazz, 74, 91
Jenkins, Gordon, 235
Jennings, Waylon, xxii, 164, 170, 172, 181, 183, 186, 191, 192, 193, 194, 196, 201, 202, 205, 228
recording with, 176–177
talent of, 182
Jerusalem Post, 262
Jesus, xxi, 110, 249. *See also* Baptist; Christians; God; Gospel Hymns; *Gospel Road*; Religion
on accepting, 125–126
film of, 124, 127–131
first century history and, 226–227
as personal, 125
songs of, 128–129
Jimmy Dean Show, The, 87
Johnny Cash Museum and Gift Shop, 228
Johnny Cash Parkway, 228
Johnny Cash Show, The, 83–86, 87, 98–101, 105, 192, 242. *See also* Movies; TV
Johnson, Robert, xvi, 55, 101
Johnstown, Pennsylvania, xiii, xiv
Jones, George, xvii, 163, 164, 223, 227, 238
Jones, Sheriff Ralph, 68, 151–152. *See also* Drugs
on free will, 69
Journal of Country Music, 251

Kansas State Prison, 79
Kansas Women's Industrial Reformatory, 79
Katz Drug Store, 236
KCIJ radio, 238
Keegan School of Broadcasting, 48, 235. *See also* Radio
Kemp, Wayne, 175
Kershaw, Doug, 98
King of America, 204
Kingland, Arkansas, 5
Klein, Gary, 168, 174

Kristofferson, Kris, 126, 128, 129, 144, 164, 196, 205, 249, 252
  recording with, 169–170
KWEM radio, 2, 236

La Farge, Peter, 56, 57, 88
  death of, 152–153
Labels. *See* Record companies
"Lady Came From Baltimore, The," 168
Landsberg Barbarians, 2
Lane, Red, 140
Las Vegas Hilton, 146
Last Days of Frank and Jesse James, The, 162
Late Burt Reynolds Show, The, 77
Laurel Canyon, 89
Law, Don, 55, 56, 67
Law suits, 96
Leavenworth prison, 77–82. *See also* Prisons
  concert at, 79–81
  country music at, 78
  friends made at, 82
  June Carter Cash at, 79
  road show to, 77–78
Leg injury. *See* Health
Legacy, of Johnny, 220, 268
Lewis, Jerry Lee, xiii, 37, 52, 147, 164, 181, 205, 221, 223
Liberto, Vivian, 1, 48, 51, 113, 151, 237
  break-up with, 59, 150, 240
  meeting of, 44, 235
Liner notes, xiv, 39, 258,
  Bob Dylan, 85
Lionel Trains, xvii, 136–137
Little House on the Prairie, 162
L.L. Cool J, 245
Loneliness, xiv, 88–89, 107, 162, 248
Look (magazine), 5
Los Padres National Forest, fire started in, 240
"Lost Highway," 177
Louisiana Hayride, 3, 41, 46, 238
Love, free, 122
Love songs, 112, 113, 118, 173, 248. *See also* Songs
Lowe, Nick (former son-in-law), 201, 204, 206
Lynn, Loretta, xvii, 161
Lyrics, 49, 93–94, 97, 107, 123, 159. *See also* Songs
  censoring, 203
  voice and, 35, 107, 146

Man in Black (first autobiography), xxiv, 26, 88, 143, 164, 166, 228, 255,
Man in White (Johnny's novel), xxiv, 202, 227
Manitoba, Dick, 221–222
Marijuana legislation, 149. *See also* Drugs
Marriage
  of Johnny and June, 60, 105
Martin, Dean, 93, 221
Mattea, Kathy, xx
McCullough, Dan
  as fan of Johnny's, xxiv, 211–215
McCurdy, Ed, 57
McDill, Bob, 201
McGibony, Richard, 69–70
Media
  on Johnny, xxi, xxii, 41–42, 73, 180–181, 218, 252, 255

serious attention from mainstream, 74
Mellencamp, John, 204
Memphis, 2, 46
Mercury Records, xx, 45, 164
Merritt, Neal, 66
Metallica, 202, 203
Midwestern Hayride, 87
Migrants, 5, 88
Mistakes, 167
Mitchell, Joni, 89, 98, 204–205
Mixing
involvement in, 174–175
Monticello, Illinois, 96
Moral principles, 121–122
Moss, Kate, xxii, 223, 253
Mother. *See* Cash, Carrie
Motorhead, 202
Movies, of Johnny Cash, xvi, xviii, xx, 41, 50, 53, 176
The Gospel Road, 110, 124–126, 127–132, 176
A Gunfight, xvi, 113
Nashville, xviii
Old Fishhawk, 133
MTV, 223, 253
Muppet Show, appearances on, xxii, 162
Murder in Coweta County, 162
Music
alternative, xxi, 222, 226, 252
dissatisfaction with, 166–168
fans in all genres of, 147
genre of, 101
video, 223
youth and, 128
Music City News, 60
Musician, 163
Musicians, 188, 267
My Old Man (Cash, Rosanne), 267

Nashville Banner, 42, 43–46
Nashville Skyline, 85, 90, 201, 205, 242, 243
Nashville Tennessean, 267–271
NBC, 42
Neal, Bob, 3, 44, 47, 49, 50, 237–238
Neal, James, 156
Nelson, Willie, 161, 164, 181, 193, 194, 205, 263
New Traditionalists, 163–164
New York Times Magazine, 58, 88, 110, 138, 143, 205, 247
Newport Jazz and Folk Festival, 58, 94, 243
Newsweek, 51, 130
Nixon, Richard, 73, 95, 137, 143–144, 154–155, 156, 231
"No Expectations," 187
Noontime Roundup, 232
Nostalgia, 164, 200

O Brother Where Art Thou?, xviii
"Okie from Muskogee," 154
Oldham, Will, 263, 264, 266
Oppression, 74
Orbison, Roy, 164, 177, 181, 205, 223
Osbourne, Ozzy, 202, 203, 223
Ostrich, attack of, 164, 251
Ozark Jubilee, 87

Pain. *See also* Songs
in country songs, 35
Parade (magazine), 25
"Paradise," xix

Parker, Tom Colonel, 242
Parton, Dolly, 108
Pearl, Minnie, 89, 182
  support of, 42, 43
Penthouse interview, 143–160
Perkins, Carl, xxv, 3, 49, 79, 112, 114, 145, 147, 154, 164, 166, 177, 181, 192–193, 197, 205, 223, 239, 257, 271
Perkins, Luther, 2, 35, 45, 49, 107, 235, 236–237, 253
  best work of, 38
  death of, 242
  as limited musician, 36, 37–38
Petty, Tom, 224, 255, 257, 262, 264, 265
Phillips, Sam, xv, 2, 3, 47, 48, 55, 66, 200, 201, 252
  changing of John's name, 237
  first meeting with, 236
  Johnny lying to, 55
  on Johnny's first audition, 36
  on Johnny's sound, 37
  tape delay or slapback of, 37
Phoenix, River, 224
Piano, 20, 38
  lessons, 139–140
Pierce, Webb, 193
Pills. *See* Drugs
Playboy, 60
Politics, 73, 103–104, 123, 144, 183–184, 195, 267. *See also* Government
  of Johnny, 118–119, 137, 143
Polygram Records, xx, 202
Poor, xv, 86, 88, 90, 91, 94, 99, 112, 123, 195
  black, 108
  Southern whites, 107, 108, 111
  of yesterday, 107
Pop music, xvi, 88, 147, 183. *See also* Music
Poverty. *See* Poor
Power, from prisoners, 75. *See also* Prisoners
Premonitions, 26–27
President(s), 137, 182–184, 195
  campaigning for, 184–185
  show taken to, 80
Presley, Elvis, xiii, xvii, 37, 42, 47, 49, 52, 108, 147, 177, 181, 182, 201, 204, 223, 236, 242
  commercialization of, 197
  competition from Johnny, 46
  erroneous crowning of, 88
  groomsman to, 2–3
  Johnny better than, 44
  opening for, 238
  as "white nigger," 42
Press. *See* Media
Press photographers, 68. *See also* Media
Press-Scimitar, 68
Pride, Charley, 85, 161
Pride of Jesse Hallam, The, 162
Prine, John, xix, 189, 201
Prison(s), xxi, 108, 157, 202. *See also* Causes; Concerts; Folsom prison; Jail; Leavenworth prison; San Quentin prison
  conversation on, 84
  Cummins, Arkansas, 84–85, 102–103
  disdain for, 75–76
  Huntsville Texas State Prison, 139
  reform, 138–139, 148–149

Prisoners, 98, 99, 101–102, 113, 147, 149, 153, 262
 on easing lives of, 76
 ecstasy of, 103
 empathy for, 81
 power from, 75
Producer(s), 55, 165, 168, 175, 194
 Rick Rubin as, 218–220
Producing
 movie, 131
 records, 135, 187, 191
Publicists. *See also* Media
 press releases of, 42

Radio, 78, 106, 107, 147, 182–183, 235
 conflict with, 231
 dreams of singing on, 235–236
 school, 1, 45, 48
 shows, 42, 145
 WMPS, 237–238
Railroads. *See* Trains
Range. *See also* Songs
 of singing, 36
Rap, xxii, 245
Ratings, 194. *See also* Charts
RCA-Victor, 2–3, 192, 238
Reading, 52–53
Rebel outlaw image, 202, 218, 251
Record(s), 194. *See also* Albums, of Johnny; Singles/songs, of Johnny
 bootleg, 205
 on breaking of first, 237–238
 crossover, 182–183
Record companies, 177
 blame on, 163
 crossover record for, 182
 influence with, 205
 switching, 39
Record sales, xv, 48, 52, 55, 92–93, 144, 164
 sagging, 162, 163, 164, 244
Record World, 193
Recording, 163, 192
 Cash as failing in, xx
 at House of Cash, 135–136
 studio, 58, 67
Redbook, 110
Rehabilitation, 101–102. *See also* Prisons
 prison, 138–139
Relationships, inattention to, 25
Religion, xxi, 121, 196. *See also* God
 and drugs, 152
 importance of, 132
 youth losing faith in, 121
Republicans, 95
Requests, 206, 260
Responsibility, 180–181
Reynolds, Allen, 201
Reynolds, Burt, 77
Rhythm, 45, 162–163, 191
 famous chigga-ching of, 37, 38, 163, 167
 section, 36
Richards, Keith, 187, 253
Riots, 138
Robbins, Marty, 56, 193, 194
Robeson, Paul, 93
Robinson, Sherman E. (Red), 95–96
Rock 'n' Roll, 42, 45, 53, 202, 218, 259. *See also* Music
 censorship in, 203–204
Rockabilly, 171, 201, 206, 248, 253, 258
Rockefeller, Governor Winthrop, 85, 102–103, 104

Rodgers, Jimmie, xvii, xxii, 2, 35, 91, 107, 144, 236
Rogers, Kenny, 204
Rolling Stone, xx, 42, 55, 57, 218, 225, 262
Ronstadt, Linda, 204
Roosevelt, Eleanor, 13
Roosevelt, Franklin Delano, 5, 145
Rorick, Dave, 248, 253
Route 89 festival, 206
Rubin, Rick, xxi, xxii, 200, 247, 251, 252, 253, 256, 258, 261, 263, 264, 265, 268
  meeting with, 244–245
  Viper Room meeting with Johnny, 224–225
Rural roots, 3, 99
  South and, 112
Ryman Auditorium, 43, 270

San Quentin prison, xv, 38, 75, 148, 179, 242. *See also* Prisons
  standing ovation at, 103
Sarver, Robert, 102–103
Satherly, Art, 55
Seeger, Pete, 99
Self-destruction, Johnny on, 59–60
Self-esteem
  lack of, 25
Sermon on the Mount, 127
Sharecropping, 10
Shaver, Billy Joe, xix, 201
Sherley, Glenn, 148
Sherman, Hal, 125
"Ship That Never Returned, The," 98
Shore, Dinah, 77
Shy-Drager syndrome, 219, 267, 269. *See also* Health, of Johnny
Silverstein, Shel, 73, 242
Sinatra, Frank, 225
Sing Out!, 56, 88
Singing, 201. *See also* Voice
  limits of, 36, 37
"Singing Brakeman, The," 91
Singles/songs, of Johnny, 59, 101. *See also* Albums, of Johnny
  "Any Old Wind that Blows," 133
  "Ballad of a Teen-Age Queen," 52, 55, 107, 168, 176, 205
  "The Ballad of Ira Hayes," 56, 58, 89, 152, 153, 231, 240, 248
  "The Ballad of Jesse James," 259
  "The Baron," xiii
  "Belshazzar," 235, 236
  "The Big Light," 204, 206
  "Big River," 35, 37, 97
  "Bird on a Wire," 168, 249, 252
  "Blistered," 73
  "Bottle of Inspiration," 206
  "A Boy Named Sue," xv, 73, 80, 93–94, 206, 242
  "Children, Go Where I Send You," 118
  "City Jail," 178
  "Cocaine Blues," xxii
  "Cold Lonesome Morning," 162
  "Come In Stranger," 37
  "Committed to Parkview," 172, 179
  "Country Boy," 3
  "Cry, Cry, Cry," 2, 3, 48, 52, 107, 145, 237, 238
  "Daddy Sang Bass," 73
  "Dark as a Dungeon," xv
  "Daughter of a Railroad Man," xxiv, 172
  "Delia's Gone," 244, xxii

"Dirty Old Egg Sucking Dog," 202
"Don't Take Your Guns to Town," 52, 56, 107
"Down at Dripping Springs," 170
"Down the Street to 301," 38
"Even Cowgirls Get the Blues," 164
"Everybody's Tryin' to Be My Baby," 257
"Fair Weather Friends," 199
"Five Feet High and Rising," xv, 57, 97
"Flesh and Blood," 175
"Flushed from the Bathroom of Your Heart," 202
"Folsom Prison Blues," xv, xxii, 3, 35, 38, 48, 52, 57, 62, 75, 81, 94, 102, 103, 145, 183, 207, 235, 237, 242, 245, 253, 259, 260
"Frankie's Man, Johnny," 56
"Frozen Four Hundred Pound Fair to Middlin," 202
"Get Rhythm," 48, 254
"(Ghost) Riders in the Sky," 162, 248
"Give My Love to Rose," 3, 35
"Green Green Grass of Home," 207
"Greystone Chapel," 148
"Guess Things Happen That Way," 38, 55, 168, 176
"Happy to Be with You," 59
"Hey, Porter!" 2, 3, 48, 107, 209, 235, 237, 238, 270
"The Highway Patrolman," 204
"I Dreamed about Mama Last Night," xxiii
"I Got Stripes," 107, 207
"I See a Darkness," 266
"I Still Miss Someone," 3
"I Walk the Line," xiii, xv, 3, 43, 45, 46, 48, 49, 52, 57, 62, 86, 107, 147, 181, 183, 239, 248, 260
"I Will Rock & Roll with You," 190
"I Wish I Was Crazy Again," 177
"I Won't Back Down," 257, 262, 264, 265
"I'll Go Somewhere and Sing My Songs Again," 209
"It Ain't Me Babe," 58
"It's All Over," 173
"Jackson," 102, 254
"Jesus, My Soul's in Your Hands," 207
"Johnny 99," 204
"The Lady Came from Baltimore," 162
"The L&N Don't Stop Here Anymore," xix
"Man in Black," 175, 230–231
"The Man Who Couldn't Cry," 224
"The Mercy Seat," 262, 263, 264, 266
"My Old Kentucky Home," 162
"The Night They Drove Old Dixie Down," 168, 169
"Nine Pound Hammer," xiv
"No Expectations," xxiv
"Oh Bury Me Not," 248
"Okie from Muskogee," 154
"One More Ride," 3
"One Piece at a Time," xix, 171, 172, 175, 178
"Oney," 133

"Orange Blossom Special," 107, 248, 260
"Orphan of the Road," 135
"Peace in the Valley," 207
"Pickin' Time," 3
"The Prisoner's Song," 81
"The Ragged Old Flag," xxi, 155
"Reason To Believe," 168
"The Rebel—Johnny Yuma," 56
"Redemption," 245, 249
"Ring of Fire," xv, 59, 107, 168, 177, 211, 215, 240, 242, 248, 254, 260
"Rock and Roll Ruby," 45, 49
"Rusty Cage," 256
"San Quentin," 207
"Singing in Vietnam Talking Blues," 144
"Sixteen Tons," xiv
"Smokey Factory Blues," 168
"So Doggone Lonesome," 3, 48
"Sold Out of Flagpoles," xviii, 179
"Solitary Man," 262, 264, 265
"Stop and Smell the Roses," 168, 169
"Strawberry Cake," xxi
"Sunday Morning Coming Down," 73, 179, 249, 260
"Tennessee Stud," 224
"That Lucky Old Sun," 265–266
"There Ain't No Good Chain Gang," 162, 177
"There You Go," 49
"Train of Love," 39, 49
"Understand Your Man," 59
"Wanted Man," 209
"Wayfaring Stranger," 263, 264, 265
"The Ways of a Woman in Love," 169
"Welfare Cadillac," 118, 143, 154
"We're Alright Now," 257
"Were You There When They Crucified My Lord," 152
"What Is Truth," 73, 128
"When He Reached Down His Hand for Me," 62
"Why Me Lord," 252
"Wide Open Road," 237
"You're Gonna Make Me Lonesome When You Go," 257
"You're Right, I'm Left, She's Gone," 177
"You're the Nearest Thing to Heaven," 38
Sir Mix-A-Lot, xxi
Skaggs, Ricky, 163
Skinner, Jimmie, 36
Slapback echo, 37, 172, 174, 190, 253
Slaves, 6, 93
Smith, Carl, 43, 56, 193, 242
Smith, Warren, 45, 49
Smoking, 226. *See also* Alcohol; Drugs
addiction to, 134
Snow, Hank, 44, 48, 182, 193, 236, 256
support of, 42
Socialism, 13–14
"Someday My Ship Will Sail," 176
Song(s), 93, 112, 144. *See also* Ballads; Charts; Gospel hymns; Music; Singles/songs, of Johnny
choosing own, 173–174
communication through, 147
first, 232, 235
gospel, 128, 152

greatest, 268
of Johnny and John Carter, 202
love, 112, 113, 118, 173, 237, 248
No. 1, 48, 175–176, 181, 182, 239, 242
No. 2, 43, 242
old, 187
pain in country, 35
request for, 206, 260
spiritual core of, 265
trouble with crossover, 183
writing of, 52–53, 132, 159, 167–168
Songwriter(s)
Johnny as, xix, 49, 52, 146, 162, 170–171, 179
other, xix, xxiv, 158–159, 188
parties, 159
Sonic Youth, 222, 223
Sound, augmenting Johnny's, 38
Soundgarden, 255, 256
South, false impression of, 185–186
South, Joe, 129
Specials, hosting, xx. *See also* TV
Spin (magazine), 227
Springsteen, Bruce, xix, 201, 204, 222
Staff, of Johnny, 53
Staff sergeant, 48, 106–107. *See also* U.S. Air Force
Stapp, Jack, 45
Stars, Inc., 44
"Star-Spangled Banner, The," 99
Statler Brothers, 79, 96, 112, 189, 271
Stereophile, 255
Stevens, Ray, 168
Stevenson, Adlai, 97
"Stop and Smell the Roses," 168
Strait, George, 163, 206
Streisand, Barbra, 146
Stuart, Marty, 200, 256, 257, 270
Studio(s), 187–188, 189. *See also* Recording
Jack Clement, 188
mistakes in, 166
other, 188
Ray Stevens', 168
sluggishness in, 200
Success, 100–101
Sullivan, Ed, 41, 48
Sun Records, xv, xxv, 2, 35, 37, 45, 46, 47, 52, 55, 107, 145, 147, 164, 167, 168, 172, 186, 190, 201, 206, 218, 223, 236, 237, 238, 251, 252
artistic high point at, 37
to Columbia Records, 55, 239
competition with Columbia Records, 39
early critical scrutiny of Johnny at, 36
first encounter with, 1
primitive recording techniques of, 36
simple sound of, 173, 177
Superiority, 118

Tape delay, 37
Taylor, Fred, 213–214
Taylor, James, 123
Tench, Benmont, 263, 265
Tennessee State Prison, 139, 148
Tennessee Three, 38, 80, 96, 107, 112, 167, 172, 173, 248, 253, 258
Tennessee Two, 2, 45, 52, 107, 255
become Tennessee Three, 38
unique sound of, 35, 36, 37

as whole greater then sum of parts, 36
"That's All Right," 236
Thorogood, George, 252
Time (magazine), xxiv, 51, 56, 218, 247
Tittle, Jimmy, 268
Tom Petty and the Heartbreakers, 255, 256, 257, 264
Tours, 68. *See also* Concerts
Johnny on, 114
various, 110–114
Tragedy. *See also* Songs
songs of, 35
Trains, xiv, xvii, 98, 112
Traveling, 113
Travis, Merle, 183
Travis, Randy, 163, 206
Travolta, John, 197
Truth, searching for, 99, 113
Tubb, Ernest, xxii, 2, 35, 36, 44, 48, 193
on limits of voice, 37
support of, 42
Tucker, Tanya, xvii, 183
Turner, Zeb, 36
TV. *See also Johnny Cash Show, The*
ads, xxiii, 125, 136–137, 167
movies, xx
shows, xvi, xx, xxiv, 41, 46, 53, 83, 89–90, 92, 93, 98–100, 157–158, 158, 162, 203, 204–205, 242, 270
20th Century-Fox, 124, 130
rights to *Old Fishhawk*, 133
Twisted Sister, 202

U2, 223, 264, 265, 269
Unfaithfulness, of Johnny, xxi
U.S. Air Force, xxi, 1, 44, 48, 52, 106, 145, 234
U.S. Air Force Security Service, 234
US Weekly, 255–260
USA Today, 271

Vallee, Rudy, xviii
VH–1 special, 225
Victor Records, 109
Vietnam War, 85–86, 137, 138, 143, 184
learning from, 174
singing for servicemen in, 99, 153–154
Viper Room, 224–225, 245
Virtues
old-time, 21–22
Voice, 218, 222, 263, 264
baritone range of, 36, 37, 49, 93, 100, 146, 162, 207, 254
blue tonality of, 93
deterioration of, 262
lyrics and, 35
speaking, 94
tremor in, 230

Wainwright, Loudon III, 218, 224
Wallace, Henry A., 13
War, Johnny on, 119, 231, 233
Warner Brothers' cartoons, 27, 28
Washington Post, 271
Watergate, 144, 155–157, 184
"Watermelon Wine," 135
Wayne, John, 50, 94, 255
Welk, Lawrence, 45, 221
Wells, Kitty, 183
White House, xvi, 154–155
"White Sport Coat," 38

Wife, first. *See* Liberto, Vivian
Wife, second. *See* Cash, (Valerie) June Carter
Williams, Bert, 263
Williams, Hank, xvii, xxii, xxiii, 35, 144, 163, 256
  Johnny as successor to, 49
  muted electric guitar sound, 36
  as quintessential country music figure, xvi
Williams, Hank Jr., 164
Wills, Bob, 55
Winners Got Scars Too (Wren), 125, 166, 228
  excerpts from, 5–23
Winston, Dr. Nat, 70, 71, 72, 117
Winters, Jonathan, 77
Wisconsin State Fair, 92
WMPS radio, 237–238
Women's Liberation, 122
Woodstock, 73
Wootton, Bob, 248, 253
Working class, xiv, xvii, 56
World War I, 234
Wounded Knee, 153
WPA (Works Progress Administration), 22
Wren, Christopher S., 5, 125, 126, 166, 228
Writer, 37, 52
  of prose, xxiv, 52
WSM radio, 42, 45, 91

Yoakam, Dwight, 206, 252
Young, Faron, 193
Young, Neil, 123
"Young Love," 38
Youth, 74, 94, 113, 206, 226, 258, 266
  on drugs, 120–121
  on Johnny, 111, 219
  and music, 128
  responsibility towards, 119
  and spiritual experiences, 121